LECH WAŁĘSA AND HIS POLAND

LECH WAŁĘSA
AND
HIS POLAND

Mary Craig

CONTINUUM • NEW YORK

FOR BARBARA AND ROBIN KEMBALL

and for Janusz, Joasia, Wojtek, Monika, Piotr – and all those others who risk their freedom to keep the crystal spirit from breaking.

1987

The Continuum Publishing Company
370 Lexington Avenue, New York, N.Y. 10017

First published 1986 by Hodder & Stoughton, London, as
The Crystal Spirit: Lech Wałęsa and His Poland

Printed in the United States of America

Library of Congress Cataloging-in-Publication Data

Craig, Mary.
  Lech Wałęsa and his Poland.

  Previously published as: The crystal spirit.
  Bibliography: p.
  Includes index.
  1. Poland–History–20th century. 2. Wałęsa Lech,
1943– . I. Title.
DK4382.C73 1987   943.8′05   87-6731
ISBN 0-8264-0390-5

ACKNOWLEDGMENTS

To all inside Poland whom I prefer not to mention by name.

To Elżbieta Barzycka; Urszula Grochowska; Irena Grzeszczak; Maciej Jachimczyk; Andrzej, Jadwiga and Krzysztof Jaraczewscy; Barbara Kemball; Ludka Laskowska; Dr Jerzy Peterkiewicz; Dr Jagodziński of The Polish Library, Hammersmith; Antoni Pospieszalski; Dr Jan Sikorski (Leeds); Jan Sikorski (London); Grażyna Sikorska; Ewa Stepan; Kazik Stepan; Martha Szajkowska.

To Dr Bohdan Cywiński, for the time he gave me, and particularly for his excellent unpublished paper, *The Polish Experience*.

To my friends, Frances Donnelly and John Harriott, whose encouragement and support were invaluable.

To Tim Garton Ash, in whose book, *The Polish Revolution*, I discovered the Orwell poem from which I have taken the title for this book and to the estate of the late Sonia Brownell Orwell and Secker & Warburg Ltd for permission to use it. To the Association Des Philatélistes Polonais en France for their generosity in helping me obtain the stamps.

To Anna Zaranko for her imaginative involvement in the book, for coming to Poland with me, and for some of the photographs. And to Eric Major, Carolyn Armitage and Ion Trewin of Hodder & Stoughton for believing in the project and supporting it.

To Dr Antony Polonsky, Olgierd Stepan and Dr Bogdan Szajkowski, who read the MS and gave me their valuable comments.

And lastly to my husband, Frank, for his unfailing tolerance, assistance and love.

ILLUSTRATIONS

Lech Wałęsa's birth entry in register[2]
The Wałęsa family[2]
The house in Popowo where Wałęsa was brought up[3]
Wałęsa's school, Chalin[3]
Wedding photograph[1]
Danuta Wałęsa[2]
Warsaw churchyard[2]
Dreams and determination[1]
Occupation strike in Lenin shipyard[1]
Bread for the strikers[1]
Confession on site[1]
Signing of agreement for independent self-governing trade unions[1]
Cardinal Wyszyński at the Gdańsk monument[1]
Western European support for the Poles[1]
The nation unites in support of Solidarity[2]
Martial law[1]
The realist[1]
Father Henryk Jankowski[2]
Father Jerzy Popiełuszko[2]
Wałęsa and Pope John Paul II in Rome[1]
V for Victory[2]
Stamps[4]
The author with Lech Wałęsa[2]
The Wałęsa family, 1981[1]

[1] Reproduced by courtesy of The John Hillelson Agency, London ©
[2] Author's photograph
[3] Reproduced by courtesy of Anna Zaranko
[4] Reproduced by courtesy of the Association Des Philatélistes Polonais en France

CONTENTS

ROUGH GUIDE TO THE
PRONUNCIATION OF POLISH

The following hints may be useful to the reader:

The vowels *a*, *e* and *o* are short, i.e. as in: c*a*t, b*e*d, b*o*x.

The vowels *i* and *u* are long, i.e. as in f*ee*t, m*oo*n.

ą and *ę* are nasal sounds, *ą* being pronounced like the '*on*' in French *monde*; and *e* like the *in* in French *fin*.

j is a half-vowel, pronounced as *y*; as is *y*, which is pronounced somewhere between a short *i* and a short *e*. Try either.

oj = *oy*, as in b*oy*.

ó is (like *u*) pronounced *oo*.

ów (a frequent combination in Polish) = *oof*.

c = *ts*, as in *tsar*.

ch is pronounced like its counterpart in Scottish *loch* or German *ach*.

c(i) = *ch(ee)*

cz = *ch*

ł = *w*

sz = *sh*. Hence the formidable looking combination szcz = merely shch.

s and *s(i)* also = *sh*. Likewise, believe it or not, *rz*.

w = *v*. There is no letter *v* in Polish, despite the frequency with which the V-for-Victory sign is made.

ź and *z(i)* = *zh(ee)*

ż resembles the -(a)ge in French *courage*.

An accent over the *ń*: merely denotes a softening of the sound.

IN POLISH THE STRESS USUALLY FALLS ON THE
PENULTIMATE SYLLABLE.

I have tried to keep the use of Polish proper names to a minimum. Of those I have used, most are easy to pronounce. Here, however, are phonetic transcripts of the most commonly used:

BYDGOSZCZ: bid-goshch.
CYWIŃSKI: tse-ween-skee.
CZĘSTOCHOWA: chen-sto-ho-va.
JASTRZĘBIE: yas-tshen-b'ye
MIŁOSZ: mee-wosh.
POPIEŁUSZKO: po-pyay-woosh-ko.
SZCZECIN: shchech-een.

WAŁĘSA: va-wen-sa.
WALENTYNOWICZ: va-len-tě-no-veech
WOJTYŁA: voy-^{kě}-wa.
WYSZYŃSKI: v^i-sh^{i}n-skee.

As with proper names, I have also attempted to avoid sets of initials. Only a few recur with any frequency in the text. They are:

KOR: the Workers' Defence Committee. Later renamed KSS-KOR, Social Self-Defence Committee-KOR.
SB: secret police, usually known as the UB.
ZOMO: units of specially trained, motorised riot police.

FOREWORD

Early one morning, in the middle of August 1980, a thirty-seven-year-old, out-of-work electrician called Lech Wałęsa scrambled over the twelve-foot-high perimeter wall of the Lenin shipyard in the Baltic port of Gdańsk, Poland. The workers there, driven to desperation by endless shortages, were about to go on strike, a shocking possibility in the "workers' paradise" of People's Poland. Standing on a bulldozer, the director of the shipyard attempted to soothe them with golden promises. They were wavering, almost ready to believe the promises that past experience had taught them were never kept. Suddenly, the air became charged with excitement, as Wałęsa, a short, stocky, young man with a huge moustache, climbed on to the bulldozer and from a higher vantage-point than the director, shouted: "Remember me? I was a worker in this shipyard for ten years. But you kicked me out four years ago . . . We don't believe your lies any more, and we're not going to be cheated again. Until you give us firm guarantees, we're going to stay right here where we are."

The director remembered him all right, and the workers' hesitation vanished. Before the next few days were out, Lech Wałęsa would be famous far beyond the confines of the shipyard, the city of Gdańsk, or even Poland. When he climbed over that wall and on to that excavator, he was entering history. The Solidarity movement which flowed from that moment will for ever be associated with his name. To the world at large, no other name is of importance. Lech Wałęsa is Mister Solidarity.

But Solidarity was much more than just another trade union movement, and Lech Wałęsa did not just spring into active life in that August of 1980. The story of the man and of the movement is a complex, interwoven one. And the story does not make any sense to the outsider unless the story of Poland is told, at least of Poland in the last forty-odd years, that is to say in the lifetime of Lech Wałęsa. For Wałęsa, unknown till 1980 outside of Gdańsk, became the voice of Poland, the man who, for all his peasant origins and uncouth accent, was able to articulate the hopes and longings of a nation which, since 1939, has been in bondage to two ruthless totalitarian systems alien to its nature. "Let Poland Be Poland," was the theme song of Solidarity, one of the few hopeful that the government would engage in dialogue with the discredited Solidarity, in order to save Poland from disaster.

When I met him again a year later, the political climate had deteriorated drastically. Jerzy Popiełuszko had been murdered, and many other supporters of Solidarity, priests and laymen, had disappeared in mysterious circumstances, or were being persistently harassed by the police. A trial that same week, conducted without even the semblance of respect for justice and truth, had resulted in long prison sentences for three men whose only crime was that they had tried to humanise the Marxist–Leninist state in which they lived. Wałęsa, under orders not to leave Gdańsk without permission, had been summoned that very morning to the Public Prosecutor's Office for questioning. There he had refused to speak. Instead he had silently placed a written statement on the prosecutor's desk. In the face of such a monstrous miscarriage of justice, the statement said, the only way to retain one's dignity *vis à vis* the courts, prosecutors or police, was silence.

Wałęsa's mood that afternoon, when I met him in a room at St Brigid's, the "shipyard church", was sombre, his face tense and exhausted – like those of most of the people I met. But not defeated, not afraid. Shadowed always by the police, his every movement watched, he can still assert that he is "the free-est man in the world", and mean it. This book is a modest attempt to shed some light on the apparent paradox.

It is also an attempt to present the story of Poland in the last troubled half-century in an easy-to-read form. It is a layman's, not a scholar's book, and I have included only as much detail as seemed to me indispensable to the overall picture. For this reason too I have cut down on proper names and have provided a rough guide to the pronunciation of those which remain. The pronunciation of Polish is not nearly as daunting as it seems.

My aim has been to give some idea of just what the Polish experience has been in this most terrible of centuries; and to clear up some of the many misunderstandings which prevail in the West. Because present-day Poland is a closed society in which information cannot be freely sought, nor interviews freely given, I have for the most part referred to my contributors by name only when they are already well-known; and am unable therefore to acknowledge my debt to them properly. To illuminate their testimonies, I have quoted also from novels, films and poems of the period, which seem to me to convey a heightened perception of a painful reality.

Many years ago, a friend of mine told me she was convinced

that Poland had the spiritual capacity to save the world from itself. I knew nothing about Poland then, and promptly forgot what she had said. But the remark must have lodged in my subconscious, and for the last few years, ever since August 1980, in fact, I have been sure that my friend was right.

MARY CRAIG, September 1985

PROLOGUE

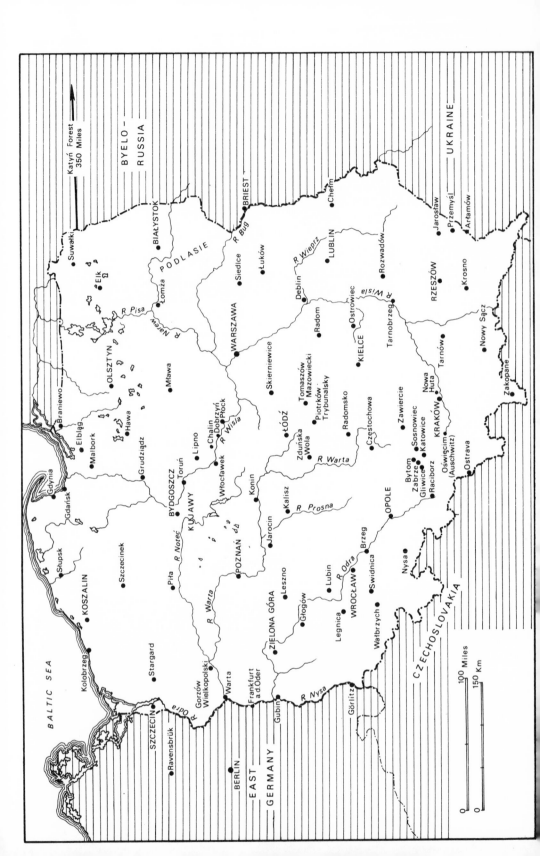

INDEPENDENCE (1918–39)

I would say this for the Poles: for every stain on the escutcheon of
the nation, I can find a concomitant act of unparalleled unselfish-
ness and heroism to lay in the balance. This is no ordinary country
– Polish history has decreed it thus. A great and enduring people
who have become thus against the most extraordinary of odds –
there you have the Poles.

Stewart Steven, *The Poles*

Wałęsa? Even the Poles had difficulty remembering the name
when they first heard it in 1980. Polish surnames usually tell you
where a person comes from or what his/her occupation is. All
those names ending in -ski or -cki are of that sort. But Wałęsa tells
a different story. It is based on a Polish verb meaning "to wander
about", and suggests a rootless individual, a restless spirit, someone pushed around from one place to another. Someone hunted
by the police perhaps? A deportee?

In 1830 a young man named Wałęsa was deported from Russian
Poland. And that is where the two stories, of Wałęsa and of
Poland, first actually coincide.

*   *   *

In the monastery at Częstochowa, the shrine which is at the very
heart of Polish nationhood, there is a storehouse of priceless
treasure. Among the royal regalia, the gold and the jewels, the
porcelain of ages past, there is an item from Poland's more recent
and tragic experience: an urn filled with ashes – the ashes of those
who died in the 1944 Warsaw Rising, or in the concentration
camps of Majdanek, Auschwitz, Stutthof and countless other
places of horror. "Gold and tears," sighed one of the monks,
pointing out these disparate treasures with equal pride. "Gold
and tears. That's the story of Poland."

The country lies in the exact centre of Europe, at a dangerous
crossroads, prone to sudden attack by enemies to north, south,
east and west, and for ever paying the price of her unenviable
geographical position. As Igor Stravinsky so graphically put it,

21

"If you pitch your tent in the middle of Fifth Avenue, don't be surprised if you are run over by a bus."

Poland was a democracy as long ago as the second half of the fourteenth century, when the other great states of Europe – France, England, Germany, Russia and Spain – were all heading in the direction of autocracy and the setting up of absolute monarchies. True enough, Poland's democracy was of the gentry only, but then nowhere else in Europe was there such a large gentry class, comprising about ten per cent of the population.[1]

In the sixteenth century, Poland was a powerful nation, but in the following one she steadily declined from that high point. Her insistence on personal freedom, so intense as to be almost anarchic, was her undoing, and by the eighteenth century, Poland had become ungovernable. Her decline came about just as the Russia of the Romanovs, the Prussia of the Hohenzollerns and the Austria of the Hapsburgs were growing in strength. In 1772, these voracious neighbours proceeded to annex a large part of Poland.

After the success of the French Revolution and the spread of revolutionary ideas in 1789, enlightened spirits in Poland attempted to stop the rot and provide the country with a worthwhile system of government. The Constitution of 3rd May, 1791, was Europe's first and the world's second (after America) written body of law to proclaim the rights of man and of the citizen. If it had been implemented, Poland would have become one of the most progressive countries of Europe. But scarcely was the ink dry on the paper than her three neighbours, alarmed by the revolutionary nature of the Polish charter, moved in to stop the cancer from spreading; and annexed all but a small fragment of Poland's territory, forcing her to abandon her Constitution. Two years later they took away even the bit that was left. For the next one hundred and twenty-three years, Poland was carved up between Russia, Prussia and Austria and disappeared from the maps of Europe. In the history books, these are the years of the Polish Partitions; to the Poles they were rather the *finis Poloniae*, the end of Poland.

Yet, during those years of oppression, when Prussian Poles and Austrian Poles and Russian Poles grew up absorbing different political, social and cultural values into their bloodstreams and had little contact with each other, Polish consciousness somehow refused to die. Whether in the Russian sector where Polish Catholics were actively persecuted by Orthodox Christians; in the Prussian where they were hounded by the Lutherans; or in the

Austrian (known as Galicia) where rule by the large Polish land-owners (magnates) preserved an outmoded economic structure which left the majority of the population extremely poor, and exacerbated religious and national tensions between Poles and Ukrainians; it was in the Roman Catholic Church that Poles everywhere could find their common ground. At times even their language was forbidden, and Polish children received their schooling only in Russian or German. But they always learned their catechism, secretly, from the priest, and he taught it to them in Polish. In this way the language and traditions of the old Poland were kept alive.

In the first of the Partitions, it was Prussia who did best out of the deal. But after 1815, the lion's share of Polish territory was acquired by Czarist Russia. As the Russian noose tightened, strangling Polish culture and language, the Poles entered a long period of struggle to preserve their self-respect along with their national identity.

On several occasions the Poles rose in revolt against their oppressors, but the revolts were always bloodily put down; and more repressive measures followed. The first of these brave but doomed insurrections was against Russia and took place in November 1830. It was spearheaded by a number of impecunious gentry who believed they had nothing to lose. The young Wałęsa, ancestor of Lech, was almost certainly one of them.

The Rising was put down by vastly superior Russian forces, and many young Poles fled the country. In the harsh reprisals that followed, many more, about eight or nine thousand in all, and including Wałęsa, were deported by the Russians, who then under-took an even more savage Russification of their part of Poland. Universities were closed down, Parliament suppressed . . . Most of the exiles went to France, where their desire for freedom had aroused the most sympathy. Paris at this time was a haven for many national liberation movements, and now became the centre from which hopes of a free Poland radiated.[1]

*   *   *

It was not, however, till 1918 that Poland regained her independence. Even then it was no more than an accident, and proved to be little more than a breathing-space. It so happened that her Russian overlords went to war with her German and Austrian masters, and in the course of that war they all three lost their empires. For six years Poland was a bloody battlefield over which their armies advanced and retreated, trampling her underfoot in

23

the process. When the Armistice was signed in the West in November 1918, German troops were still victoriously in place on Polish soil. Then, almost by default and hardly able to believe her good fortune, Poland was declared free. Free, indeed, but still a cat's-paw; a stick with which the Western allies could belabour the defeated Germany. The Treaty of Versailles which restored Poland to the map of Europe aroused deep fury and resentment in Germany and sowed the seeds of the next World War and Poland's virtual destruction. Germany and Russia, Poland's traditional enemies, were for the time being impotent. But they would not long remain so. Poland's resurgence may have seemed like a miracle to the newly-liberated Poles, but in the light of history that resurgence was foredoomed to be short-lived.

Poland in fact was bleeding and helpless from the war which had raged over her and she needed a powerful shot in the arm if she were to survive. But self-interest governed Western policy. It was only French fears of both Germany and newly Bolshevik Russia that had tipped the balance in favour of creating a free Poland as a useful buffer between those two potentially dangerous aggressors. A strong and vigorous Poland was no part of the Allies' post-war strategy. Only reluctantly did they agree to her request for an outlet to the sea, at Danzig, on the Baltic Sea. Then, almost as if regretting such generosity, they made Danzig (known to the Poles as Gdańsk) a Free City, belonging neither to Germans nor Poles, yet inhabited by both. The Prussian part of Germany was now divided into two by what became known as the Polish Corridor. A recipe for disaster, if ever there was one. It was a positive invitation to future German adventurism.[2]

Over the next few years, until 1923, Poland fought six wars to establish her frontiers. French fears were proved to be only too well grounded when, during the Russo-Polish War of 1920–1, the Bolsheviks came near to taking Warsaw, from where they hoped to sweep on over the Oder River and into Germany. A new Communist leadership of Polish revolutionaries was all ready to take power and had begun addressing manifestos to the nation. Anticipating victory, the Russian General Tukhachevsky gloated: "Over the corpse of Poland lies the road to worldwide conflagration. We shall drown the Polish Army in its own blood." Trotsky was certain that Europe was about to be set ablaze. But for once the gods were with Poland. By a miracle (attributed by the Poles about equally to Marshal Józef Piłsudski and the Virgin Mary), the Russian troops were turned back at the eleventh hour, and Europe gained an eighteen-year reprieve. The Battle of

Warsaw, one of history's most crucial battles and known to the Poles as the Miracle on the Vistula, put an end to whatever sympathy Poles might have felt for Russian Communism. The relationship between the two countries suffered a terminal blow. And from now on, Joseph Stalin, the new master of Soviet Russia, would brood on revenge just as ominously as did the Germans.

By 1921, Poland's frontiers were as secure as they were ever likely to be, given her precarious geographical situation, like a nut lying in the hollow of a temporarily out-of-action nutcracker. She could at last address herself to the awesome problem of self-government. As one commentator put it, it was "as though she had been handed a six-inch nail, which she had to bang into a concrete wall with her bare hands".[3] The Western allies left her to it, though she was financially exhausted and lacked all experience of political independence. Government after government fell, as politicians wrangled and failed to find common ground.

The new Poland was a mishmash of ill-assorted ethnic groups with little or no understanding of each other's problems and plenty of ambition and mutual dislike. Ukrainians, Byelo-Russians all dreamed of unilateral independence and resolutely refused the federation that might possibly have saved them.

Frighteningly insecure as she was, Poland became defensive and jittery about the hostile minorities in her midst, and in particular about the Jews, who now represented ten per cent of the entire population (a far higher percentage per head of population than anywhere else in Europe), who seemed to present the biggest threat to Polish autonomy. "Poland for the Poles" became a popular slogan, as the Jews' unpopularity increased.

In earlier centuries, Poland had been renowned for her religious tolerance. No religious wars were ever fought on her territory, and, during the Reformation period, she was a recognised haven for those who were being persecuted elsewhere. Not least for the Jews. Poland, for example, had been the only country in Europe to welcome them, when they were expelled from Spain and Portugal. By the eighteenth century, more than seventy-five per cent of the world's Jews were living in the Polish–Lithuanian Commonwealth.

During the nineteenth-century Partitions, however, Polish Jews had come under more openly anti-semitic rule and were subjected to frequent pogroms by all three occupying powers, particularly by Czarist Russia. It followed that many Poles had been born and bred in an atmosphere which encouraged and provoked anti-semitism. Moreover, many of the Jews in Russian-occupied eastern Poland had joined revolutionary groups, and it was their identification with Russian Bolshevism which was the main cause of their unpopularity in independent Poland. In 1918, the Polish Communists opposed Independence, arguing that the country should remain part of the new Soviet Russia. And as Jews formed the nucleus of this Communist Party, the Poles chose to believe that the entire Jewish community was plotting a Russian take-over. This was unfair, since the Jewish Communists, as avowed atheists, were disliked by their orthodox fellow-Jews almost as much as by the Polish Catholics.

There were economic reasons, too, for the Polish mistrust of the Jews. At a time when the Poles were desperately trying to stave off economic collapse, Jewish control over much of the industrial and commercial life of the country, and Jewish domi-nance in medicine and law, aroused furious national resentment. During the dictatorship of Marshal Józef Piłsudski (who had as-sumed emergency powers in 1926 in order to lift the nation out of chaos), the Jews were relatively protected. But after Piłsudski's death in 1935, the "government of the colonels" which succeeded him was obsessed with national unity and became stridently chauvinistic.

A tide of nationalism and anti-semitism was sweeping across Europe, and Poland was not exempt from the madness. Outbursts of anti-semitism became frequent, all too often approved and accepted by the powerful Roman Catholic Church, for whom the Jews were not only Communists but freemasons and secularists bent on destroying the fabric of society. The boycott of Jewish shops and businesses became an accepted part of Polish life.

Four hundred thousand Jews left Poland at this time – with feelings of bitterness which are still strong half a century later. Such bitterness is understandable. Nevertheless, as Isaac Cohen of the Anglo-Jewish Association was later to insist, Jews who believed themselves persecuted in Poland "did not have long to wait for conditions which made Poland look like paradise".

Poland's pre-war intolerance of her minorities would cast a long shadow over her post-war reputation. Angry charges, both justified and unjustified, are laid against her. But it can at least be pleaded in extenuation that in those inter-war years she was struggling to learn democracy the hard way, alone and unaided, after a century and a half of being enslaved; and that she lacked the political maturity to handle wisely those who seemed to threaten her survival. Whatever her faults, and they must not be brushed aside, Polish society was basically healthy, and was a more likely breeding ground for true democracy than for either of the ugly totalitarian tyrannies which lay in wait for her. She needed more time. But time would not be given her.

It is said that, just before his death, Marshal Józef Piłsudski expressed the fear that one day Russia and Germany would unite. And in that hour of mortal danger, he prophesied, Poland would stand alone and defenceless. Britain and France, he was quite sure, would not lift a finger to help her.

[1] Marek Wasowicz, *Idea Demokratyzmu i Tolerancji Religijnej w Historii Ustroju Polski*, Almanach Polonii 1980.

[2] From an article in *Poland One*, January 1985, Volume 1, Number 8, "Polish Independence: How Lloyd George Failed To Stop It", by Józef Gintyllo.

[3] *Idem.*

PART ONE

THE WILDERNESS YEARS

1   A DOUBLE HOLOCAUST (1939–43)

I think that Solidarity has really been in existence in a latent form
since the last war. It was forged in the Polish resistance movement
and, to the end, thanks to what you call the "intransigence" of the
Poles, it was preserved. Otherwise, we would not have Solidarity
today.

Jan Nowak, 1980

Germany had made no secret of its intentions. "Poland's existence
is intolerable, incompatible with the essential conditions of Germany's life," wrote a German general in 1922. "Poland must and
will go." Taken in conjunction with Russian – by now it was Soviet
Russian – resentment of a "bourgeois" Polish buffer between
herself and her plans for carrying the revolution into Germany,
the signing of the Nazi–Soviet pact in 1939 sounded Poland's
death-knell. A new Partition, worse than those of the nineteenth
century, was about to overwhelm her. And when the coming war
ended, more than six million Polish citizens, including approxi-
mately three million Jews, would be dead. That is to say, one in
five of the country's population.

Stalin congratulated Ribbentrop, the German Foreign Minister,
on the new friendship between the two erstwhile enemies. "A
friendship cemented by blood," he called it. By Polish blood. In
a speech to the Supreme Soviet on 31st October, 1939, Russian
Foreign Minister Molotov bluntly spelled out the nature of this
friendship: "A short blow at Poland from the German Army,
followed by one from the Red Army, was enough to annihilate
this monster-child of the Treaty of Versailles."

By then it was over. Assured of Soviet collusion, Hitler had
attacked Poland on 1st September. Barbara N., fifteen years old
at the time, remembers: ". . . the paralysing terror, the sensation
that the whole world was falling about one's ears, the shock of
seeing shot and bleeding people lying in the roads. Everything
that once had seemed eternal simply collapsed."

The Polish Army fought bravely, in the belief that they would
soon see the British and French launch a counter-offensive across

31

the Rhine. It simply did not occur to them that those two countries, who had finally declared war on Germany on 3rd September, would abandon them to their fate. Earlier that summer the Allies had even prevailed on Poland not to mobilise, for fear of provoking the Germans. As a result of this disastrous decision, Polish volunteers were wandering round in a shocked and futile search for arms and equipment. "Surely we are not going to die for Danzig" summed up the Western attitude, and, as Piłsudski had foreseen, not a shot was fired in Poland's defence by her allies.

Just how hopeless Polish resistance was became clear on 17th September, when the Red Army marched into eastern Poland, on the pretext of liberating those territories which the Russians had never ceased to claim as theirs. To the Poles it seemed like a new variation of the old Russian expansionism.

The Nobel poet, Czesław Miłosz, compared those desperate days to a fire in an ant-hill: "Thousands of hungry and frightened people clogged the roads: soldiers of the beaten army trying to get home, policemen getting rid of their uniforms, women searching for their husbands . . ."

A vicious persecution began, not just of landowners and "class enemies", but of millions of ordinary people. (Not even Polish Communists were safe. Stalin had liquidated all those he could lay hands on in 1936, accusing them of being Trotskyists. The future leader, Władysław Gomułka, saved at that time by virtue of being in a Polish prison, was taking no chances now. Communist or not, he preferred to try his luck in the German zone.)

To the Russians, all Poles were dyed-in-the-wool counter-revolutionaries. Ludka L.'s story is typical of thousands. Her father was a policeman, therefore a "class enemy". Day after day he was summoned by the NKVD (the Russian Secret Police, later called the KGB) and interrogated. Returning home after one of these interrogations, bruised and beaten, with several teeth missing, he confided to his family that he would try to "escape" into the German zone. That was the last they heard of him, until years later they were told that he had died in Auschwitz concentration camp.

Meanwhile, the Russians were arresting army officers, judges, policemen, teachers, civil servants and anyone who might conceivably stand in their way. Children at school were arrested for refusing to stand to attention during the singing of the Internationale. While the prisoners were deported to Siberia, their wives sold everything they could find in the house, to get money for food. Rumours were rife that they were to be deported too, to make room for the families of the Russian soldiers. Ludka takes up the story:

> And then it came, the night of 13th April, 1940. We were in bed when the knocking on the door started and Russian soldiers with guns burst in and told us to pack. We had to leave immediately. My mother was given papers to sign, while the soldiers searched the house looking for guns. They found a little jewellery (not much; she had sold most of it already) and took that . . .

> We got to the station by hay-cart. There we saw a long train of cattle-trucks waiting for us. It was a terrible sight. Masses of people and Russian soldiers prodding everyone with their guns. Cries and callings for help and curses. It was a nightmare.

> They packed us about sixty to each truck. At each end of the truck there were sort of shelves. Some of us children were told to lie down on these at once, otherwise there would have been no room for others even to stand. There were two tiny windows at the top of the wall, and huge sliding doors at each end. We were kept at the station for two days until all the trucks were full of people. We left at night and travelled for over two weeks. Now and then we stopped to get food, mostly thin soup, bread and hot water. Nobody was allowed to leave the cattle-truck, except the people who were bringing the food. There was a hole in the floor for a toilet. Most of us had either diarrhoea or constipation.

> I remember the moment when we crossed the border into Russia. We all cried. Some people had a premonition then that they'd never see Poland again . . .

Their destination was Siberia. From the station they travelled by ox-cart for three days and three nights before reaching the collective farm where they were to stay with a Russian family. At the farm (*kolkhoz*) Ludka slept in one bed with her mother and sister; her brother, Marian, slept on top of a large stove; and the other member of their group slept on top of their combined suitcases. For this accommodation they were ordered to pay forty roubles a month:

> Everyone had to work. Mother made bricks; Mila and Marian worked in the fields (we children had to go to school). We were given bread, skimmed milk and seasonal vegetables in small quantities. At the end of the season we were supposed to be paid, but as we hadn't fulfilled our "quota", there was no money for us and we were told that we owed them for the food we'd received.

When winter came it was terrible. Our clothes were far too thin, and we were hungry. Mother swapped whatever we could spare for potatoes and bread. When we complained to our work-foreman, he said, "You'll either get used to it or die." We were not prepared for such bitter cold and so much snow. That snow, even our houses were covered with it. Those who died during that dreadful winter had to be buried in the snow and then reburied when the thaw came.

By despatching between one and two million Poles to the arctic wilderness, Stalin could confidently leave typhus, dysentery, starvation and freezing cold to do the work of extermination for him. Of those deported, about a fifth died. A miner, trade unionist, who survived a work-camp in the regions of northern Siberia, described the appalling conditions in which the prisoners worked – in sixty-five degrees of frost, and with no day of rest:

The prisoners suffered from exhaustion after a very short time and were easily attacked by disease. Yet a man only got sick-leave when he had at least forty degrees of fever and then only if the sick-leave quota for that day was not filled . . . Out of a camp of some ten thousand men, two thousand died every year. Every morning there were some prisoners who could not be roused, having died in the night. In the first two and a half months of my time at Kolyma, out of the total of twenty Poles in my group, sixteen died.[1]

Among the thousands of deportees was a sixteen-year-old high-school boy, Wojciech Jaruzelski, despatched to the north-eastern part of the Soviet Union with his parents.

The towns and villages which the deportees had left behind were being thoroughly bolshevised.[2] The secret police were given free rein, the Polish language was banned, Polish currency abolished, publication of Polish newspapers abandoned. Crucifixes and statues were removed, churches were converted into social clubs. Stalin was seeking to ensure that never again would Poland dare to assert her independence from Russia.

Almost certainly for political reasons, the world has learned little to this day of Russia's part in the crucifixion of Poland. Yet in the first two years of this, one of the most brutal occupations in human history, the savagery of the Russians probably exceeded that of the Germans. The Russians had long experience (in a

34

tradition inherited from the Czars and enthusiastically continued) in the effective application of psychological terror.

*   *   *

Like Stalin, Hitler wanted his revenge for Versailles; he too wanted to exterminate the Poles. He admitted to his military chiefs[3] that Danzig had been only an excuse for invading Poland: he wanted the destruction of Poland, living room for Germans and a source of cheap labour for the Reich. In a document later read to an International Military Tribune, he suggested killing without mercy "all men, women and children of Polish race or language". Hitler's persecution differed from that of Stalin in that it was along racial rather than class lines: the Jews were confined to ghettos; the Aryans themselves were divided into categories of Reichsdeutsch (those born in Germany), Volksdeutch (those of possible German ancestry) and Nichtsdeutsch (everybody else).

On the western side of the border agreed beforehand with Russia, the Germans established a General Government area with its administrative centre in Kraków; while many areas of Prussia and Silesia were simply incorporated into the German Reich. From Kraków, Governor Hans Frank directed the plunder and exploitation of a captive people. "The Poles," he told his subordinates, "will work. They will eat little. And in the end they will die. There will never again be a Poland." All potential leaders – which meant all those who had received a higher education – clergy, teachers, doctors, dentists, vets, writers, journalists, students, along with landowners and businessmen, were to be liquidated. Blonde and blue-eyed Polish children were kidnapped on the streets and sent to the Reich to be brought up as Germans; hostages were rounded up and shot in scores or hundreds. It was not only the Jews for whom a Final Solution was being prepared.

But the full force of German hatred for Poland had not yet been unleashed. The knell sounded on 22nd June, 1941, when Hitler attacked his erstwhile ally, the Soviet Union, and drove the Red Army out of eastern Poland within a few days. Hitler was at the peak of his power; his grip on Eastern Europe was now complete. He was free to carry out the ambitious social engineering he had planned: where possible, the Poles were to be Germanised; and where it was not possible they were to be expelled to settlements beyond the Urals; a mere residue of the population was to be kept as a pool of semi-educated slaves, their education limited to a little reading and writing, and counting up to ten. "Sub-human" or useless human beings, such as Jews and gipsies, were to be eliminated.

They had already begun to implement these plans in west Prussia where seven hundred and fifty peasants had been driven out to make way for incoming German families; now they began to do the same in central Poland. Within a year they had cleared over three hundred villages with unspeakable lack of humanity. The whole world later heard of the massacre which took place in the Czech village of Lidice in reprisal for the murder of SS General Heydrich; and of Oradour-sur-Glane, the French village whose inhabitants were burned to death. But such massacres were commonplace in Poland, and few outside that country have been told of it.

This "pacification" of more than three hundred Polish villages is a statistic that numbs the mind. Yet even that was only part of the horror. Poland, wrote one historian, became "the home of humanity's holocaust, an archipelago of death-factories and camps, the scene of executions, pacifications and exterminations which surpassed anything so far documented in the history of mankind".[4]

The concentration camps for political and racial enemies of the Reich, which now proliferated throughout Poland, soon became the setting for wholesale slaughter. Life expectancy for a working inmate of Auschwitz, for example, was three months: many were simply killed on arrival. The very name of Auschwitz became synonymous with horror, the distilled essence of man's inhumanity to man. Irena G., a former Polish inmate there, will remember for ever what she saw on the morning after her arrival:

> It was a beautiful morning and as I came out of the barracks opposite the crematoria the sun was shining on what I took to be a pile of firewood. When I drew closer, I could see that in fact it was a huge heap of human bodies waiting to be shovelled into the ovens. As I stood there, dazed with horror, I found myself looking into a pair of imploring eyes, and realised that some of these pathetic "corpses" were still alive. They were putting the sick as well as the dead on those piles.

Like many other survivors of Auschwitz, Irena speaks of "a sky without birds". How could there have been birds, she asks. "There was nothing for them to eat. We prisoners had devoured every last blade of grass, every worm . . ."

The one ray of light was that the two tormentors were now at each other's throats. To the Poles in the eastern territories, the rout of the Russians was welcome; and to the deportees it brought an unexpected release. For the Soviet Union now became devotedly anti-Nazi, and what had once been denounced as the "imperialist war" had now been transmogrified into the "Great Patriotic War", in which the Russians' own survival was at stake. Stalin reached an agreement with General Sikorski, leader of the Polish government which since 1940 had been functioning in exile from London, made up of representatives of *all* the recognised pre-war political parties.

An amnesty was granted for the (non-existent) crimes of the deportees, and Stalin called on all Poles in the USSR to volunteer for a new Polish army unit which he hoped to incorporate into the Red Army. General Anders was released from the infamous Lubjanka prison in Moscow to lead it against the Germans. Thousands poured out of the slave-labour camps in the north and rushed south. Czesław Miłosz wrote: "The corpses of these ragged beggars littered the streets of the cities of south-eastern Russia, and out of the totally exhausted, half-dead people who survived the trek, an army was formed."[5]

Ludka L. and her family could scarcely believe their good fortune when they received the documents declaring them to be free. Eager to do something, anything, they joined the rush to the south in search of the new Army. Ludka's sixteen-year-old brother, Marian, eagerly joined up. They never saw him again; he died at Monte Cassino, fighting the Germans.

Stalin's hopes of bringing this Polish Army under his control came to nothing. It was the London government-in-exile which assumed control. In this lay the seeds of future trouble, for in Stalin's eyes, this was the army of the class enemy, and one day he would declare all who fought in it to be "enemies of the people".* The accusation would tragically blight the lives of their brothers, sisters, uncles and cousins who had remained behind in Poland.

* In March 1942, after much stalling and prevarication on the part of the Soviet authorities, Anders' army, together with the families of the fighting men, crossed into Persia, from where General Anders joined up with another Polish brigade to form the Second Corps. These men fought with distinction alongside the British Army in North Africa. In the ranks of Montgomery's Eighth Army, the Poles fought and died at Gazala, Tobruk, Monte Cassino, Ancona and Bologna. The Second Corps, together with the Polish Armed Forces which were already in the West, made a massive contribution to the Allied cause, one that ought never to be forgotten or undervalued. In the Battle of Britain of 1940, twenty per cent of the RAF's fighter pilots were Polish airmen.

An alarming discovery was then made. Among all the thousands of deportees flocking south, there was no sign of the fifteen thousand Polish officers deported in 1939. These men were, for the most part, reserves, professional men in civilian life: doctors, teachers, scientists, businessmen regarded with special loathing by the NKVD. As the "cream of the class enemy",[6] they had been segregated from the other deportees and sent to three special camps in western Russia.

Two years later, in April 1943, four thousand, three hundred and twenty-one corpses were discovered by the Germans in Katyń Forest outside Smolensk. They were the officers from one of the three camps. Most had their hands tied behind their backs and a bullet in the back of their necks. Goebbels made propaganda out of the discovery; Russia hastened to accuse the Germans. But, whatever the record of Nazi bestiality, few believed that the Germans were guilty of this particular crime. The evidence (the summer uniforms worn by the murdered men; the age of the tiny saplings growing on the mass grave) all pointed to the deed having been done in April 1940 when the area was still in Russian hands, rather than in the winter of 1941 when the Germans had conquered it.

Because no one has ever admitted to the crime, it has remained a great unsolved mystery, a festering interrogation mark over future relations between Poland and Russia. The fate of the other eleven thousand officers can still only be guessed at. But few people doubt that a realistic search would bring to light other Katyńs.

*   *   *

The Jewish community was already wasting away from terror and near-starvation in the ghettos. In Warsaw, on 4th May, 1942, Chaim Kaplan wrote in his diary: "The hour of twilight is harder to bear than the hour of total darkness. We are on the eve of great events – perhaps decisive ones."[7]

On 30th May he wrote: ". . . outside – annihilation; inside – terror. Woe unto us, for we are lost. You are certain that the death sentences have been drawn up; it is merely a matter of awaiting your turn – your turn to die. Perhaps it will come tonight, perhaps in a few more nights, but you will not escape your fate."

As Jewish settlements all over Poland were being wiped out, their inhabitants murdered, Jews from other cities were being driven into the already bursting ghetto of Warsaw. By July 1942 the deportations from Warsaw had already begun, and Kaplan's diary becomes more and more anguished:

27 July . . . the ghetto has turned into an inferno. Men have become beasts . . . People are being hunted down in the streets like animals in the forest . . .

1 August: Families become frantic. Where will you go? What can you save? What first, what last? They begin to pack bundles in haste and fear, with trembling hands and feet which refuse to do their bidding and to take their belongings outside, for they no longer have a home. Hundreds of women and swollen infants rend the heavens with their cries. The sick are taken outside in their beds, babies in their cradles, old men and women half-naked and barefoot . . .

On that day alone ten thousand people were deported from the ghetto. Jewish Warsaw was in its last agony – the death camps were operating at peak capacity. In April 1943, in a final act of glorious heroism, the survivors of the ghetto went down fighting, as once their ancestors had fought at Masada. Seven thousand Jews were killed in that Ghetto Rising – its fifty-six thousand survivors were transported to instant death at the Treblinka Camp outside Warsaw. Hope died. The insurgents sent a last accusing message to the world outside: "The world is silent. The world *knows* (it is inconceivable that it should not) and stays silent . . . This silence is astonishing and horrifying."[7]

The accusation of silence – and worse – is today often levelled against the Poles; and in some cases the charges are undoubtedly true. There were fanatical anti-semites among them, and there is appalling evidence that some of them rejoiced in this butchery of the Jews. But it is tragically unfair to blame the majority. One woman in Warsaw must surely speak for thousands of decent ordinary Poles when she recalls her horror at what was done: "For me and for everyone I knew, these things put an end, once and forever, to whatever anti-Jewish feeling we had had. I for one felt ashamed even to be alive in a world where such things happened."

People travelling through the ghetto area in sealed trams would throw food parcels out of the tram windows. One woman who worked in a packing factory whose windows overlooked the ghetto also threw out parcels when she had anything to put in them. "It wasn't much," she admits, "but there wasn't much to give. The Jews were starving. But we Poles were not far from starving either."

In providing any help at all to the stricken Jews, every Pole put his life at risk. It is not generally realised that Poland was the only Nazi-occupied country in which even to offer a Jew a glass of water merited instant death – not only for the offender but for his or her entire family too. In the face of such appalling retribution, who can stand in judgment on those Poles who turned away? The amazing thing, however, is that thousands of Poles took the risk, and paid the penalty. If between fifty and a hundred thousand Jews survived four years of Nazi occupation in Poland, it is because many were hidden by individual Poles or by religious orders throughout Poland. Many others actually survived the concentration camps.

Those Poles who were guilty of betraying Jews to the Gestapo were invariably sentenced to death by the courts set up by the Home Army resistance groups, and the sentences were faithfully executed. When Jews were betrayed in this way, not only they but the Polish family sheltering them were shot.

The Home Army resistance movement set up special units to help Jews, and organised various escape routes, a difficult feat with the Gestapo always in evidence. "We got hundreds of children out through underground sewers," says a Home Army man whose home for four years was in the vast Kampinos forest outside Warsaw. "I wish it could have been thousands. But we did our best."

When the Warsaw Ghetto rose in its last defiant stand, the Poles gave what help they could. Later they would be charged with not doing enough, with not, for example, providing the insurgents with enough guns. But they didn't have the guns. The Home Army at that period was not as self-sufficient as it later became; and the only ammunition at their disposal was: what the British managed to send them; what they had managed to save from the September 1939 campaign; and the little they were able to manufacture for themselves. Very occasionally a Polish resistance fighter would manage to persuade a friendly German to supply them with guns; but such an arrangement was dangerous, and discovery always meant death. "Would it have helped," mused a Polish woman, "if all of Warsaw had risen then, in support of the ghetto? I honestly don't think so. The result would have been the same. It might have taken a little longer, that's all."

Outside the ghetto area, Warsaw was surviving, but only just. While the men fought in the Home Army, the women worked to help them and to keep starvation from their families. Not only starvation but fear. "A ring at the door and the sight of the police after curfew terrified us. We were never free of fear." But, afraid or not, they were utterly convinced that one day the Germans would be driven out and Poland would once again belong to the Poles. Faith in the future was strong. The churches were fuller than ever they had been before the war. "For my generation," a young woman said, "it was the time when our religious faith was reborn."

[1] Quoted by Norman Davies in *God's Playground, A History of Poland*, Volume II, Clarendon Press, Oxford, 1984.

[2] Czesław Miłosz, *The Captive Mind*, Chapter 4, Secker & Warburg, 1953.

[3] Nicholas Bethell, *The War Hitler Won*, Allen Lane, Penguin, 1972.

[4] Norman Davies, *op. cit.*

[5] Czesław Miłosz, *op. cit.*

[6] Norman Davies, *op. cit.* Chapter 20: "Golgota, Poland in the Second World War."

[7] *Scroll of Agony: The Warsaw Diary of Chaim H. Kaplan*, Hamish Hamilton, 1966. Found intact on a farm outside Warsaw twenty years after the events it describes.

Reference has been made in this chapter to three papers given at an international Conference on Polish–Jewish Relations held at Somerville College, Oxford, in September 1984:

I. "The Problem of Polish Anti-Semitism," Jerzy Turowicz.

II. "Polish Society in Confrontation with Jewish Fugitives in Hiding 1942–1944," Shmuel Krakowski.

III. "Polish–Jewish Relations in Occupied Poland 1939–1945," Władysław Bartoszewski.

2 WAŁĘSA

For Freedom's battle once begun,
Bequeath'd by bleeding Sire to Son,
Though baffled oft is ever won.

Byron: *The Giaour*

The young Wałęsa who had been deported by the Russians after the 1830 Rising had made the most of his opportunities in France; he had married and bought some land there. But as time passed, the position of the Polish *émigrés* in France changed. Towards the end of the 1870s, as a result of international agreements reached between France and the Russian, Prussian and Austro-Hungarian occupiers of Poland, it became clear, beyond the faintest shadow of doubt, that Poland could not gain her freedom in the foreseeable future. From then on, France no longer made even a pretence of support for the Polish cause. "The Poles in emigration grew older and died," says one historian.[1] Some remained in Paris, brooding on Poland's lost greatness and dreaming impossible dreams. But in some, disappointment bred a new realism. They returned home to Poland, there to work, quietly but doggedly, for the creation of a free Poland at some time in the far-distant future.

It was the son and grandson of that earlier Wałęsa who now returned to Russian-occupied Poland to look for a suitable place to live. The father and his son, whose name was Mateusz, concentrated their search on the area between the Vistula River and the vast Kujawy plain, an area to whose myriad tiny villages the Poles give the collective title of Dobrzyń. "The landscape," wrote Halina Mirowska,[2] over a century later, "is full of Mazovian melancholy which foreigners reared on Chopin call Polishness. White ducks dive sleepily on overgrown ponds, storks, willows weeping into the ditches, and isolated farms among dusty raspberry patches."

It is a lonely area, miles from any large town. "I think my great-great-grandfather wanted to be as far away from the towns as possible," speculates Lech Wałęsa's sister, Izabela. And far away from the secret police who would no doubt be aware of his return. Izabela agrees: "He seems to have been afraid of someone or something, and only in the depths of the country could he feel safe."

Mateusz Wałesa's father bought the tiny hamlet of Popowo, about fifty hectares, and set himself up as a gentleman farmer. (There are several villages called Popowo in Poland, but this one is too small to feature on any map.) He was minor gentry – not a great landowner, but grand enough to ride to church in his own horse-drawn carriage. A pious man, he walked his fields each day, rosary in hand. The village inn which he owned and rented out did a thriving business, because in those days the busy trade routes from the Baltic ports to the south of Poland ran through Popowo, and the traffic was constant.

Every so often, Mateusz and his father returned to France for a visit. But Poland was now their home, and after a while the visits ceased. When Mateusz married, he had two sons. One of these became one of the first Polish Communists and was disowned by his father. The other son, Jan, Lech Wałesa's grandfather, inherited the whole estate. Jan was something of a legend in the village. He had twelve sons and twelve daughters; was reputed to have belonged to a Polish military organisation, and to have sheltered Józef Piłsudski, the future Marshal of Poland, in his house. He was a well-informed man, who would not burn a newspaper until he had read it from cover to cover, though he always tore off a corner of it to roll round his tobacco for a cigarette. The First World War rolled over the Kujawy plain, though the destruction there was less than elsewhere. The final outcome of the war, however, the rebirth of Poland in 1918, must have been a deeply moving experience for Jan Wałesa.

When Jan died, the Popowo property was divided into twenty-four neat but very small parcels. Poland has no law of primogeniture, whereby the eldest son inherits everything, and the others learn to fend for themselves. In a system in which every member of a gentry family inherited *some*thing, the villages of Poland were in those days full of proud but utterly pauperised gentry.

Like his brothers and sisters, Jan's son, Bolesław, who was to become the father of Lech, farmed his inadequate morsel of land. It was not only inadequate but very poor, and nothing would grow there but wheat and potatoes. In addition, he kept a few pigs, two cows and some hens; and travelled weekly to market to sell his butter, milk and eggs. Bolesław, usually known as Bolek, and his brother Stanisław, had learned carpentry from their father, and

43

it stood them in good stead. They were skilled craftsmen, the best for miles around, and were in much demand by local farmers, for building barns and cowsheds.

Bolek married a girl from another Dobrzyń village, Feliksa Kamińska, whose family had lived for generations in the area. Her father, Leopold Kamiński, was a peasant farmer, poor but extremely intelligent, and, despite his lack of education, well-read and a mine of information. In his spare time, Leopold kept the parish records up to date.

After their marriage, Bolek and Feliksa settled down in what was little more than a cowshed on Bolek's share of the Popowo land – a mere hectare and a half (about three acres), barely enough to feed the two of them, and even more woefully inadequate when the children began to arrive. When the war came to blast their lives to hell, the couple had two children, Izabela and Edward, with a third, Stanisław, on the way.

Their part of Poland was incorporated into the German Reich and systematically stripped of all traces of Polishness. Place-names were Germanised, Polish flags burned, Polish books and libraries destroyed, and Polish schools closed. In the country, only the poor farms – like that of Bolek – were left in the hands of the Poles. All larger farms were handed over to German farmers – and the local women were required to work for them on demand. Feliksa Wałęsa (and even her small daughter, Izabela), worked for two farmers, by name Proch and Krempitz. On the whole, the German farmers in this area were kind enough; and only one of them seems to have inspired terror.

But the peasants had to provide food for the Germans. Everything they produced had to be delivered to the Germans at a stipulated time and a stipulated place. In exchange they were given black bread, sugar, oil for their lamps, coupons to exchange for clothes. They were not allowed to keep any of their own grain. If they did so (and most did), they would grind it in a coffee grinder to avoid detection. Possession of a grindstone or quern for grinding wheat was punishable by hanging, or by being sent to a concentration camp. The same fate awaited those foolhardy enough to keep a pig, chickens or geese for their own use. To kill a food-animal was a capital offence.

And if the peasants were unable, by their own efforts, to fulfil the quota set for them, they simply had to acquire the stuff somehow on the open market. No excuse was accepted.

Almost without exception, as in every part of Poland, the peasants either belonged to or supported the Home Army partisans, who lived in the forests by day and came out at night to collect food and sabotage the German communication lines. In sheltering and feeding them, the peasants ran almost as much danger as the partisans themselves, and arrests were frequent. A mass grave for twenty-four unnamed Poles in Sobowo churchyard where the Wałesa family worshipped, tells its own sombre story.

Izabela Wałesa (now Młynska) recalls putting out food for the partisans at dead of night. She would be given bread and meat by her mother and told to place them under a certain tree. In the morning they would be gone. The exercise was almost routine for the child. But there is one day in particular which she will never forget. Her father's brother, Stanisław, had been deported to a labour camp in Germany, but had managed to escape, wearing a stolen German uniform. In the late summer of 1943, he had reached Popowo and hidden in Bolek's barn. Someone – perhaps because of the German uniform – must have informed; and next day the Gestapo came. They did not find Stanisław, who had already gone to join the partisans in the forest. He must have gone in the German uniform, since they did not find that either. (It must have been tricky explaining that away to the partisans, and it is a wonder he was not shot on sight.)

But the Germans did not go away empty-handed. Failing to find one brother, they took the other. Bolek was taken away for questioning. At his interrogation, he was beaten so badly that his skull was damaged. Then he was sent off to forced labour, leaving his wife, twenty-six-year-old Feliksa, far advanced in pregnancy, to look after the farm and the family single-handed.

At 9 a.m. on 27th September, 1943, her fourth child, a boy, was born. Stubbornly asserting his Polish heritage, she gave him the old Slavonic name, Lech, after the legendary founder of the Polish race. Perhaps because of the circumstances surrounding his birth, perhaps because of the poverty and hopelessness into which he was born, he would always be her favourite child.

To Feliksa's sorrow, the baby could not be christened in her own church at Sobowo, four kilometres away across the fields. For the parish priest, Father Zaremba, like most of the other priests in the area, had been sent to a concentration camp and had been killed there in 1941. Instead, the christening took place, on 3rd November, at the big church of Mokowo, and a neighbour lent the family a horse and cart for the occasion.

Lech Wałesa would never know his father. Bolek, seriously injured after his beating, was sent to a labour camp at Młyniec near Toruń, and put to work digging trenches and building bridges.

The work was beyond his strength, and he made little pretence at doing his share. When the job was done, and the other prisoners were moved to another site, Bolek was left behind, to endure the freezing winter of 1944–5 in an unheated barracks, with no more than a sheet to cover him at night. "Can you imagine: to lie on the bed under a single sheet in that cold? Your hair froze to the wall!"[3] It was a death sentence, and Bolek knew it.

[1] *The History of Poland since 1863*, ed. R. F. Leslie. C.U.P., 1980.
[2] Halina Mirowska, *Lechu*, Glos Publications, New York, 1982.
[3] Neal Ascherson, *The Book of Lech Wałesa*, Chapter 1, Penguin, Allen Lane, 1981.

3 THE EDGE OF THE CYCLONE (1943–5)

Communism for us is not what it is for the great majority of people in the world, an idea, a project, good or bad, true or false, orientated towards the future. It is a reality. A reality which no one in the country chose; a reality imposed on us by force against our will and in spite of our struggles.

Bohdan Cywiński, 1984

The Germans pressed on towards Moscow. But, like Napoleon before them, they had overreached themselves. The six-month battle for Stalingrad proved to be the turning-point of the war. It marked the beginning of the end of the Third Reich; and it was now that to all intents and purposes the post-war period began, as Stalin took out of cold storage his earlier plans for the subjugation of central and Eastern Europe.

Already he had re-activated the Polish Communist Party, which he had determinedly destroyed in 1936. A three-man team, chosen from comrades who had survived the purges in the Soviet Union, was parachuted into German-occupied Poland. In January 1942 this group established itself in Warsaw under the name of the Polish Workers' Party. They were soon to be joined by Władysław Gomułka and others who had never left Poland. Avoiding the name "Communist", so detested by the majority of Poles, and all mention of class war or revolution, the group appealed for a broad national front to defeat the Nazi invaders. For the most part, their appeal fell on deaf ears. The Poles, who already had a perfectly satisfactory resistance movement, were well aware that only since the Soviet Union had been attacked had the Communists (whether they used the name or not) been willing to take a part in the struggle for freedom. By June 1942 only four thousand had joined them, plus three thousand partisans in the Communist militia, the People's Guard.

The Polish Workers' Party continued its conciliatory stance right through 1942 and for the first part of 1943. But after the discoveries in the Katyń Forest, followed by the London-based Polish government's demand for an International Red Cross enquiry, Stalin broke off relations with the Poles, and the Party went on to the offensive. It became stridently hostile to the London government and turned its People's Guard into a People's Army intended to be a direct rival to the London-led Home Army.

By the middle of 1943 it was abundantly clear that Poland would eventually be "liberated" by the Red Army and not by the West. In a bid to keep control of the Polish Communists, Stalin now sent a Polish-born NKVD security police official, Bolesław Bierut, to Poland to keep the Party on the right pro-Soviet lines. Bierut immediately clashed with the Polish leader, Gomułka, who wanted to establish a socialism specifically geared to Polish needs and who, for that purpose, wished to seek help from other left-wing parties. To Bierut such considerations were irrelevant: if support was not forthcoming, then coercion would have to be used.

The Communists now set up a National Council for the Homeland, which claimed to be "the real political representative of the Polish nation", qualified to take power and establish a government when the moment came. But to Gomułka's disappointment, the regular left-wing parties would have nothing to do with it.

Stalin was worried both by the Polish Workers' Party's conspicuous lack of success and by its unwelcome spirit of independence. As an insurance, he set up a rival, more trustworthy, body of Polish Communists in the Soviet Union itself. This group, the Union of Polish Patriots, immediately called for a Polish military force under its control.

So the Kościuszko division of the Red Army, under General Berling, came into being. It was Stalin's own, unlike the Polish armies in the West. For it, he had unearthed Soviet citizens of Polish origin; and large numbers of Polish refugees and deportees, who had not been able to reach Anders' army in time, and who now saw this new unit as their only hope of ever escaping from Russia. Polish Jews, whom Stalin judged unlikely to have much sympathy for the Polish population as a whole, represented by far the largest single group of deportees, and were drafted in large numbers into the political and security sections. Together with the pseudo-Poles (many of them Russians or Ukrainians drafted in their thousands, though they could not speak a word of Polish) and with the Polish Communists who had settled in the Soviet Union after 1917, these inexperienced "soldiers" were to enter Poland with the Red Army and act as a prop for the pro-Soviet government to be established there. Over half of the officers had previously served in the Red Army, and all the highest ranks were filled by Russians. The security police and the Union of Polish Patriots were in overall control. In the ranks of this army was Wojciech Jaruzelski. His father, an agricultural engineer, and his mother, Wanda, had disappeared somewhere in Soviet Russia, and Wojciech had been working as a labourer. In the circumstances, the creation of Berling's Army must have offered him a heaven-sent opportunity of securing a future for himself. He was enrolled into the army as an "orphan soldier".

The people of eastern Poland watched in horror as the Russian tide advanced. They wanted to be rid of the Germans, it is true; but they had always recognised that the enemy had two faces, and that the threat from the east was, if anything, more to be feared. They had no illusions. After all, they had only recently emerged from a century and a half of Russian domination, and memories were still raw: "With the Russians there is no hope. Only the dead hand of oppression, the unrelieved weight of Russian insensibility . . . Do it their way or die . . . Russians can make an entire nation a tomb. They're geniuses at building tombs."[1]

The nightmare began to take shape. On 2nd January, 1944, the Red Army crossed the pre-1939 frontier of Poland, which Stalin was also laying claim to. From this moment the Polish Home Army partisans launched their long-prepared Operation "Tempest". Believing that the Red Army intended to co-operate with them in the liberation of Poland, large groups of Polish partisans (the Home Army had 300,000 members and the peasant battalions at least half that number) began attacking German garrisons and freeing large areas of the country. In these towns and villages they set up a Polish administration. The partisans' success enabled the Russians to advance with lightning speed, encountering little opposition from the already demoralised Germans.

But the Poles' joy was short-lived. NKVD units had entered Poland with the Red Army and immediately on arrival set up a Polish section, the UB security forces. Their only task was to arrest anyone associated in any way with pre-war Poland, especially those who had fought in the underground resistance. All those who had recently assumed administrative duties in the liberated villages were arrested. And the partisan units, far from finding the Russians grateful for their assistance, were disarmed, arrested and sent to concentration camps in the Soviet Union. Many senior officers were executed on the spot.

When an area had been thoroughly "liberated", Soviet-style, hardly anyone was left who might be capable of independent thought. In his novel, *Seizure of Power*, Czesław Miłosz recounts

the feelings of a young man who has returned home in this way
with the conscript Polish army:

> My country. Everything on a small scale, clutching at bits of land –
> small fields, small gardens, narrow boundary strips, a peasant with his
> only horse, an old woman with her cow, an inn, a village shop,
> neighbours leaning against fences, small girls with bare red feet driving
> geese – a world innocent of mechanised warfare and books on political
> theory . . .

> What did the peasants think? Their land had been crushed by tanks
> built in the Ruhr; they had known terror and man-hunts and blue-
> eyed, fair-haired children taken from their mothers by force . . . Now
> at last they saw tanks built beyond the Urals. Everything reached
> them from the outside: a punishment, a calamity, the edge of a cyclone
> whose centre was always somewhere else, somewhere far away in an
> unknown country or in the minds of unknown people.[2]

The Red Army's summer offensive swept all before it. But the
Stalin-inspired Polish Workers' Party was having much less joy,
as neither the peasants nor the political parties in the liberated
areas would succumb to its honeyed promises. Then on 21st July,
1944, the Red Army captured Chelm near Lublin, which lay 130
miles west of the Polish border as the Poles knew it, but which in
Stalin's eyes was where Poland began. Once again, the glowing
promises were dropped in favour of coercion. On the following
day, without so much as a nod in the direction of the populace,
and without consulting any of the other interested parties, Stalin
set up a Polish Committee of National Liberation, composed
entirely of Communists and fellow-travellers, though the fact was
carefully disguised and it was made to look like a genuine, Popular
Front government, with Bolesław Bierut and Władysław Gomułka
at its head. Posters proclaiming the Committee's Manifesto had
been printed in Moscow beforehand. The Committee's spectacular lack of popular support seemed not to matter, as anyone who
opposed it was promptly dealt with by the security forces.

Right up to 29th July, Moscow Radio was calling on the citizens
of Warsaw to rise, and on 30th July a Soviet military station called
them to arms: "People of Warsaw, strike at the Germans. Help
the Red Army cross the Vistula." Soviet planes over Warsaw
dropped leaflets urging an immediate uprising. By now, six million
Poles had been "liberated" by the Russians. The Home Army
resistance forces in the city, under the leadership of General
Bór-Komorowski, had a terrible decision to make. It was already

clear that Warsaw would make a last stand against the Russians, in order to preserve some sort of base for a future Polish state. The agonising question was: when? But, with the Red Army already at the gates, there was little freedom of manoeuvre. The order was given to start Operation Tempest in Warsaw.

In the first days of August the Red Army and Berling's Polish Army crossed the Vistula in several places south of Warsaw, and then suddenly came to a halt. Few people today doubt that they did so for political reasons. Communist historians claim that the Red Army met heavy German resistance hereabouts and was forced on to the defensive. This claim does not bear much examination: the Russian forces were many times larger than the Germans', and the German defence lines were weak. When, on 1st August, the Rising actually broke out, the insurgents gained some considerable successes in the first few days, liberating most of the city in fact, apart from a few isolated pockets of stiff German resistance. If the Soviets had wished to, they could easily have invaded at that time. But, from the moment that the Rising began, the radio stations went quiet, as did the Russian tanks and guns. They simply stayed on the outskirts of Warsaw, while the citizens, despite their initial success, were systematically butchered by the Nazi troops and the city itself was razed to the ground.

Even at this eleventh hour, the Home Army counted on some sort of help from Britain and America. But the Western allies dared not offend Russia. Relations between them had deteriorated, but Russia's help was still believed necessary for the final defeat of Germany and the continuing war with Japan. At a meeting in Teheran in November 1943, the three wartime allies had already agreed in principle to divide Europe into separate "spheres of influence"; and on a new outline of the Polish–Soviet frontier, which would ratify Russia's present gains and which was to all intents and purposes the same as the Nazi–Soviet demarcation line drawn up in 1939. The Poles did not know it yet, but Britain and America had already left them to their fate. Apart from a couple of attempted parachute drops (see next page), no help was forthcoming to the Warsaw insurgents from the West.

After a few days' silence, Moscow spoke again but this time with a very different voice. On 6th August, an article in the Soviet army newspaper made the absurd claim that the Home Army insurgents were collaborating with the Germans! On the 8th, Radio Moscow said that it was not the Home Army but the Communist People's Army which had sacrificed itself in the slaughter – in spite of the fact that there were only six hundred or so Communist fighters in Warsaw, compared with over forty thousand Home Army soldiers.

Beleaguered and desperate, the people of Warsaw continued to hold out: without water, gas, electricity, food or medicines, reduced to eating dogs and stray pigeons to stay alive. A survivor has left this record:

> German bombers rampaged over the city day and night, burying the living beneath the rubble. People sought shelter from the air-raids in basements, but found no safety there; the Germans dragged them out and conducted mass-executions – of men, women and children. Everyone took part regardless of age or sex. People did not sleep, eat or wash for days on end. No one knew whether he'd be alive five minutes later. Corpses lay about in the streets and the stench of rotting bodies rose from the ruins.[3]

The odds were hopelessly unequal. In that last act of defiance over one hundred and fifty thousand died, and among them were the flower of Poland's youth, the young men and women who might have given leadership in a reborn Poland. Many others, regardless of whether they were resistance fighters or civilians, were rounded up and forced to march to Pruszków, a transit camp about thirty kilometres outside Warsaw, from where they were despatched to Auschwitz and other concentration camps in Poland or Germany. A woman civilian recalls bitterly: "They arrested my mother and me, and said we were bandits. Then they put us in cattle trucks and sent us to Ravensbrück. Well, I came out of there alive, but my mother didn't. She died in the camp at the age of fifty-five."

With some help from the West, in the shape of parachute drops of equipment – largely carried out by the Polish Air Force with much loss of life – the insurgents held out for sixty-three days. But with no help coming from outside, further resistance was hopeless. With despair they heard their commander, General Bór-Komorowski, give the order to surrender. Yet, though this decision was a painful one, the General had wrung one important concession from the Germans. Members of the beaten Home Army were to be treated not as bandits but as regular prisoners of war, in accordance with the Geneva Convention.

All this while, the Russians played a waiting game, watching impassively from the south bank of the river. "They wanted us to die," say the survivors, while, in spite of the official surrender, the Germans, on the express orders of Hitler himself, proceeded to the stone-by-stone demolition of what had been one of Europe's most beautiful cities. Other European cities suffered devastation; but what was done to Warsaw was without parallel. Many had not obeyed General Bór's instructions to come out and surrender to the Germans. They were still there, in their houses, when the Germans started on the final demolition – blowing up the houses, throwing flame throwers or cylinders of explosive gas into the cellars.

What remained was a smouldering moonscape of debris and ash, a graveyard of Polish dreams. When the vandals had done with Warsaw, they had destroyed not only some ninety per cent of the city, but also the nerve-centre of "the most widespread and determined of Europe's resistance movements".[4]

Stalin's ruthless determination had been clearly demonstrated. So too had the Western allies' helplessness. The shock to the survivors cannot be overestimated. They knew that it was all over, that the Communists had only to walk into the city and claim it. The Lublin Committee proclaimed itself the Provisional Government on 31st December, and within it the Polish Workers' Party was predominant. In January, Berling's First Polish Army, under its Russian command, took possession of the stricken shell of the capital, and staged a victory parade amid the ruins.[5]

When the Germans had gone, one hundred thousand people crossed the Vistula River to Warsaw, by boat or over makeshift temporary bridges. Some were returning from Germany, as the concentration and labour camps yielded up their victims; others from different parts of Poland. They came by cycle, by horse and cart, or on foot, walking barefoot and in rags towards what they could not recognise as Warsaw. No streets, no houses, no landmarks of any kind.

> We walked through the snow, with tears streaming down our cheeks, hoping to avoid the unexploded bombs [remembers a survivor], and wherever we looked, there was nothing but rubble and little wooden crosses in the dust. Then, through the curtain of snow, we saw a wisp of smoke and moved towards it. Some enterprising person had started a fire over some planks and was selling hot soup.

Ninety per cent of those who returned would have nowhere to go and no families to find, and a feature of that time was the countless little notes, left on stones or in the porches of surviving churches, giving information about where the writer was to be found.

The Nazis left, convinced that Warsaw would never rise again.

The city looked, as Bolesław Bierut observed, "as though a great earthquake had shattered it". Living in caves, like troglodytes, in holes in the ground, in ditches, sewers, underground tunnels and shelters; in wooden shacks or the staircases of demolished houses, without water or light, roofs, doors or cooking stoves; without transport, schools, hospitals, or communications of any kind, the people of Warsaw were consumed with the desire to rebuild their city as it had been.

But first the Army would have to defuse the bombs. The whole area was a minefield. And next the people must perform what for them was the most sacred of all duties. They gathered the ashes or remains of those who had been executed by the Gestapo, and gave them burial. Only when that was done, could the work of reconstruction begin.

They would rebuild the city. And for the first two years they would do it by clawing the earth with tiny shovels or with their bare hands. Wrapping their hands and feet in rags to keep out the bitter cold, with brick-dust silting up their mouths and noses, the inhabitants of Warsaw set to with incredible vitality. They gathered and sorted bricks, salvaged pieces of wood from charred window-frames. They dug up stones, levelled the earth and took away the rubble in horse-drawn carts. And beneath every heap of stones they would find a corpse.

And when they at last had some sort of roof over their heads, a shelter from the wind and rain, however makeshift, they would ask to rebuild the churches of Warsaw and the mediaeval buildings of its Old City.

[1] James A. Michener, *Poland*, Secker & Warburg, 1983 and Corgi Books.
[2] Czesław Miłosz, *The Seizure of Power*, Abacus, 1985.
[3] Anna Świrszczyńska in *Anthology of Post-War Polish Poetry*, selected and edited by Czesław Miłosz, University of California Press, third edition, 1983.
[4] M. K. Dziewanowski, *Poland in the Twentieth Century*, Columbia University Press, 1977.
[5] Because he attempted to help the Warsaw insurgents in September 1944, General Berling was hauled before his Russian superiors and sent to the Soviet Military Academy for "further education". His post was taken over by someone more "reliable".
Also: "Poland's Aftermath", article by Thomas Field in *Poland One*, 1/12.

4 TOWARDS A BETTER TOMORROW? (1945–7)

Many people were spiritually prepared to rebuild the system. Had it not been for their narrow atheism, Polish society with its cultural, historically democratic tendencies, would have been a most fertile field for a wise government to work on. Unfortunately, observation proved how little talent for social work this government had; how very much it relied on physical oppression and force. This in itself negated a good part of the positive results, since the people, oppressed, stood up in opposition even against many legitimate goals. If Marxism had come directly from the West, without Eastern intervention, it would undoubtedly have been accepted with greater trust.

Cardinal Stefan Wyszyński: *A Freedom Within*

Letters went out to the men who had fought in the West. "Your country is free. Come back and build the new Poland." But in May 1945, as the men from the Western armies returned, they found all too often that the homes they had left no longer existed. Many of the exiles in Britain and France were unable to return as their home towns and villages were now incorporated into Russia. The harvest of war had been bitter; the people were shattered. One fifth of the population of pre-war Poland had been killed, and of these almost ninety per cent had been shot, hanged, or murdered in the concentration camps. Six million, twenty-eight thousand Polish citizens dead, of whom three million were Jews. In spite of their magnificent resistance, the people had a crushing sense of failure.

"Do you know what it's like to be twenty-five and to find no one who knew you as a child?" The speaker, a returning soldier, had lost twenty-two members of his immediate family: parents, brothers and sisters, uncles, aunts, cousins, friends, all shot in 1940 in the house where they were celebrating a wedding.

Among the half-dead survivors of camps such as Auschwitz and Majdanek, Buchenwald or Ravensbrück, were the "guinea-pig" victims of medical experiments, people like Wanda P. who had bacteria injected into her legs and spine, and petrol into her veins. Or Małgosia K., a child of three subjected to such gross internal

55

experiments that she would spend most of her childhood in a hospital bed. Hanka L., a baby liberated from Auschwitz and delivered to an orphanage, was, like Małgosia, among the many who would never discover who they really were:

> I don't know exactly when I was born [she has said]. My mother was taken to Auschwitz and gave birth to me there. She died in the camp, and my father was executed. It seems from the camp archives that I had an older brother who died from typhus in the camp and it's thought that my family were previously in Majdanek camp. I was prisoner number . . . which was tattooed on my arm by the SS.

As Stalin's winter offensive of January 1945 drove the Germans out of their last footholds in western Poland – the territories they had incorporated into the Reich itself – it seemed as though the "liberators" were even more intent on terrorising the local population than on expelling the Germans. In these lands which were to be taken from Germany and given to Poland, the Russian army wreaked unbelievable havoc: "Arson, battery, murder, group-rapes and family suicides marked the passage of the liberating armies on a scale unparalleled elsewhere in Europe."[1]

The roads were jammed with refugees. The Russians plundered machinery from factories, cut down the dockyard cranes and sent them to the Soviet Union for scrap metal; they confiscated food from the peasants and removed railway works, locomotives and trains. Two weeks after the end of the war, Russian soldiers from the garrison at Lębork went on a drunken rampage and burned down the whole town. Danzig, once again called Gdańsk, was also effectively razed to the ground.

Old familiar landmarks had disappeared – Poland had suffered a sea-change. "Wherever we went," said a survivor of the camps, "it was as though we were in another country." The old territorial boundaries had changed and, enclosed now on three sides by Russia, Poland was effectively cut off from all contact with friendly countries. Her ethnic mix was reduced: the Byelo-Russians and Ukrainians had been absorbed by Russia; the Jews had vanished into the ovens*; her intelligentsia had been liquidated. The whole

---

* At the beginning of the 1950s, the Jews accounted for 0.2 per cent of Poland's population. A high percentage of Jews had returned from the Soviet Union in 1945 where they had spent the war years. These Jews were former inhabitants of Poland's eastern territories annexed by the Soviet Union in September 1939. This fact saved them from the gas chambers to which their fellow-Jews in Nazi-occupied areas were doomed. *See* Peter Raina: *Political Opposition in Poland, 1954–1977.*

country was a seething mass of migrants, as the hordes of refugees, expellees and repatriates clogged the railways and roads. As millions of hapless Germans fled westward, millions of equally hapless Poles trekked from the east to take their place. Marek Korowicz, returning from the West, described the nightmare journey by slow train from Gdynia and a meeting with some of these refugees:

> At one station we talked for a couple of hours with these unfortunates. Their transport had been on the way for two weeks. For two weeks, women and children, old people and countless adult men had been travelling in cattle trucks on straw. Half of these trucks had no roof. In the cold, rain and snow, people were huddling under sheets; emaciated children were crying; old people, lying on the straw in hopeless apathy. They had to survive as best they could.[2]

In this climate of unimaginable misery, Yalta was perhaps the bitterest pill of all. For it was at Yalta in the Crimea that Poland was handed over to the Soviet Union. In February 1945 the Big Three, Roosevelt, Churchill and Stalin, had met at Yalta to consolidate the understandings reached at Teheran about the fate of Europe and to re-establish the balance of power. Stalin had the upper hand, since Roosevelt believed that he still needed his help against Japan (the A-Bomb had not yet been tested) and did not want to antagonise him. Churchill had his hands tied: "Uncle Joe" Stalin was popular with the British public and there would be an outcry if he was thwarted now. Besides, the West was impatient with Poland for putting "unnecessary" difficulties in the way of a post-war settlement with Russia. In Britain this resentment was increased by a totally unfounded belief that enough British money and energy had already been spent on Poland. The stark truth that, after her initial gesture of declaring war, Britain had not struck one blow in Poland's defence was conveniently forgotten, as was the enormous contribution made by the Poles to the British war effort. (When the Victory in Europe parade marched through London in May, the Poles did not even receive an invitation to attend.) Russia, who had in any case "liberated" most of Poland by this time and was not intending to leave, was felt to have earned a stake in Poland, a fair compensation for her own undoubted sufferings during the war. Westerners did not know or care to recall that, in the course of that war, the Russians had sent over a quarter of a million Poles from the captured eastern provinces to their deaths.

Ignoring the undeniable fact that Russians and Poles are as

different from each other as the proverbial chalk and cheese – the Russians with their long experience of despotic tyranny and their blindly obedient people, the Poles with their fanatical love of independence – Roosevelt and Churchill handed Poland over. In all their history the Russians had never known freedom; the Poles had valued it above all else. Marxist-Leninism would strike at the roots of everything the Poles held most sacred.

Stalin appeared to make a concession to his allies by agreeing to "free and unfettered" elections in Poland, as soon as she had straightened herself out; and by allowing representatives of the London Poles to take part in the government and to be eligible for election. To be fair, Roosevelt and Churchill did not understand the enormity of the threat to Europe's freedom, nor realise that when Stalin talked of "democracy" he did not even know what it meant. They trusted Stalin to be a man of honour on their terms – though Roosevelt died a disillusioned man and Churchill later wondered how history would judge his naïvety. "The Eagle should permit the small birds to sing," he had suggested to Stalin, and foolishly had hoped that the small birds of Eastern Europe would soon be at full throttle.

In spite of Russian claims to the contrary, only a small minority of Poles welcomed the Red Army with undiluted enthusiasm. The huge relief that the Nazis were on the run was tempered by dark fears for the future. "We had gone on telling ourselves," said a survivor, "that if only the Germans would go, then we'd be free. But the day the Russians came meant the end of hope." Irena G., escaping from the death march out of Auschwitz camp*, heard the news as she was hiding in a farmer's hayloft:

> Two soldiers wearing Polish uniforms but with slant-eyed Russian faces, came to the farm, yelling at us to come out. "You're free. The Russians have come," they shouted. I came out of the barn where I'd been hiding, and stood looking at them, tears streaming down my face. But they weren't tears of relief. "No, we're not free," were the words I wanted to say, but dared not.

At the Peace Conference at Potsdam in July 1945, the decisions made at Teheran and Yalta were finally ratified. The Soviet Union was allowed to keep the Polish eastern territories which she had annexed. This meant almost half of Poland's pre-war territory,

---

* All those who were able to walk were evacuated from Auschwitz before the Red Army could arrive. They were destined for other concentration camps in Germany itself, but many of them died on the way.

and included the cities of Wilno and Lwów, which had played a large part in her cultural and religious history. Compensation was given to Poland in the shape of a huge chunk of territory taken from Germany: land which had once been Polish but which was now overwhelmingly German in population. The Oder–Neisse frontier was accepted as Poland's western border, and the country found itself shifted bodily two hundred miles westward.

With the signing of the peace, the legitimate Polish government in London was written out of existence and the Communist-dominated Provisional government was given legal status as the Polish Government of National Unity, with Bierut as acting President and Gomułka as first Vice-Premier. To keep Britain and America sweet, Mikołajczyk, the left-wing Prime Minister of the exiled London government, with two other London Poles and two non-Communists from Poland, were allowed to join the sixteen hand-picked Communists in the government. But Gomułka made sure that they knew the score: he had no intention of sharing power with them in any real sense:

> . . . We will never surrender the power we have seized . . . If a government of national unity cannot be established, perhaps several hundred people will be killed, but this will not frighten us . . . We will ruthlessly destroy all reactionary bandits. You may cry that the blood of the Polish people will flow, that the NKVD is governing Poland, but it will not divert us.[3]

If free elections had been held in Poland, the vote would have gone overwhelmingly to Mikołajczyk and his Peasants' Party. For Polish society was ready and even eager for some kind of Socialism. Even before the war it was becoming more radical, and there is a distinct chance that, if Hitler had not invaded when he did, there would have been a social upheaval in the country. The war had taken the process further. The Nazis had broken up the old estates and destroyed or scattered the gentry who had owned them. Scarcely anyone was still in touch with his pre-war source of income. Shared danger and suffering in the Occupation years had washed away the old class distinctions and bred a comradeship between the different social groups. As a result, there was now a deep longing to see this comradeship given a lasting political expression. "There was a wonderful unity during those years of Occupation. Anybody at all who spoke Polish was simply a member of the family," says Basia N. Like most countries in war-ravaged Europe, Poland in 1945 was experiencing a lurch to the left, and a real longing for change.

The Communists lacked the imagination to channel this general yearning successfully. Had their policies not been applied by force (and by Russian force at that), matters might have been different. But to the average Pole there was nothing to choose between the Soviet invaders of their country and the Polish lackeys who did their bidding. Gomułka was heard to complain that in the eyes of the Poles, the Party was nothing but an extension of the Soviet secret police. The Polish security force had, in fact, been strengthened and brought under the control of the Party. Repression of political opponents had been stepped up. It seemed that coercion was the only political method that this government understood.

Many of those who now returned from service in the Polish or British Air Forces in the West were arrested as spies and given long prison sentences. But the most shameful treatment was reserved for the resistance fighters of the Home Army. When this army was disbanded by its own High Command in January 1945, the partisans found themselves outlaws. These men and women who had spent years fighting the Nazis and who in normal circumstances might have expected a heroes' return, were now accused of being German spies and of sabotaging the Russian war effort. They were the class enemy, murderers, fascists, traitors, and an instruction had gone out to the UB (Polish security police) chiefs that they must be ruthless in liquidating them. "The Home Army, dribbling reactionary dwarf," sneered a poster.

Thousands of those who came out of the forests and voluntarily laid down their arms were arrested forthwith and deported to the Gulags of Soviet Russia or to concentration camps left empty by the fleeing Germans. In March 1945, a brand-new camp was set up by the NKVD at Rembertów near Warsaw, a transit camp whence prisoners were sent to Russia. In this year alone, fifty thousand Poles were sent to camps inside Russia. Conditions were terrible. In one transport of fourteen thousand prisoners, over three hundred died on the month-long journey to the Arctic. And with supreme cynicism, the Russians frequently put Home Army fighters in the same prison cell as Nazi murderers. Kazimierz Moczarski, for example, a young Home Army lieutenant, shared a cell with Jurgen Stroop, the butcher of the Warsaw Ghetto. Both were equally described as "war criminals".[4]

In June, sixteen leaders of the Home Army, who had been tricked into a meeting with the Russians and had then disappeared, were put on trial in Moscow as war criminals and sentenced to penal servitude in the Gulags. Several of them

60

would die there. There was much anger in the West, but no real protest.

Not all the rank and file obeyed the order to stop fighting, when the new wave of terror struck. Some of the units of the Home Army took to the woods and hills yet again, to fight a new enemy. About 80,000 armed anti-Communist partisans (some of them small semi-fascist groups), were active in the first half of 1945.[5] For them it was a fight for survival, they had nothing to lose. One of these units made a night-attack on the concentration camp of Rembertów and set free eighteen hundred of their former companions who were about to be transported to the Soviet Union.

But the people as a whole were exhausted by suffering and weary of fighting, particularly when it meant that Pole was killing Pole in a civil war which had no future. The novel *Ashes and Diamonds*, published in 1948, caught the confusion and despair of the months that followed, in which "the worst years had passed, but now, at the beginning of a new day, it looked as if so much had been destroyed, so much laid waste, so much crushed down and afflicted, that the destructive force, as though still unappeased, was encroaching upon the present, poisoning even the future".[6]

One reason why so many were prepared to go on fighting, however, was the universal conviction that Britain and America would soon invade, to prevent Russia from swallowing the whole of Eastern Europe. It took at least two years for this illusion to fade and for the heart to go out of the struggle; but with their antiquated (or non-existent) arms the partisans had no real hope. Thousands were killed; thousands more were arrested and forced to sign pledges of loyalty to the Soviet Union. Some caved in and joined the Party; some were deported, others put on trial as bandits and fascist collaborators.

What support the Party had came by and large from the ambitious sons and daughters of the peasants and of the uprooted post-war refugees who needed education and encouragement. The Communists had wooed the peasants from the first moment, by dividing up the old estates and presenting a strip to each peasant. "They'll waste a lot of land that way. On the other hand, the paupers and farm-hands will start to feel human," says an honest idealist in the TV film, *Friends*.[7] But the horses, he said, should be given to the best farmers. And for ideological reasons they were not.

This agrarian reform which was welcomed by almost all sections of Polish society, brought the Communists a certain amount of popularity for a while, although not all the peasants were convinced of the regime's good intentions. Dark suspicions were entertained that the Communists would soon repossess the land and turn it into collectives. And there was never the faintest chance that Polish farmers would willingly join such enterprises. But there was no denying that life was improving for the peasants, with education for the first time freely available for their children, and social advancement a possibility. Seven million of the young and active were persuaded to abandon the villages and to seek their fortunes in the towns, mainly in the returned western territories of Silesia and Pomerania, and along the Baltic seaboard where Poland's economy was being revitalised and efforts were being made to turn her into an industrial nation.

The "better tomorrow" of which the young peasants dreamed was also the dream of a minority of Polish intellectuals who, in the face of much hostility, were hailing the new dawn. In the new society, writers, journalists, media-men, lawyers, were needed as missionaries, to spread the gospel and exert control over vital communications and the judiciary. Czesław Miłosz, a writer who before the war had belonged to radical left-wing literary and political groups, was one of those who wanted a break with the old romantic, tradition-haunted Poland, with its clericalism and extravagant nationalism. In the eyes of Miłosz and his like, Western-type democracy was disgraced or dead; only through the Marxist vision was a new world possible. It was, they believed, not only the best but the only possible solution. The brilliant young philosophy student, Leszek Kołakowski, shared their hopes for a better Poland. "Illusions, to be sure," said Kołakowski, many years later, when exiled to the West, "but not absolutely foolish, I think."

Miłosz watched in horror at the ruthless imposition of the new order, but comforted himself that it might be a necessary first stage: "What's one to do . . . if there's a rock-bottom – of poverty, oppression, humiliation – and if it is only by reaching those depths that people can change the world."[8]

Miłosz and his friends genuinely sought Poland's good; but many others joined the Party for less altruistic reasons: out of fear, weariness, vanity, the desire for power, or for the privileges that went with membership. For good or ill, Poland was going to remain in the Soviet Union's orbit, and that fact in itself caused many of Poland's intelligentsia to throw in their lot with the ruling Party.

TOWARDS A BETTER TOMORROW?

Miłosz was soon to realise that reality did not match up to the theory, that paradise was as far away as ever, if not further:

Our nation [he would write], was going to be transformed into a nation of workers and peasants, and that was right. Yet the peasant was not content, even though he was being given land; he was afraid. The worker had not the slightest feeling that the factories belonged to him, even though he worked to mobilise them with much self-denial and even though the propaganda assured him that they were his.[9]

Everyday life continued in a state of suspension. Fighting continued, the economic situation got worse. There were strikes and demonstrations in towns and cities all over Poland. People survived by bartering whatever goods they still possessed, and small private traders set up in business. Wives frequently had stalls in the market-place, to supplement their husbands' inadequate wage. Marek Korowicz reported the following conversation overheard in Kraków:

First man: What do you live on?
Second man: I'm in the Post Office, my wife's a teacher, one daughter works at the Town Hall, the other's a factory official, and my son's out of work.
First man (horrified): What, you allow your son, a grown man, to be out of work?
Second man: My dear chap, if he had a job, we couldn't possibly make ends meet. He has to earn the money to keep us all. If it weren't for him, we'd all starve.[10]

"Times are hard and are bound to get harder," sighed the heroine of a film[11] set in a small provincial town in 1946, where small-time racketeers and speculators were busy ripping off their helpless compatriots. The Polish authorities complained about this view of post-war Poland as poor, depressed and hopeless. "What about all our efforts to build a glorious Socialist Poland?" they asked. "What about all the optimism?"

*   *   *

One Polish institution remained intact – the Roman Catholic Church, restored to the affections of the people by its wartime record. Over three thousand priests had been shot or killed in the concentration camps, the most famous of these being the Franciscan, Maximilian Kolbe, who had given his life for another in Auschwitz, and who had already become a national cult figure. The Church had shared the agonies of the people. Its reputation accordingly stood higher than before. The sufferings of the Occupation had broadened and deepened the religious beliefs of the Poles, who now turned to the Church as the champion not only of their religious freedom but of all their freedoms. The shifting of the Polish borders (400 kilometres/200 miles) westward also meant that Poland, for the first time in its history, had lost its ethnic and religious minorities and become truly homogeneous. "A nation of thirty million people," said the wags, "twenty-nine million of whom go to church."

As long as the Church was prepared to go along with plans for rebuilding the country along Socialist lines, the authorities were willing to pay lip-service to the idea of co-existence. They confined themselves temporarily to anti-clericalism – priests, for example, who had belonged to the Home Army, had to change their names or go underground; and to accusing Pope Pius XII of harbouring pro-German sentiments. But the faith itself they left alone. Religion was still being taught in the schools. The Feast of the Immaculate Conception of the Virgin Mary was declared a public holiday. In those days even high-ranking Communist dignitaries went to church on Sundays or at least took part in the annual Corpus Christi procession. Even Bierut, in July 1945, took part in a ceremony during which a statue of Christ was placed in front of the Holy Cross Church in Warsaw.[12] And though Communists took care to address each other as "Comrade", older habits of speech died hard:

> "May God keep you, Comrade." Szczuka opened his mouth to speak but hesitated.
> "Thanks," he said. "May God watch over you too."[13]

Some Catholic newspapers were allowed into print and churches were rebuilt with State assistance. On the Church's part, although the hierarchy frequently thundered against the more inhuman aspects of Communism, they agreed with the proposed agrarian reforms and with the drive to turn Poland into an industrial nation. Like their opponents, they were prepared to wait and see. As Cardinal Wyszyński was later to remark, Polish society at this time could have been "a most fertile field for a wise government to work on".[14]

---

[1] Norman Davies, *God's Playground*, Volume II, *op. cit.*
[2] Marek Korowicz: *W Polsce Pod Sowieckim Jarzmem (1955)*.
[3] Dr Antony Polonsky in an article: "Stalin and the Poles, 1941–1947."

TOWARDS A BETTER TOMORROW?

[4] Kazimierz Moczarski, *Rozmowy Z Katem*, Panstwowy Instytut Wydawniczy, Warszawa, 1977.

[5] Dr Antony Polonsky in an article: "Stalin and the Poles, 1941–1947."

[6] Jerzy Andrzejewski, *Ashes and Diamonds*, Penguin, 1980.

[7] *Friends*, Telewizyjna Wytwórnia Filmowa, Poltel, 1981.

[8] Czesław Miłosz, *The Captive Mind*, op. cit.

[9] Ibid.

[10] Marek Korowicz: *W Polsce Pod Sowieckim Jarzmem (1955)*.

[11] *Year of the Quiet Sun*, directed by Zrzysztof Zanussi.

[12] *Dramatyczny Rok, 1945*, Tadeusz Zenczykowski, Polonia, 1982.

[13] Jerzy Andrzejewski, *Ashes and Diamonds*, as above.

[14] Cardinal Stefan Wyszyński: *A Freedom Within*, Hodder & Stoughton, 1985.

5 THE REVOLUTION THAT NEVER WAS (1945–8)

> So often are you as a blazing torch
> with flakes of burning hemp falling about you.
> Flaming, you know not if flames
> freedom bring, or death,
> consuming all that you most cherish;
> if ashes only will be left and
> chaos and tempest shall engulf.
> Or will the ashes hold the glory
> of a starlike diamond, the
> Morning Star of everlasting triumph?
>
> Cyprian Kamil Norwid (1821–83)
> Translated by Bolesław Sulik, for
> the film *Ashes and Diamonds*

In the late spring of 1945, while Stalin's army rampaged slightly to the north, thirty-seven-year-old Bolek Wałęsa returned to Popowo, to "cough his lungs up" and die. The pneumonia he had caught in the draughty barracks at Młyniec, added to the severe skull injuries inflicted on him by the Gestapo, left the outcome in no doubt. But in the little stone cottage in Popowo, he resolutely clung to life, until his younger brother, Stanisław, should return home from the forests. When Stanisław came, in June, Bolek begged him to take care of Feliksa and the children; and, having extracted the promise, died. He was buried in the little churchyard at nearby Sobowo, where so many of the graves seem to bear the name of Wałęsa.

A year later, Stanisław honoured his brother's last wish, and married Feliksa. "He was our father," says Izabela, the oldest. "We none of us really knew Bolek."

Even with his own piece of land added to Bolek's, Stanisław had to support his new family on only four hectares. It was poor, sandy ground, and nothing would grow there except potatoes and low-grade wheat. On the edge of a little birch wood, Stanisław built a new house for them all, bigger than the tumbledown hut in which Bolek had lived with Feliksa, but still not much larger than a dolls' house. Like his brother, Stanisław was a skilled craftsman, but there could have been few comforts in that little two-roomed stone croft for two adults and four children. And when, before long, three more children, Tadeusz, Zygmunt and Wojtek, were born, the poverty of the family went from abject to unbearable. "We weren't just poor," recalls Zygmunt, "we were paupers."

Bigger than the house was the adjoining cowshed, which Stanisław also built. The two cows, ten pigs and one hundred chickens were the family's ticket to survival. There was no money coming in. They had only what they could provide for themselves.

When he killed a pig, Stanisław would fill a suitcase with joints of pork, butter and eggs, and go off to the nearest market. He was too poor to own a horse, and on these occasions had to borrow a horse and cart from a neighbouring farmer, in exchange for three days' work by himself or his sons.

From the time they could walk, the children had to help "with everything". They would take the cows out to graze, and help with the milking. They worked for the horse-owning farmer, weeded the ground, made hay, and helped their mother make bread and the huge variety of sausage, brawn and black puddings into which Polish country-women convert their slaughtered pigs. They would go into the woods to gather the juniper branches needed for smoking the sausage, and afterwards they would help pack the meat in salt and store it in the large space under the cement floor of the house.

In the woods too there were the delicious mushrooms, which all Polish children learn to identify at an early age. And on winter days, when they were able to borrow the horse (two days' borrowing meant five days' work for the farmer) they would gather firewood and bring it back on a home-made sledge.

"They were difficult times," says Zygmunt, "but we weren't unhappy. It was a different atmosphere then. We respected our parents, and trusted the neighbours. People hadn't started yet to be afraid of each other."

Elsewhere in Poland, armed resistance had almost petered out.* But the people were still restless, and Stalin used the

---

* Parts of the resistance movement continued fighting until 1948. Some forty thousand are believed to have died on both sides. In July 1985, a monument commemorating members of the security forces who had died in the defence of People's Poland was unveiled in Warsaw. It depicted soldiers, militia, security police, workers and peasants raising aloft the (uncrowned) Polish eagle. The monument is deeply resented by the vast majority of the Polish people, as is the one unveiled earlier in the same year, which, while commemorating the Polish officers murdered in the Katyń Forest, describes them as "victims of Hitlerite fascism". Someone secretly scored out the word "Hitlerite", but left "fascism" in place.

unsettled state of the country as an excuse for postponing the "free and unfettered elections" he had promised the West at Yalta; and to intensify the ruthless Sovietisation of the country. The scales at last fell from Western eyes. This brutal dehumanisation of Polish life was the last straw which caused the breakdown of the wartime alliance with Russia and the start of the Cold War. Churchill spoke of an "iron curtain" descending on Europe and both he and the Americans declared Poland's new western border to be anything but final. This caused great consternation in Poland, where the question of the western frontier was just about the only issue on which government and people were united. A great hopelessness engulfed the country, a state of mind which Gomułka took care to encourage, reminding the people over and over again that Russia was the only true protector of their interests. At this point Stalin exerted pressure on the government to refuse the Marshall Aid from America which was helping Poland in the daunting task of reconstruction.

One way or another, the anti-Communists lost heart and, in the face of the overwhelming odds, decided, for the time being, to bow to the inevitable. Many of them reluctantly threw in their lot with the regime, in the hope of salvaging something from the wreckage of Poland. It was still almost possible, in spite of everything, to believe in the prospect of better things to come. Rebuilding was proceeding at a steady rate. The Russians had sent what Bierut called "fraternal, heartfelt and selfless help", in the shape of some economic assistance.[1] A little basic machinery was now available for the work of rebuilding, and lorries had taken the place of handcarts. The towns were taking shape again. All freedoms were not yet completely abolished. The people could still move about freely, worship where they pleased, choose where they would work, criticise the government in the privacy of their homes, and listen to the radio, even to foreign stations. The opposition Peasant Party, led by Mikołajczyk, was a major political force, with a membership far larger than the combined numbers of the Communists and their allies. Mikołajczyk was genuinely hopeful that Poland might yet become a real democracy, for in a genuine election campaign, the Communists could hope for less than five per cent of the national vote.

But the peasant leader (and almost everybody else) had reckoned without the crucial fact that the Communists could impose their will by armed force. "Was anyone so naïve as to expect that a revolution carried into this land at bayonet point would yield before a ballot-box?" a Party boss later asked a

Western journalist.[2] In that icy winter of 1947, when the Poles had no coal because the Russians had taken it all, the farcical elections took place after a fierce and bloody campaign which was a continuation of the civil war by other means. If the elections had really been "free and unfettered", an overwhelming victory would have gone to the immensely popular Peasant Party. But there was nothing either free or unfettered about them.

The Communists used every trick in the book to keep Mikołajczyk out, secure in the knowledge that at every step of the way they could call on the support of the Russian armed forces. They disfranchised at least a million voters, raided their opponents' offices, cut off telephones, planted weapons, threatened, kidnapped, murdered. They isolated Poland from her friends in the West by setting up a bloody pogrom of Jews in the town of Kielce, four days before the elections. When the results were finally declared, they were quite clearly faked. The popular Mikołajczyk and his party were declared to have received only ten per cent of the vote, and the government bloc eighty per cent. The people received the news with undisguised dismay, understanding too late that they had been tricked, and that their fate was now upon them.

Almost immediately the regime began to tighten the screw, enlarging the security forces, imposing stricter censorship, and staging a long series of political trials designed to crush any remaining opposition. At the end of 1948, the Polish Workers' Party forcibly swallowed up the Socialists; and the pro-regime Peasant Party did the same to Mikołajczyk's party which was far larger than itself and far more representative of the Polish peasants. The peasant leader realised then that no more lip-service would be paid to carrying out social change in accordance with the needs and wishes of the people; and that Poland was to be brought, lock, stock and barrel, into the Russian system. Knowing that his own arrest was a matter only of time, Mikołajczyk fled to the West in October. As Bierut put it, all too clearly, in 1948: "People's Democracy did not arise as the result of an armed uprising, but as the result of victory by the Soviet Union."

Indeed, Poland had had no revolution. Power had passed smoothly and inevitably from the Nazis to the Red Army and from them to the Provisional Government established at Lublin. The Poles had never at any stage been offered a choice. Yalta had handed them over on a platter to the Russians, who had cynically chosen to devour the small birds rather than let them sing.

Gomułka was now intent on developing a specifically Polish road to Communism. Being at once a Pole and a realist, he did not believe that the Polish peasants would ever accept the forcible collectivisation of their land. But his plans for the future were overturned by dramatic events in Yugoslavia. In 1948, Tito's defiant rejection of Russian dominion over his country sent shock-waves through the Communist Parties of Eastern Europe. Stalin clamped down hard, forcing a uniform discipline upon them all, determined to ensure their total obedience, and to prevent the emergence of new Titos. He had never much trusted Władysław Gomułka, who was not one of the Russian-trained and therefore "reliable" Polish Patriots. In the light of Tito's shocking betrayal, independence of mind was not to be tolerated; any man who challenged Soviet supremacy in his own country was a danger to Stalin's grand post-war plan for reshaping the history of Europe.

So, in September 1948, on the grounds that he had been too conciliatory towards Tito and had had the temerity to act as though Poland were an equal partner with the Soviet Union, Gomułka was dismissed as a nationalist deviationist, and his job was taken over by President Bierut. The Revolution, as always, was devouring its own children.

With the purge of all those who shared Gomułka's views, and their replacement by men subservient to Stalin's wishes, Poland's subjugation to the Soviet Union was complete. To underline just how unequal she was, Poland's forces were reorganised on the Soviet model; her soldiers were made to swear an oath of allegiance to the Soviet Union and, bitterest insult of all, the Soviet Marshal Rokossovsky was brought in as Commander-in-Chief of the Polish Army; and all major units were put into the charge of Soviet officers. Such a stinging affront has no parallel before or since, even in the tiniest, most insignificant dependent states, anywhere else in the world! Poland, like the other countries of Eastern Europe, was put on a war footing. Her frontiers were closed, her economy given over to the demands of war. Her shops were empty, her people hungry. And the worst was still to come.

[1] Bolesław Bierut, *The Six Year Plan for the Reconstruction of Warsaw*, Książk i Wiedza Report, 1949.
[2] Stewart Steven, *The Poles*, Collins/Harvill, 1982.

6 ASHES, NOT DIAMONDS (1948–56)

The Party denied the free will of the individual – and at the same time it exacted his willing self-sacrifice. It denied his capacity to choose between two alternatives – and at the same time it demanded that he should constantly choose the right one. It denied his power to distinguish good and evil – and at the same time it spoke pathetically of guilt and treachery. The individual stood under the sign of economic fatality, a wheel in a clockwork which had been wound up for all eternity and could not be stopped or influenced – and the Party demanded that the wheel should revolt against the clockwork and change its course. There was somewhere an error in the calculation; the equation did not work out.

Arthur Koestler: *Darkness at Noon*

By the end of that year, the circumstances for the Party were particularly propitious. The Church's leader, Cardinal Hlond, the Primate of Poland, had died in October and been replaced by Stefan Wyszyński, the young bishop of Lublin. At a crucial time in its affairs, then, the Church had as leader an inexperienced bishop who had been running a relatively uncomplicated diocese for less than three years.

But even if, in these circumstances, the way seemed open for the Party to destroy its chief rival, in the short term a certain amount of caution was still necessary.

Sooner or later the shaky truce between the Church and the State was doomed to break down; and by 1948 it was already doing so. As Miłosz was to write:

In its own fashion, the Party too is a church. Its dictatorship over the earth and its transformation of the human species depend on the success with which it can channel irrational drives and use them to its own ends . . . No other church can be tolerated; Christianity is Public Enemy Number One. It fosters all the scepticism of the masses as to the radical transformation of mankind. If, as the Gospel teaches, we must not do harm to others, then perhaps we must not harm the kulaks?[1]

71

It would be foolish as yet to close down the churches and forbid the practice of the faith, for such a course might provoke the people to renewed armed resistance. Far better to divide and rule, to accuse some of the priests and bishops of being reactionaries and foreign agents, while encouraging the PAX groups of "patriotic" priests sympathetic to the regime.*

PAX did the Church a lot of harm. The "patriotic" priests were few in number, but they were manoeuvred into positions of importance, despite the hierarchy's objections. Meanwhile, a new martyrdom was beginning. Bishops and priests were placed under strict surveillance and a wave of radio and press propaganda accused them of every crime under the sun. By the end of 1950, more than five hundred priests, monks and nuns were in prison, some of them in Siberian work camps.

Still a bit wary of the people, the regime embarked on a campaign to encourage atheism. Atheistic societies were formed, and in schools, colleges, places of work and tenement blocks the Poles were made to listen to interminable lectures on "scientific" Marxism, designed to prove that religion was nonsense. Crosses were taken down from public buildings; and the serving of fish was encouraged on every day except Friday, the Church's traditional day for abstaining from meat: "Today there is fish," remarks a character in a later novel about the period. "That is because it is not Friday. No fish is allowed to be served in restaurants on Friday. You see, they are rather childish sometimes, the people who look after us."[2]

Pilgrimages, processions and all public meetings were banned and Catholic newspapers were forced out of print. *Universal Word*, however, the PAX "Catholic" daily which, in the words of the Polish Primate, "might as well have been written by Stalin", was given all the newsprint it needed. Employees in state enterprises were compelled to work on Sundays, and "voluntary" work brigades were organised to ensure that young people would not get to church. On church feast days, official parades or special

---

* A pseudo-Catholic group, under the leadership of Bolesław Piasecki, began to emerge as early as 1945. Piasecki, the pre-war leader of the anti-semitic Falanga group, had fought the Russians during the war in his own underground unit. Arrested by the NKVD in 1944, he turned his coat and offered his services to the Russians. He was released immediately and set up the group of pseudo-Catholics which would become known as PAX. Until his death in 1979, Piasecki remained one of the most hated men in Poland.

See Tadeusz Zenczykowski, *Dramatyczny Rok 1945*, Polonia, 1982.

football matches were carefully scheduled to coincide with church services.

Some were taken in by all the propaganda, but a contemporary observer records that on the whole the attacks on religion only provoked resentment. "The threat nourished devotion to the only source of warmth, of spiritual peace, of comfort and of hope that was left."[3]

The Party could hardly fail to be aware that the churches were fuller than they had ever been – not just on Sundays but every day; and not just at the time of religious services. They guessed, probably correctly, that at least in part this fervour was an outlet for a hatred towards Russia and towards Marxism–Leninism, which had no other means of expression. So, in an attempt to trap its arch-enemy, the regime proposed an agreement with the Church. Such an Agreement was signed in the spring of 1950, with the Communists offering more tolerance in exchange for positive Catholic support. It had the appearance of a hopeful charter, but hardly had it been signed than the regime reneged on its part of the bargain and started attacking the Church again:

> Priests are constantly spied on, placed under surveillance, provoked. A whole network of Communist agents surrounds them. Every careless word uttered by a priest is reported, twisted, exaggerated out of all proportion. Because, as a result, priests are cautious about what they say, informers simply invent whatever they please and always manage to provide witnesses.[4]

Whatever good Bierut's regime carried out in the early fifties – the rebuilding of houses, schools and hospitals; industrial development; the provision of social, sports and cultural amenities, of kindergartens and crèches; the loving care with which historic buildings were reconstructed – was lost in the orgy of horror into which the Polish people were now plunged; and which owed less to Marxism–Leninism than to the traditions of the hated Czars.[5] Brute force prevailed. Stalin had once said that imposing Communism on the fiercely independent Poles would be like trying to fit a saddle on to a cow. And so it proved. Where argument had failed, police terror was let loose. It was said[6] that Stalin was addicted to terror and understood that it was most effective when applied in a random, chaotic way, creating an atmosphere in which no one felt safe and everyone was afraid.

The noose tightened; the Party moved to establish control over every aspect of life. Repeatedly told that they did not exist as individuals, that their only function was to work and to serve the

Revolution, the people felt themselves more and more isolated and helpless. Poland was fast becoming an imitation Russia, with red flags and banners fluttering, and compulsory mass parades on vast public squares; while from office walls and hoardings stared outsize portraits of Lenin, Stalin and Bierut. Grey concrete apartment blocks rose from the rubble and hideous, Soviet-style architecture began to dominate the skyline of Polish cities; all the old values – of religious faith, parental authority, patriotism and high moral standards – were denounced and ridiculed. Life became more and more intolerable.

Writers who in the early days of the regime had written pretty nearly what they pleased, so long as they refrained from criticising the Soviet system, were now ordered to give positive support to the Revolution (that never was), to devote their talents to the construction of Socialism. The more cowardly among them began to produce books which were little more than strings of quotations from Lenin or Stalin, and were quite unreadable. The better ones remained silent. Only works which praised Socialism and wrote in glowing terms of its achievements were allowed to be published. An Orwellian "doublespeak" swamped the elegant Polish language. Wherever people went, whether shopping, waiting for a bus or train, or attending one of the unavoidable public meetings, their ears were assailed by a crude propaganda which poured out of the public address system:

The – train – for – Chelmno – will – leave – from – platform – three – beware – of – bacteriological – warfare – by – the – foreign – imperialists – the – train – from – Kraków – is – arriving – on – platform – number – two – long – live – socialism – and – workers' – unity . . .[7]

All contact with relatives and friends who had remained in the West was a punishable offence, as was any mention of those who had died at Tobruk, Monte Cassino, Arnhem or the Battle of Britain. The singing of patriotic songs such as the popular "Red Poppies of Monte Cassino" was rigorously forbidden. The war was said to have begun only in 1941, and had been won by the Soviet Union alone. Only the Eastern front had been important. While every Polish town had its war memorial to the Soviet dead, there was none to the Poles who had died in the fighting of 1939, or on the Western fronts. As for the Home Army partisans, Stefan D.'s experience was common: "In the Stalinist years," he says, "I had fourteen different jobs. Every time they discovered that

I'd been in the Home Army, the police ordered the employer to get rid of me."

A totalitarian society demands the full, round-the-clock co-operation of all its members. To ensure such co-operation, the secret police were given full rein. They acted on the principle that it is a far, far better thing to punish the innocent than to allow the guilty to go free. In any case, few people any longer knew how to distinguish the innocent from the guilty, since only the Party had the power to decide what was right and what was wrong. Good and evil could be defined only in the context of the Revolution (it was dangerous for a priest to speak of them in the pulpit); conscience was an irrelevance; and the end justified the means, however ignoble. Law had acquired a new meaning – in Humpty Dumpty fashion, it meant whatever the Party wanted it to mean.

This departure from the rule of law increased the uncertainty and fear. People trembled at the mere mention of the UB (the secret police). Eye-witness accounts tell of hundreds of thousands arrested, till the prisons were bursting and the overflow was being crammed into the cellars of ordinary houses. Every word or act was potentially dangerous, even chance remarks made in private could be reported and lead to arrest. The citizen's only duty (he did not have rights) was "watchfulness against the enemies of the people". Denunciations were encouraged: they were the mark of the good citizen. Informers supplied the UB with material for personal dossiers on every single person. These were said to be for reference only, but in fact they labelled a person as politically reliable or unreliable and at the very least determined his chances of a decent job, since almost all personnel officers were under the control of the UB. "At work you were continually watched," said a factory-worker, "who you worked with, who you talked to, what you were talking about."

Tadeusz B., arrested in the early hours of one morning was taken to police headquarters, where he was first of all ordered to write a summary of his life. The investigators wouldn't accept what he wrote the first time, nor the second, nor the third, fourth, fifth, sixth . . .

This went on for hours [he remembered]. Then I was put into solitary, to "contemplate my destiny". After midnight I was questioned again, and again was ordered to write the story of my life. I sat on a stool placed about two metres from the large table where the interrogators sat. On the table was a reflector with a spotlight trained on my face so that I was blinded by the light and could see nothing. The interrogation went on and on until I was totally drained and exhausted. Then, when I was expecting the worst, they unaccountably sent me home. But they sent for me again, and the whole procedure was repeated. It happened several times.

The terrifying pressure of daily life made people mentally and physically ill, and soured their personal relationships. Since nobody knew whom to trust, tensions became unbearable. Uncertainty about whether they would still be free, in work, with a roof over their heads, or even alive, reduced many to such a state of neurotic terror that they were ready to save their own skins by accusing their neighbours or colleagues on demand. In many ways this mental suffering caused by fear, guilt and shame was worse than the Nazi Occupation. In this poisoned atmosphere, "people were rushing to join the Party, take on safe jobs, planning, preparing themselves against some unimaginable Day of Judgment. A movement of their eyes, a sudden blush, an unexpected bowing of the head, betrayed the inner chaos and anguish that inspired their conduct."[7]

One consolation – and this in spite of the risks involved – was listening in to Western radio stations – BBC, Voice of America or Radio Free Europe – for a true account of what was happening in Poland. Many a parent locked himself into the bedroom with the set, away from the prying eyes of the children. Andrzej Gwiazda, a future leader of Solidarity, was a child at the time and remembers his parents keeping a primitive radio set hidden under the blankets.

I can remember how friends went pale, how their hands shook, if I forgot to switch off the receiver before inviting them into the room. But despite the fear there were many who listened . . . People in the free world will never understand the significance those broadcasts had for us. Only one who has been in prison, hemmed in all round by concrete, can appreciate what the tiny slit in the wall, through which a tree or a passing car can be seen, means to the prisoner. It is proof that a normal world still exists outside the iron bars and the concrete.[8]

In the prisons, beatings, injections, hypnosis, long terms of isolation, day-and-night interrogations under blinding lights destroyed the nerves and will of even the strongest and could reduce valiant men to submission in twenty-four hours. Not many were heroes, not even those who had a record of gallantry in more than one war. It was a leading Communist who in later years was to describe the horror of:

> people who were caught in the streets and released after seven days of interrogation, unfit to live. These people had to be taken to lunatic asylums. Others sought refuge in the asylums to avoid the security police. Men in panic, honest men, were fleeing abroad to escape our system . . . The whole city knew there were cells in which people were kept for three weeks standing in excrement . . . cold water was poured on people who were left in the cold to freeze.[9]

This was the time of those mockeries of justice, the show trials which were being held all over Eastern Europe as Stalin consolidated his hold on his empire. Though less bad in Poland than elsewhere, they nevertheless inspired terror. The courts were corrupt, a great many of the judges being in the pay of the secret police. Pictures of those accused (who would soon be mouthing an abject public confession, whether guilty or not) were printed in the official dailies. When Marek Korowicz saw the picture of a man he knew, he was appalled: "In place of the virile, stocky, rather muscular chap I knew I saw a grey-haired old man, thin as a skeleton. What had they done to him?"[10]

The exemplary trials also included among their victims several well-known clergy. One priest was condemned to death; another to fifteen years' hard labour because photographic equipment, some yards of cloth and a few bottles of wine (the possession of which was not illegal) were found in his house.

No one was exempt from the Terror. Workers who did not fulfil the norms laid down in the Six Year Plan were held just as guilty as those whose crimes were political. In fact the UB eventually succeeded in having this failure to produce the goods pronounced a political crime. The fact that norms were always being raised, so that workers were being paid less and less for more and more work, made no difference. Those who "sabotaged" the Plan were sent to work-camps attached to the coal-mines, stone-quarries or steelworks in the industrial areas. "It's come to this," said a disillusioned worker, "that every steelworks and every mine will soon have its own slaves, and getting coal and steel will cost the authorities almost nothing."

When the regular miners and steelworkers saw the half-starved prisoner-workers embarking on their sentences, the braver among them spat and swore and cursed those who had sent them there. But many of these paid for their temerity by being themselves arrested and sent to similar camps elsewhere.

"He who works eats." In these camps the Orwellian dictum was applied as a matter of course. Whoever did not fulfil his work norms was deprived of food. People would return from those camps pale, nervous, silent, afraid of their own shadows. Suicide became common, but more often the survivors became helpless tools of the UB, informers, prepared, however shamefacedly, to do anything rather than be sent back to the camps.

If, in the early dawn of "liberation", some at least of Poland's industrial workers (including the many thousands of former peasants) believed that a new era of happiness was at hand, they were discovering the hard way that they had been conned. Certainly there were good things: full employment; education for the children – and evening classes for the adult workers; occasional expenses-paid holidays in a rest-home. But, though the increasing productivity of the worker was the basis of the Communist achievement, the worker was not his own man. He belonged to a State, which claimed to know what was best for him, and to speak in his name.

> Workers are told that a strike is a crime. Against whom are they to strike? Against themselves? After all, the means of production belongs to them, the State belongs to them. Such an explanation is not very convincing. The workers who dare not state aloud what they want know that the goals of the State are far from identical with their own.[11]

The unions had no teeth. They had been taken over by the Party in 1949 and their former officials had been purged. The new leaders were quite clear as to their duties: they were taskmasters in the drive for increased production; it was definitely not part of their brief to try to defend their members' interests.

Poland's current Six Year Plan committed her to producing jet planes and spare parts for Russian tanks. Nowhere did it take into account the basic needs of the people. The government set wage-scales over the heads of the unions, increased the working week, passed laws which bound workers to their present jobs and imposed a draconian system of time-keeping whereby even a few minutes' lateness was severely punished. "Heroes of Socialist Labour", super-quota workers akin to the Russian Stakhanovites (and a great many of them fictitious), were urged to perform prodigious miracles of production, so that work-norms might be raised even higher. Since building workers were in such demand, some of them became famous for their efficiency, especially when they began to increase their output by means of teamwork. The incident in Andrzej Wajda's celebrated film, *Man of Marble*, in which one team lays thirty-eight thousand bricks in a single eight-hour shift, is based on a true statistic, which Bierut himself quoted in the Six Year Plan for 1949. For this feat, Wajda's film-hero, the idealistic Mateusz Birkut, is showered momentarily with rewards and bouquets from a grateful Party, and earns the furious loathing of his fellow-workers. The rising work-norms and the accompanying exhaustion and despair caused further breakdowns in health among the workers; and in spite of the strict surveillance and the terrifying punishments involved, absenteeism mounted steadily and standards of work – and honesty at work – went to the wall.

Apart from everything else, the Poles were well aware that the Russians were milking them. Not only were they forced to produce military hardware for the Russian war build-up, but in so many other ways the "fraternal ally" was taking far more than it gave. In the middle of freezing Polish winters, for example, there was no coal, not even in Katowice where it was mined (but from where a railway line ran direct to the Soviet Union). Thank God for our Polish railway workers, went a bitter joke of the period. If it weren't for them, we'd have to carry the coal to the east on our backs. Poland had to import sugar from Czechoslovakia, then sell it at less than half the market rate to the Soviet Union; for railway engines they were paid little more than the cost of materials, and for manufactured cloth not even that.

In George Orwell's satire on Communism, *Animal Farm*, Mollie the mare pines for sugar and is rebuked by Snowball the pig who tells her she doesn't need sugar because under the new dispensation she will have all the oats and hay she needs to keep her alive. Polish women under Stalinism did not even have the human equivalent of oats and hay, let alone the sugar. Frequently they had nothing to eat but potatoes. Badly housed, under-nourished, exhausted, their nerves stretched to breaking-point, housewives forlornly trailed their shopping baskets to empty shops or joined the long queues for bread or meat which started at dawn or even earlier. And as few families could exist on one man's wages, on leaving the queue many of the women would set off for a day's work in office or factory. Sometimes mothers sent their children out to queue. One man, a child at the time, remembers:

queues for everything . . . In the morning before going to school I had to queue for bread and milk, the essentials which were our staple diet, under different guises, at every meal. My parents who both

79

queued at different shops would send me to the baker's rather than anyone else, because as a boy I was more likely to wriggle myself to the top of the queue and return home with a loaf of bread and a litre of milk.

Even such items as sewing thread and nails had long since vanished from the shops. In fact the only commodity not in short supply was alcohol. Excessive drinking was officially discouraged; but it was widely believed that the regime preferred the workers to spend what money they had on drink rather than attempt to save it. Not that savings were of any use. Twice in this period currency reform wiped them out altogether; and as prices went up on everything except heavy industry, people joked that the only bargain for the working man to buy was a railway-engine.

Food was strictly rationed but the number of coupons available depended not, as in less inhuman societies, on the age or health of the individual, but on his job status, his degree of usefulness, his political purity. Special-status workers, such as miners, and, of course, the highly productive super-quota workers, received a greater allowance of coupons. In any office or factory the boss received more coupons than his underlings. The Communist slogan, incorporated into the new Soviet-style Polish charter of July 1952, "from each according to his ability; to each according to his work" was cynically interpreted to mean that a full stomach depended on a person's willingness to serve the Party unreservedly.

A new élite had sprung into being, wealthier and far more powerful than its pre-war predecessors. Managers of firms, factories and mines; top civil servants; heads of schools and universities; directors of hospitals; leading members of the judiciary; army officers; media people – all owed their jobs to the Party which had hand-picked them on the basis not of their talent for the job but of their slavish adherence to orthodoxy. These were the urbane, smooth-suited, privileged elect who could be trusted to stick to the rule-book; the grey, faceless men who would never be tempted by compassion to make an exception to the rule. The rewards for such as these were numerous and sweet, and for the greater number of them were the whole *raison d'être* of their loyalty.

Known as the *nomenklatura* (the trusted ones), these were top people, set apart from their countrymen, cut off from real life by the extent of their privileges. They had their own private hospitals, sanatoria, luxury holiday hostels, priority in housing, pharmacies, kindergartens, cinemas. And in this land where even the smallest private traders had been forced out of business, where people were "uniformly grey and uniformly poverty-stricken",[12] the new élite flaunted their special "yellow-curtain shops" – so-called after the yellow-curtained doors which hid their bulging shelves from the hungry passers-by.

Thus was the old quasi-religious Communist fervour corrupted. Thus was "the ethic of war founded on co-operation and brotherhood" transformed into "an ethic of war, pitting all men against all others and granting the greatest chance of survival to the craftiest".[13]

In bringing this new class into being and surrounding it with the luxuries that would inevitably corrupt it, the Party had bought itself servants, and had knowingly created a hydra-headed monster with a vested interest in preserving the system which was so generous to them. These men and women would continue to talk in glowing phrases about the working classes and blame industrial unrest on "enemies of the people". But they no longer shared the experience of the common people and increasingly forfeited their right to speak on their behalf:

Jakubik, a Party functionary: It's not the working classes who are restless. It's the enemies of the people who provoke them.

Piotr, his former friend: You don't know a thing about the working classes any more. You only know how to carry out the bosses' orders.[14]

It was the *nomenklatura* who had most to lose if the system came under attack. It was they who made a Communist society possible. It was to protect their privileges that the powers and prerogatives of the UB security police were expanded. Almost thirty years later, it was this same group which saw its lifestyle threatened by Solidarity and which undermined all efforts to create a dialogue between regime and people. By then, of course, the new élite, with the pharisaical morals which characterised it, had become a hereditary caste.

[1] Czesław Miłosz, *The Captive Mind, op. cit.*

[2] Frank Tuohy, *The Ice Saints*, Macmillan, 1964.

[3] Flora Lewis, *The Polish Volcano: A Case-History of Hope*, Secker & Warburg, 1959.

[4] Marek Korowicz, *W Polsce Pod Sowieckim Jarzmem*, London, Veritas, 1955.

[5] Nicholas Bethell, *Gomułka: His Poland and His Communism*, Longmans, 1969, Penguin, 1972.

[6] Ewa Fournier, *Poland*, Vista Books, 1964.

[7] Czesław Miłosz, *Seizure of Power, op. cit.*

[8] Article: "Radio Free Europe": "A Window on Sanity", in Gdańsk underground publication *Skorpion*, published in UK in *Polish Affairs*, number 110, Spring 1983.

[9] Konrad Syrop, *Poland in Perspective*, Robert Hale, London, 1982.

[10] Marek Korowicz, *W Polsce Pod Sowieckim Jarzmem*, London, Veritas, 1955.

[11] Czesław Miłosz, *The Captive Mind, op. cit.*

[12] Ibid.

[13] Ibid.

[14] Film: *Friends* (*Przyjaciele*), dir. Andrzej Kostenko, Telewizyjna Wytwórnia Filmowa. Poltel, 1981.

7 FIGHTING BACK (1951–6)

The Church in Poland has become synonymous with the Polish
nation . . . he who harms the one harms the other . . . So those
who criticise the Church . . . for meddling in politics fail to understand that in Poland temporal politics have imposed themselves
upon the Church and not the Church on politics. To understand
Poland, you must understand that.

Stewart Steven: *The Poles*

When old Cardinal Sapieha died in 1951, half a million mourners
lined the streets of Kraków, weeping and singing hymns, while the
UB melted into the background and refrained from interference.
"They couldn't have stopped us on that day and they knew it,"
people have said. The Roman Catholic Church continued to be
the people's main support – "our help and our rock" – lining
up behind those values which would one day be embodied by
Solidarity.

With the death of Cardinal Sapieha, the whole fury of the battle
fell on Stefan Wyszyński, the new Primate, a tough and pragmatic
patriot, a worker-priest who had signed the 1950 Agreement with
the regime, in the belief that the Polish Church had already shed
too much blood in the Nazi death camps and that a new bloody
martyrdom should be avoided if possible. Had the regime not
been intent on destroying the Church, it might have been able
to reach an accommodation with Wyszyński. But how could
aggressive atheism coexist with religion? The smear campaign
against the Church had now reached a high peak of hysteria, and
Wyszyński was powerless to stop it. His overriding aim was to
preserve the unity of the Church, but such unity had to be paid
for in the human suffering he had sought to avoid. By the end of
1952, eight bishops and over nine hundred priests were in prison.

A government decree in February 1953 made all ecclesiastical
positions dependent on the State. Whereupon the Cardinal and
bishops of the "Church of Silence" made an anything but silent
protest at this violation of the recent Agreement. They openly
opposed the ruthless methods of the regime and defended the

83

nation's right to its own religious tradition. It was "the most energetic and at the same time the most dignified challenge to Communist rule in Poland – a truly historic testimony in Poland's contemporary trial".[1]

The Cardinal's own arrest in 1953 was the government's response. It was intended to be the *coup de grâce* for the Church, but the action did not have the desired effect. Although the shock of the arrest drove many to despair of the Church's chances of survival, it was also salutary. The arrest of the Primate – traditionally the ruler of the Polish people in the interval between the death of one king and the election of another – increased his popularity overnight, alerted the people to the extremity of their danger and gave them a new determination to stand firm against the total enslavement that now threatened to overwhelm them.

That autumn, as the imprisoned Cardinal scribbled in his diary, he recalled that in the first church he had entered en route to being installed as archbishop of his diocese, the people had presented to him a painting of Christ, hands bound, a soldier grasping his shoulder. It was, he now realised, a fitting symbol not only of the Polish Church but of the whole Polish nation: a Christian people must share Christ's way to the cross. They must also follow Christ's example of forgiveness, giving witness to the power of good to overcome evil. When the newspapers, in a frenzy about enemies within and without, had urged the people "to train ourselves to hate more", Wyszyński had responded that "the Poles do not know how to hate, thank God." And when the regime had denied the right of the individual to a private conscience, he had left his congregations in no doubt that "the voice of conscience is the voice of the greatness of man".

Conscience was all the people had left. "Capitalism," went the Polish joke, "is the exploitation of one man by another. Socialism is the reverse." A sense of humour had always, even in the dark days of the Occupation, been a safety valve for the Poles in their struggles with a malign fate. Forbidden to voice any complaint, they took refuge in jokes with a core of political bitterness – like the endless ones about the hated Palace of Culture and Science, the monstrous edifice which dominates the Warsaw skyline and was solemnly presented as a gift to the Polish people by Stalin, at a time when the housing situation in Warsaw was acute. It has been described as "a monument to arrogance, a statue to slavery, a stone layer-cake of abomination".[2] Who's the luckiest man in all Warsaw? went one version of the joke. And the answer: "the caretaker on the top floor of the Palace of Culture. He's the only one who can't see it when he looks out of his window."

This kind of low-key joke was relatively safe and probably made its point better than the serious political articles which could not be written.

By the 1950s armed resistance was out of the question, given the ubiquitous presence of the UB and the nearness of the Russian tanks. Most active opposition had fizzled out, to be replaced by the more passive but none the less heroic tactic of refusing to join the Party. In Poland, no one was ever compelled to join, but every worker was given the chance. To refuse effectively meant an end to all hope of promotion and invited a black mark on to one's personal dossier. It was a high price to pay, and some could not find the courage. "One must live after all," they said. But the majority stood firm, and one should not underestimate the value of this type of resistance to totalitarian enslavement:

It was a question, really [said a woman from Warsaw], of trying to keep hold of one's interior identity and, even more importantly, that of one's children. You had to choose between bringing them up in a lie, in order to make life easier for them, or in the truth. It was so very complicated. We had to tell them things like, 'Well, that's the truth, but you must not say so at school.' We had to teach them to lead a double life.

In the country areas, resistance took a different form. After Gomułka's removal from office (and subsequent arrest), the regime had launched a full-scale onslaught to drive the peasants into collectives and production co-operatives on the Russian model. Poland, long known as the "granary of Europe", was to be taught to emulate a nation which had never, in all its history, known how to feed itself. Lenin's three-pronged policy for the rural areas: rely on the poor peasants, neutralise the in-betweens and scourge the kulaks (the richer peasants), was about to be put into effect.

"Now was the time of the great post-war degradation of the villages," remembers Bohdan Cywiński:[3]

. . . when singing brigades of young people from the towns in khaki shirts and red ties rode into the country on open trucks for the so-called summer campaigns, whose aim was the requisitioning of agricultural products. This witch-hunt was dignified by the name of "social work", and a contemporary filmed chronicle showed squads of these noble social workers ransacking barns, dismembering haystacks in search of the sacks of grain or sides of bacon that might be hidden there. The owners stood by and cursed or begged to be allowed at least to keep the seed-grain for the next sowing. In vain. Any peasant who tried to be efficient and plan for the future was lampooned in the press as a capitalist, a "kulak" – and everyone knew what had happened to the kulaks in the Soviet Union.

But the Polish peasants were a tough breed and, after the first shock, they had rallied. All but a few by now regarded the Communists as mortal enemies who had proffered them the carrot of a strip of land and were now intent on taking it back. Not only the "kulaks" but the poorer peasants gave the thumbs down to this rape. When they were forced, like their compatriots in the towns, to attend lectures on Marxist theory and Socialist agriculture, they came and listened in stolid disdain and continued as before.

In the film *Friends*, specially made for Polish TV in the Solidarity era, there is a scene in which peasants are attending just such a meeting. At the first pause in the political harangue from the Party official, one toothless old man breaks in: "Why didn't you bring nails? The war's been over five years and we still have no nails."

The official pours out the usual jargon: "The old expropriators are still in place; the kulaks lord it still in the villages. They'd like to take our bread, starve us out. They're trying to stop us joining co-operative farms."

The man may have been convinced by his own slogans, but the peasants were unimpressed. Mention of the nail shortage releases a chorus of complaint: how can we make bread? There's nothing to light a fire with. Why can't we get buckets? We can't even carry water. There are no saucepans . . .

Since the State paid far less than the market value of their produce, most of the peasants continued to give them only a bare minimum, while continuing to sell their surplus hay, potatoes, meat, milk and eggs on the free market at a much more profitable rate of exchange.

At first the regime was baffled and angry at their attitude, but realising that they could hardly undertake a massive repression of the peasants – the fruit of whose labour was needed for the regular quotas sent to the Soviet Union – they soft-pedalled on collectivisation. As a result, six years later only thirteen per cent of arable land in Poland had come under State control. But the regime did not stop imposing huge fines and prison sentences, managing at one and the same time to turn the peasants into implacable enemies and to send Polish agriculture hurtling down to ruin.

Such was the background to Lech Wałęsa's childhood. For the Wałęsa family too, these years from 1951–6 were the worst of all, though, as Lech's brother, Zygmunt, says, "our land was so poor that nobody even tried to confiscate it." Nevertheless, the brothers remember that "the Communists took our food, and we had to do whatever they told us." Like all peasant-farmers, they had a quota to fill, in accordance with the current Six Year Plan. If they had the audacity to kill a pig, without first fulfilling their quota to the State, they could be sent to prison for five years.

Though their stepfather, Stanisław, was a stern disciplinarian, it was their mother who ruled the household. "Small and round like an apple," a friend described Feliksa, "with that shrewdness which belongs neither to town nor village, peasant nor industrial worker, but which is born of a long apprenticeship to providing bread for the family."

A quiet woman, thrifty, an excellent housewife, is how others describe her. And in the opinion of one of the priests at Sobowo, she was, for all her lack of formal education, "one of the two cleverest women in the parish".

In Feliksa's family tree, the religious tradition was strong. For generations there had been a priest or nun in the family. She herself was very devout – "too devout", says her youngest son, Wojtek, with memories of being dragged unwillingly to church. Refusal was unthinkable. Every Sunday (in two relays because the farm could never be left unattended), the family trudged the four kilometres to Mass in the hill-top church at Sobowo, which massively overlooks the low-lying farmland. And in the evening, when the day's work was done, evening prayers were a ritual that was never dispensed with. The whole family had to say prayers before they were given supper. "And if we said them too quickly, we had to start again from the beginning," remembers Izabela.

Experience had taught Feliksa to expect little from life, and perhaps she had found her only consolation in religion. There were seven children now, all of them crammed into the little stone cottage with its damp earthen floor. Stanisław still went off to market, whenever he could borrow a horse, there to sell his butter, eggs, milk and meat. But there was little enough to keep the family on. Not enough for shoes, for trousers, for exercise books or pencils. A picture of Lech in his first year of primary school shows him with trousers far too long and a jersey far too short.

Ragged they might have been, but dirty never. Feliksa would

no more tolerate dirt than disobedience. Her children would not have dreamed of disobeying their mother, nor of arguing with her edicts. A single glance from those flashing eyes was enough to quell even the bravest. But if any of them was hurt, they ran to her for help, and then it was a different story. Of them all, Lech was most like her. Perhaps both of them had in full measure the characteristic traits of "the land of Dobrzyń". Tough, stubborn and hot-tempered, at the same time the people of Dobrzyń are reputed for their openness, their courage, and above all for their perseverance against impossible odds.

Whatever the reason, the bonds between Lech and his mother were exceptionally close. He loved to bring her presents, mushrooms or hazelnuts, or the last of a batch of apples he had stolen from a neighbouring farmer.

Though he was, according to Izabela, "the most religious of us all", he was a normally mischievous child, who went bird-nesting and caught frogs in the numerous ponds. He played with toy soldiers too and dreamed of becoming an air force pilot. Small for his age, he was always something of a loner. "He walked by himself, like a cat," says Izabela. "He was always different somehow. He used to think about things more than we did." Though close to his older brother, Stanisław, he preferred to be alone and to look at the world with eyes wide open. "Ever since I was a child," he told the Italian journalist, Oriana Fallaci, "I've taken note, listened, watched. I've always spied on life, and I think I've come to know something about it."

From the age of seven he attended the primary school in the village of Chalin, three kilometres away. Chalin is a village out of time. A "proper" village with a recognisable street and a handful of shops; but also a village which plunges the visitor back into an earlier age, where women with kerchiefed heads gather to discuss the day's events; where the cart filled with hay or firewood is a much more common sight than the motor car; and where farmers in blousons and black berets peaceably till the fields with a horse-drawn plough. Nestling among plane trees, Chalin boasts a large and very beautiful lake. Before the war, the mansion house overlooking the lake was privately owned, and the village children have been instructed what to think about the owner. "A wicked man," they say, "he didn't give the villagers anything to eat." But he was driven out by the Germans, and later the Communists took possession of the estate, so that now the house is the village school. For years, it has been falling into disrepair, and the wooden tiles on the classroom floors are rotting away. But a more idyllic setting can scarcely be imagined.

Each day the Wałesa children made their way in wooden clogs along the sandy cart-track from Popowo, beside waving fields of wheat, punctuated by little ponds with their croaking frogs. In summer it must have been delightful, in the Polish winter, exposed to the cruel winds, a nightmare. At times, when the snow lay too thick on the ground, the school, which was unheated, remained closed.

Lech never played truant. He says modestly that during his first years at school, he was "damn gifted", with a good memory and an intuitive grasp of most subjects. His teachers remember him as no better than average, though they admit that the cramped conditions in the Wałesa home were not conducive to much studying. That he was better at crafts and sport than at academic work is generally agreed.

Schoolfriends say that, true to his name, he was a "restless spirit", brave but inclined to show off. When, after school, the others would be fooling around with home-made fishing rods, Lech was the one who always caught his fish. "He'd always swim faster and further out into the lake than anyone else. It was as though he had an inner compulsion to succeed."

His bravery, however, had its limits, and did not extend to large dogs. "The trouble was, I was a little kid, and all the dogs were bigger than me. There was one in particular that seemed to know I hated him, and he hated me back."

"Ducks, too," adds Zygmunt with a grin. "He once had a very unfortunate encounter with a duck."

Did he also feel a compulsion to lead? Loner though he was, he seems to have been conscious from an early age of a natural capacity for leadership. "People have always been interested in what I say and think. Somehow, they've always followed where I've led."

For all the grinding poverty, Lech was happy as a child:

There's a saying that the poor man is a devil without a soul [he smiles]. But we had souls, so we must have been rich. In one sense, we had nothing, but you can't judge poverty by material standards. Prosperity and greed go together. Well, we weren't well-off, and so we weren't greedy. We didn't have television, or even radio, but we had books, and the whole world of nature was open for us to read. We were rich in the things that mattered.

That he was an outspoken child seems fairly clear; and it was a dangerous characteristic in Stalinist Poland. When still quite

89

young, he was warned by a priest that he would end up in prison if he didn't watch his tongue. By 1952, when he was nine, church schools throughout the country had been closed down or taken over by the regime, and the Russian language had become a compulsory subject. No one could escape the indoctrination classes, the classes in citizenship, which began for children at the age of twelve. If the factories, barracks, workshops or sports clubs were centres for political propaganda, the classroom was even more so. For that was where the new generation of Socialist citizens was being nurtured. The main objects of education were three: to make the young aware of the class struggle; to make them good Marxists; and to encourage friendly feelings towards the USSR. Any fact or event that did not portray Russia in the most amiable light was taboo. The Russo-Polish War of 1920, the 1939 Russian invasion of Poland, Katyń or the Warsaw Rising were simply never mentioned. The world, the children were taught, was divided into two: the heaven of enlightened progress that was the USSR; and the hell of reaction and privilege exemplified by the USA.

A syllabus dictated what was to be taught and left no scope to the teachers. Many of the teachers were lukewarm in their enthusiasm for the syllabus, but they had to follow it, if they wanted to keep their jobs. Some confined themselves to lectures on honesty in human relations, or duty to family and country. But there were always a few who were crudely propagandist:

> In my school [said a girl], the history teacher turned the lesson into a vulgar comparison between the "peaceful" Warsaw Pact countries and the "war-mongering" Nato states; between the poverty of the poor exploited workers in the West and the prosperity of our socialist society. Even at our young age, we knew he was talking rubbish. Any and all shortcomings in Poland were blamed on American capitalist plots. And it sometimes seemed that if it rained for the May Day parade, the Americans were to blame.

Even the youngest pupils gathered daily round an enormous portrait of Stalin, twice as large as life, to sing songs about his wise leadership and kindly nature. One of them, sung to a fairly lively tune, contained the lines:

> For ever will live our beloved Uncle, Stalin,
> Whose lips are sweeter than raspberries.

"None of us really believed it," says a contemporary of Lech

Wałęsa, "but it was something we had to pretend about. Otherwise our parents would have received a letter from the school, followed by a visit from the police." A few children were more impressionable. One remembers getting a beating from his father for referring lovingly to Stalin at home as "our grandpa".

This sort of thing did not go down too well with the young Wałęsa, though he liked some of the scarlet and white banners – with slogans like WYWALCZYMY TRWAŁY POKÓJ, We shall fight with all our might for enduring peace – which always festooned the classroom walls. "I had problems with the teachers," he admits. "They taught us Communism and I didn't pay any attention. Once I was sent to the headmaster and he broke a cane over my head. The trouble was, if I could see very well that something or other was white, no one was going to persuade me that it was black."

Later, when he was older, he saw this teaching in a different light: "We were ordered to be atheists, and we were taught atheism, and look what happened. Almost the whole nation is religious. We learned good things in a bad school."[4]

The official Marxist indoctrination of their children was resisted head-on by the peasants. With the tenacity of their kind, they joined the ideological struggle, but not in the way Stalin intended. When the children were taught at school that there was no God; when they learned in biology that Christianity was outmoded and unscientific, and that the whole idea of man being created for a purpose was false; when their history and geography textbooks were discovered to be revamped editions of Russian models, their mothers, fathers, uncles, aunts, grandmothers and grandfathers moved on to the attack. Often unable to read or write themselves, they would explain to the children that everything they had heard during the day – except perhaps in mathematics and physical science – was a lie. Grandparents in particular, highly conservative and regarding all Communists as the brood of Satan, had an answer for everything the children had learned in the classroom.

As a result, the only village children likely to succumb to the propaganda were those who did not receive an alternative education from the family; and some of the cleverer ones who knew well that the best opportunities were open only to those who accepted the Party version of reality.

Felik sa, like most of the village women, sent the children once a week to the church at Sobowo for religious instruction, while at home she set them firmly on the right lines. Life in the villages was slower, closer to the earth than life in the towns. Family life was more intense; and in the long evenings when the oil-lamps were lit, the children gathered round to imbibe a very different philosophy of life from their elders. In both town and country, the real moral and ethical education took place in the heart of the family.

In the Wałęsa family, it was Feliksa from whom they learned. She had never lost the lively, enquiring mind that she had inherited from her father, and she read everything she could lay hands on. "My mother," says Lech, "was the best-read woman I have ever met. I think she had read every book, not only in our house, but in everyone else's, including the church library; and every paper, even old pre-war ones that neighbours had kept."

Feliksa talked to her children about Poland's history, and read aloud to them from the Polish classics. It was from her that Lech first heard the great epic work of Sieńkiewicz, which told the story of the Cossack Wars and praised the chivalry of the Polish knights. As he played with his toy soldiers, did he ever see himself (as later he was most certainly encouraged by others to do) as the Little Knight in that epic – fearless, resourceful and strong, who loved argument and fighting for their own sake rather than for any craving for violence; impatient for action and adventure, but calm in a crisis – "a great soul in a little body"? Was he intrigued by the physical description of the Little Knight, easily recognised by his long, twirling moustaches?

In towns and villages alike, people avoided the Marxist books. Classics, like those of Sieńkiewicz, were in great demand. (As they portrayed the Germans in a bad light, they were among the few classical novels still in print.) At times such as these, there was need to remember that Poland had once been great. Feliksa lost no opportunity of getting the message across to her family. Lech, consequently, viewed the official teaching with mistrust. He was argumentative in class, sometimes giving in when he was getting the worst of it, only to return to the fray next day with fresh ammunition from home. "I always had a lot of problems," he recalls. "You could say that my whole life has been one long turmoil."

[1] O. Halecki, *A History of Poland*, chapter 28, Routledge & Kegan Paul, 1978. "Ten Years of Trial".

[2] Tadeusz Konwicki, *A Minor Apocalypse*, Faber & Faber, 1983.

[3] From an unpublished article: "The Polish Experience".

[4] *Time* magazine, 4.1.82.

8 SPRINGTIME IN OCTOBER (1956)

A Soviet writer asked me what the Poles' real concern was in October 1956. He used the term "petit bourgeois revolt". I answered that the concern was for moral law. "Well, that's a provincial point of view," [he] said, laughing indulgently. "Judaea was a province too," I said, "a little province that gave the world the Old and New Testaments."

Kazimierz Brandys

In March 1953 Stalin died. On the day of his funeral, a three minute silence was observed throughout Poland. Those Poles who had bought the official line that Stalin was a kindly uncle to whom all good things were owed, duly grieved. Grażyna S., four years old at the time, wept, because "we got sweets at Christmas in our kindergarten, and we were told that Stalin had sent them to us. Now, I imagined, there would be no more sweets. My grief was very real."

Outwardly nothing changed. The man was dead, but his system lived on, even though the personality cult he had represented had been repudiated in Moscow, where collective leadership was now the mode. Malenkov ruled for a while in the Kremlin, and when he fell, Krushchev replaced him. It seemed like the mixture as before. Yet underneath the surface, something *was* changing. There was movement under the ice, though nobody could have imagined that within three years the ice would actually crack and give way.

In Poland, the rot set in faster and went further than in any other country in the Soviet bloc. The process began in October 1954 with the broadcast revelations of Józef Światło, a former Lt-Col. in the secret police who had fled to the West the previous December. Światło, the man who had arrested Gomułka in 1948, had organised Department 10 which had kept tabs on the ideological purity of Party members themselves. Accordingly he had a wealth of information about every member of Party and government from the lowest to the highest. He could make or break any or all of those who held power. When he began to tell all he knew on Radio Free Europe he had a fascinated and captive audience among millions of Poles, and what he said instilled terror into the hearts of the powerful. He blew the gaff on corruption and intrigue in high places and on police brutality. He spoke of torture chambers and what was done there. And when he referred to the informer system, he gave chapter and verse, naming names and quoting from actual reports. The portrait of top Communists emerging from these revelations was of "utterly ruthless and utterly dishonest men who stopped at nothing in order to obey the orders of their Soviet masters and to foster their own private interests".[1]

In the first flush of anger, embarrassment and dismay, the regime issued indignant denials. But though the people hated what Światło had stood for, they knew that he was speaking the truth about what was happening in Poland. In the end, the government admitted that mistakes had been made and promised that the guilty would be punished. The secret police apparatus was shaken to the core.

The effects of Światło's broadcasts were earth-shattering. Realising that the Terror must now surely end, people began at last to emerge from the zombie-like trance of fear in which they had been frozen. As life returned, a number of emotions which had been kept submerged for years rose violently to the surface and overflowed.

It was the young people who began it – the new generation that had inherited the Communist paradise. The white hopes of the Party, untainted by the past. They had free schooling, access to jobs, training in sports, medical care, all the things their fathers had dreamed of. But the advantages did not conceal the fact that the life they had to lead was not only bleak, with no outlet for youthful high spirits, but, even more importantly, schizophrenic, with a yawning gap between the official gilded view of reality and the grim reality itself.

In the summer of 1955, the government had staged a Youth Festival for Communist youth from all over Europe. Their aim was to display Polish achievements; but, not surprisingly, the event backfired disastrously. For the first time, the majority of Polish youngsters met their counterparts from the West, and discovered that they had been told a monstrous lie. Far from starving, the Westerners had more to eat than they did; their clothes were more colourful, their music and culture more vibrant and alive. Contrasting the lifestyle of their visitors with their own drab and colourless existence, the Poles were angry at the con-trick that had been worked on them. Ironically, the Youth Festival gave the youth of Poland an impetus to seek change. For the first time since the war, a Western craze, in this instance jazz and rock 'n' roll, seized hold of them.

After the Youth Festival, the authorities began to be seriously alarmed about the young "troublemakers" and "agitators" who were calling for change. They blamed the jazz craze and stamped down hard on its adherents. But there was more to it than jazz. Youngsters began demanding not only more lively entertainment but better food and, in the workers' hostels attached to the new industries and mines, better living conditions.

In the hostels too, a growing number of youngsters, freshly liberated from the restraining influence of parents and parish priests, were showing their frustration by brawling and heavy drinking. Juvenile delinquency in a Marxist state! It was a contradiction in terms, not to be thought of. Or was it an early sign that the morality of that particular kind of Socialism did not work?

Out of curiosity, some younger Party officials set up an enquiry into conditions in the hostels. Predictably they discovered that the buildings were sub-standard, the food inedible and the management inefficient and corrupt.

What had started as a storm in a teacup quickly became a deluge. "Pioneers" on State farms complained about *their* food, pay and housing, while students seized the opportunity to attack the compulsory Marxist–Leninist courses, the fact that entrance to higher education depended on Party membership, and that pro-regime students got the best grants, the best grades and the best jobs.

Young Party activists now took up the cudgels. Writers and journalists who till now had been afraid of repercussions from the police began at last to ridicule the absurdities of the system and to write the truth as they saw it. First in the field was Adam Ważyk whose *Poem for Adults*, published in a literary weekly, had all the force of an earth-tremor. It expressed the disillusionment of the young with the false paradise that had been promised:

> They ran to us shouting
> Under Socialism
> A cut finger does not hurt
> They cut their finger
> They felt pain
> They lost faith.

Ważyk's poem was a protest on behalf of all those whose fingers had bled and festered under the Stalin-directed regime: the hungry, the over-worked, the badly-housed, the boys and girls who were forced to spy on their parents. It ended with a rescue call for a nation that had already known too much suffering:

> We should make demands on this earth,
> Which we didn't win in a game of chance,
> Which cost the lives of millions,
> Demands for the plain truth,
> For the bread of freedom,
> For fiery good sense.
> We should make demands daily
> We should make demands of the Party.[2]

The mood of the younger intellectuals was made clear in the student newspaper, *Po Prostu*, which proclaimed: "We are a group of the discontented; we want more things, wiser things, better things."[3]

Living conditions in Poland were so bad that even Krushchev, in an address to the Polish Central Committee, had said that something ought to be done to keep the workers sweet. The workers, he said contemptuously, don't care about politics, they just want to live better. "If we don't soon manage to give them better conditions than they can get in a capitalist country, we might as well shut up shop."

A few months later it was Krushchev who dropped a bombshell. In February 1956, at the XXth Party Congress in Moscow, he demolished the Stalin myth. Non-Communists did not need to be told that Stalin had been a murderous lunatic, but to the Party faithful Krushchev's revelations came as a blow between the eyes. Many resigned on the spot, others wrestled painfully with the revelation. In the midst of all this confusion came the news that their leader, Bolesław Bierut, had died of a heart attack while in Moscow. Few would believe that version of events; but few would mourn him either, although attendance at his funeral parade was compulsory, in spite of the freezing cold. The Polish people had always thought of Bierut as an NKVD stooge. In his prison notebook, Cardinal Wyszyński noted wryly that "by now Bolesław Bierut is convinced that there is a God, and that His name is indeed Love", before listing the crimes which could be laid at the dead man's door. Of the hatchet job being worked on the Stalin legend he wrote: "How rapid is the decline of gods wrought by human hands. And it is for such a god that the Living God has to step aside."

Stalin's era in Poland was firmly coming to an end. Hastily, his jovial image was taken down from hoardings and walls. A cartoon in a new satirical weekly, showing an office wall bare except for a nail and the dusty outline of a large portrait, carried the caption: SPACE TO LET. Criticism poured out in a flood, especially within the Party itself, where hard-liners found themselves faced with a majority eager for reform.

In May 1956, thirty thousand were released from prison, and Władysław Gomułka from house arrest. Some of the most resented secret police officials were removed, and their most prominent victims rehabilitated. Among them were the men and women of the wartime Home Army. The Soviet-style history books had continued to denounce the Home Army as a nest of traitors; former Home Army members were still unable to get jobs, places to live or higher education, even if they had not been arrested and sent to one of the special camps reserved for them near the Russian border. At least a partial re-appraisal was called for. The authorities rose to the occasion. While continuing to lambast the wartime leaders as reactionary fascists, they generously admitted that the rank and file may have been inspired by love of their country. And though the subject of Katyń remained utterly taboo, a simple memorial – a tin helmet lying on a stone – was allowed to mark a spot where Home Army partisans had been executed in a group by the SS.

It wasn't a great deal, but it was a big boost to Polish morale. It also released a great wave of pent-up hatred of the Russians, so that it became next to impossible for the regime to go on maintaining that "eternal gratitude and undying love for Moscow fill every Polish heart". Disillusioned Communists led the field. They had most cause to hate the Russians, they claimed, because they knew a lot more about them.

A flood of letters to the papers now demanded the release of priests and nuns from prison. Crucifixes were taken from their hiding places and worn openly to work. In the face of clamorous popular demand, the government began to weaken. Travel restrictions were relaxed; theatres began to offer Western plays and Western music. Jazz became respectable. The Communist press ceased to rave about the exploits of the super-workers, those largely imaginary "proletarian Tarzans who happily carried out the Plan with two hundred per cent achievement". People allowed themselves to hope that a tolerable existence was possible after all! But few realised that what lay round the next corner was a genuine full-blooded proletarian revolution.

Tension had been growing. The new sense of freedom had done nothing to lessen the miseries of everyday life. "The public," wrote one commentator, "was obliged to wait longer, push harder and crowd more, to buy less and less."[4] Life was reduced to an unending struggle for existence. Apart from the chronic shortages and the queues that began at dawn, "too many people lived in dank basements or half-rotting buildings with poor or no hygienic facilities; and it is wrong to imagine one ever got used to it. There was no privacy, no comfort."[4]

"They ask us about the things we promised," says a union member in the film *Friends*, "the washing-machines, fridges, cars. Where are the miracles?"

For a privileged few, hardship and shortages did not exist. The scandal of the packed shelves and the discount prices of the "yellow-curtain shops" became so outrageous that the authorities decided to abandon them and convert them into ordinary State retail outlets. But the gesture did not help the Party, for now its lower ranks, deprived of their special status, were just as under-privileged as everybody else. Their complaints swelled the general discontent.

*   *   *

June 1956. An explosion of despair and hatred. In Poznań, sixteen thousand workers went on strike and took to the streets, singing religious and patriotic songs, and demanding bread and freedom. Shots were fired and a boy of thirteen was killed. The Army was called in, but refused to shoot at the workers. Some of the soldiers even joined the protestors. The riot was not quelled until the arrival of more politically reliable troops with tanks and heavy artillery. Fifty-four were killed, hundreds wounded, hundreds more arrested. Prime Minister Józef Cyrankiewicz hurried to Poznań and blamed everything on a counter-revolutionary capitalist plot, threatening that "every agitator or madman" who dared lift a hand against "the power of People's Poland" would have that hand cut off. The crassness of such a threat at such a time was an indication of government nerviness in the face of this unprecedented challenge. The old-guard Stalinists were urging a crack-down; the reformers wanted to release the pressure.

In the end, the reformers won the day. In July, the vast majority of collective farms were returned to private ownership. Events moved fast that summer. On 15th August, over a million and a half pilgrims converged on the hill-top monastery of Częstochowa, for the 300th anniversary of the defeat of an all-conquering army (Swedish not Russian) by a handful of resolute Poles. It was perhaps the greatest religious demonstration ever seen, and thousands had walked hundreds of kilometres to get there. In the procession at the monastery on the Hill of Light, the Cardinal's throne, empty but for a huge bouquet of red and white roses, was carried high above the crowd. With passionate intensity the pilgrims prayed for just such a miracle as had happened in 1656. And a few weeks later they were convinced that their prayers had been answered.

*   *   *

The name of Władysław Gomułka – dismissed and arrested by Stalin in 1948 – was on everyone's lips. His recall was the one subject which united the rival factions within the Party, and even to the people it seemed as if the days of his former misrule had been "the good old days". Everything had been so much worse since then that a golden haze now surrounded the memory of the post-war era. He had the aura of a martyr, punished by Stalin because he had sought a "Polish road to Socialism".

Since the first post-Stalin relaxation, however, the Russian leadership had grown increasingly alarmed and was belatedly trying to stem the tide of change. On Friday 19th October, 1956, Krushchev and a formidable array of Soviet top brass descended on Warsaw to deal with the recalcitrant Poles. Krushchev had been drinking and was purple with rage, refusing even to shake hands with the Poles.[5] At the same time Soviet troops stationed in Poland began to march on Warsaw, while the Soviet fleet staged menacing manoeuvres in the Baltic. A conference took place immediately, with a furious Krushchev accusing the Poles of selling out to the imperialists. The Poles kept cool, told Krushchev there was no crisis, but that some degree of liberalisation was absolutely necessary and long overdue. They referred to the Russian troop manoeuvres and warned that the Poles would fight if necessary. Angry talks went on for hours.

Gomułka stood his ground, insisting that if the Russian troops were not called off, he would personally broadcast to the nation – an action which would have triggered an armed uprising. The people were already out on the streets and their mood was steely and uncompromising. Workers in one factory were preparing to take up arms.

At this late hour, while three columns of Soviet-officered Polish tank units were surrounding the city, Krushchev backed away from confrontation. Ordering the troops not to advance further, he and his delegation went home.

At next day's meeting of the Central Committee, all the hard-liners lost their seats, and Gomułka was formally elected First Secretary of the ruling Communist Party. The internal revolution in the Party had been resolved. Now they had to unite and establish control over the revolution outside.

That afternoon, it was announced that Gomułka would broad-cast to the nation. Bogdan S. will never forget that day:

> We clustered round our radio sets in real terror [he recalls]. We knew nothing of the Central Committee meeting, in Warsaw, nor of Krushchev's unexpected arrival. All we knew was that Russian tanks had surrounded all the major cities and were actually on our streets. There could have been nobody in the whole of Poland who did not realise how serious the situation was.

Gomułka's speech to the nation was masterly, one of the most powerful addresses ever given by a Communist leader. He deplored the excesses of the police; promised a return to the rule of law and a certain democratisation of the Party; rejected the imitation-Soviet economy and promised one that was at least partially open to the market forces of supply and demand. To everyone's astonishment, he also admitted the unequal trading arrangements with the USSR, under which the Russians were taking best-quality Polish coal in return for obsolete machinery which had been discarded by the Russian factories.

He promised more, and more truthful, information. The system must be changed, he agreed, even if only gradually. Workers must be given a share in management; peasants must not be forced into co-operatives. He opened his arms wide and begged everyone listening to take a share in creating a new society, admitting that: "It is a poor idea that Socialism can be built only by Communists . . . What is constant in Socialism boils down to the abolition of man's exploitation by man. The roads to this goal can be and are different."

There would, he promised, be no more submission to Moscow.[6]

In the light of hindsight, one can perhaps see that he promised too much. "Maybe we were fools for believing him," says a Warsaw woman, "but we had been so long without hope. We had thought they would go on for ever getting away with all their lies.

Then suddenly there was hope. We believed that Gomułka was an honest man. So we trusted him."

The Cardinal was released forthwith. Giving his support to Gomułka, he appealed to Catholics to stand by the new regime. There was much that divided Gomułka and Wyszyński, much that would soon drive them apart again. But they were both Poles, and both had fallen victim to Stalin. Both were pragmatists who knew that at this hour, Poland's very survival depended on their pulling together.

Carried away by Poland's apparent success, the Hungarians rose in revolt. But Krushchev was not going to tolerate a re-run of what had happened in Warsaw. This time the tanks really did crush the revolution. The mood of euphoria in Poland turned rapidly to stunned dismay as the Hungarians were beaten into submission and the West proved unable to intervene. Plane loads of drugs, provisions and medicines were flown from Poland to the insurgents, every window seemed to be flying a Hungarian flag, and on every wall a graffiti dove shed tears of blood.[7] Once again the Poles returned to the brink of armed revolt which would certainly have been bloody and certainly doomed. It was Wyszyński who saved the situation. In the first sermon he had preached in three years he reminded his countrymen that it is sometimes easier to die than to go on living. "It is that greater heroism that this day calls for, this day so pregnant with events, so full of anxious speculation about the future."

The people allowed the moment to pass. Peace returned to the streets, and hope surfaced again. Though in reality they knew little about him, their enthusiasm for Gomułka bordered on hero-worship, because they believed that he had defied the Russians and got away with it. History had played one of its wry jokes, since for this new Communist regime the Poles were giving vent to an outburst of naked nationalist fervour. Few leaders in history have received such spontaneous acclaim, few have been trusted with so many hopes. And, in fourteen years of rule, few have squandered the opportunity so unimaginatively as did Władysław Gomułka.

[1] Z. J. Błażynski, "The Światło Affair", article in *Poland One* magazine, Volume 1, Number 11, April 1985.
[2] Poemat dla Dorosłych, *Nowa Kultura*, 21.8.55.
[3] O. Halecki, *A History of Poland, op. cit.*
[4] Flora Lewis, *The Polish Volcano, op cit.*

[5] Peter Raina, *Political Opposition in Poland 1954–1977,* Poets and Painters Press, London, 1978.

[6] Konrad Syrop, *Poland in Perspective, op. cit.*

[7] Ewa Fournier, *Poland, op. cit.*

9 LOST ILLUSIONS (1956–70)

A man may have great dreams about coming to power. But when he actually achieves power, he comes up against the triviality of daily life . . . He gets bogged down . . . He gets used to having power . . . Ideals and dreams go by the board . . . You have to administer Socialism and you begin to identify Socialism with the number of screws produced. Oh, don't misunderstand me, screws are very important. But Socialism is also a spiritual idea. And when that is forgotten, discord begins to outrank Truth . . . It becomes a matter of ruling rather than administering. And then even those who are not demoralised by this can at least see that we are facing a crisis.

From *Friends* (*Przyjaciele*) – film shown on
Polish Television in 1981

"I was not yet thirteen years old when, in June 1956, the desperate struggle of the workers of Poznań for bread and freedom was suppressed in blood," wrote Lech Wałęsa in his Nobel speech many years later. Even then he had been aware of "all the wrongs, the degradations and the lost illusions" suffered by the majority of the people.

His was the generation on whose wholehearted support the State was counting. Untarnished by the past, they were the regime's stake in the future. Like everybody else, Lech's older brother, Stanisław, had joined the Organisation of Polish Youth, and, at the age of fifteen, was still young enough to retain his youthful idealism about it. Quieter and more stolid than Lech, he had become the secretary of the Organisation in his school; and when it was dissolved in 1956, felt a sense of betrayal. "I was of no use to anyone any more." The oldest of the brothers, Edward, had already left school and was helping his stepfather on the land. But it was frustrating work, with few rewards, and after a year he got a job at a nearby brickworks. Stanisław took his place for a time, before going to the trade school in Lipno to train as a lathe-turner. The Union of Polish Youth helped him out with clothes, money and free lodging, and Stanisław felt a deep gratitude

103

towards them. "People's Poland helped us get out of that village," he said, years later, when he was a long-standing but disillusioned Party member himself: "How can you tell the young about earthen floors, and about there being no work even when you were starving? There *were* achievements then."

Wojtek, the youngest, agrees, though with less enthusiasm: "People's Poland gave us our trades, rescued us from poverty and promised that things would get better. So we were patient and worked as hard as we could. But the better days never came . . ."

Their mother, Feliksa, wanted them all to have as good an education as possible, so that they could get out of the village and have a more rewarding life. These were the days when the young people were deserting the villages in droves for the newly rebuilt Baltic towns. The more ambitious among them would become Party functionaries with some chance of a successful career. The majority would simply join the workforce and become the new proletariat of the Coast.

Lech too was longing to get away and work in the shipyards. He even had hopes of becoming a qualified engineer. For he was now showing promise in maths and physics, and his headmaster had proposed him for the College of Technology, which offered a five year course with a professional qualification at the end of it. The idea was attractive, and the family wanted Lech to go ahead. He took the entrance exams and passed. But in the end, lack of money prevented him. The course had to be paid for in advance, and as Wojtek fell ill with diabetes and needed specialist treatment, the money was simply not available. Lech's plans had to be abandoned.

Bending the rules somewhat, in order to help the family, his headmaster agreed to take him back for the rest of that school year, since it was already too late for other arrangements to be made. So, swallowing his disappointment, Lech returned to school for another year, taking a part-time job at the brickworks, and continuing to work on his stepfather's and other people's farms. But he regarded farm-work with some disgust: "It is hard work but stupid," he says. "You never knew whether something would grow, or whether it would get eaten up by insects or pecked up by birds."

He lost interest in school work, and his marks began to suffer. "I felt less and less like opening the books; there were always so many other things to do." Yet he didn't sulk over his lost opportunity, consoling himself in words that are typical of him: "It isn't really good to be too gifted. I think I prefer to be like the bee, which knows it is perfectly well able to collect the honey, but which doesn't rush headlong for the big beehive, where it could fall in and get stuck.''

Leaving school at last, he followed his brother Stanisław to the trade school at Lipno, a small town on the River Mień, twenty or so kilometres away, the nearest town of any size. As number 1488, he registered for the course in mechanised agriculture in September 1959. The then director remembers Lech particularly because even by current standards he was desperately poor, and everybody was very sorry for him. All the teachers knew to make allowances for him, because whatever spare time he had was taken up in farm-work on behalf of the family. The course, which included metallurgy, technical drawing, maths and physics, involved three days' study and three days (paid) in the workshops. The money he earned went to pay his hostel fees.

He seems to have been a quiet, hard-working student, with a reputation for stubbornness. "He was determined. If he set his mind on doing something, he would do it." One teacher describes him as "friendly and open. A bit of a bully but a likeable one." Another recalls his penchant for practical jokes and his complete absence of fear. On one occasion he accepted a dare to go and sit in the cemetery all night. In the end the dare was called off, but Lech had been quite prepared to go.

The present director of the school, then the newly-appointed warden of the hostel, affirms that Lech has stayed in his mind more than any of the others:

> . . . because he had such an amazing gift for organisation. In charge of any group, he was worth his weight in gold. To give you an example: the hostel students had to sweep out the corridors, and each hall took turns, a week at a time. When it was the turn of Wałesa's hall, the teacher-in-charge would just leave them to it. Lech would wake the others at six each morning, set some boys to washing the floor, others to polishing it. By the time the teacher got up, the floor was shining.

An entry in the hostel conduct book on 17th November, 1960, however, records: "Wałesa, Lech: troublemaker and smoker." No amount of bad conduct marks cured him of this habit. Three times he was summoned before a disciplinary committee and ordered to stop smoking. But his room-mate reports that to avoid detection, they simply went up on to the roof to smoke.

26th January, 1961: "Lech Wałesa walks about with his head bare, though he has a cap in his pocket." 17th April, 1961: "I suggest that Lech Wałęsa should receive no more than four points for behaviour." (A somewhat rare mark of disapproval, indicating that he was still the "restless spirit" he had always been.) A report for January 1961 gives him an overall academic assessment of "Fair", declaring him to be "sound in morals and politics", good at economics and sport, fair at Polish language studies. His worst subject appears to have been history – perhaps it was because of the distorted way in which it was taught and with which he refused to go along. But at least he passed the exams each year, and finished the course successfully. "For ten years," a commentator was to write, "the regime had been busy educating the man who would become its most formidable opponent."

Having got his certificate from the trade school – a necessary piece of paper for any Pole wanting to become a skilled worker – he worked for a while as an electrical mechanic at a State Agricultural Machinery Centre, mending electric trailers. Then, in 1963, he was conscripted into the Polish Army.

Poles traditionally have a great respect for their soldiers, a respect only slightly diminished even in People's Poland, where the military was subjected to the Party. Polish conscripts were required to swear an oath of loyalty not only to Poland but to Socialism; and a special political Youth wing of the Party was put to indoctrinating the new recruits. Bogdan S., who was in the Army at the same time as Wałęsa, says that for many of the conscripts the experience was unique:

> It was the first chance they'd ever had of living away from home and of enlarging their horizons. On another level, it was like a fish-tank, where a political indoctrination could be applied very effectively, at a critical stage of one's life. We were told that Germany alone was Poland's traditional enemy, and that the NATO powers were intent on destroying the countries of the Warsaw Pact. Some absorbed the propaganda. After all, the Army offered an opening to a secure and well-paid job, a privileged position in society – for those who were prepared to pay its price.

But, in spite of the pressures, most of the conscripts emerged unscathed, the majority of them being well and truly inoculated by their families and parish priests against such propaganda.

Wałęsa, working as a morse-code operator, enjoyed being in the Army and rose to the rank of corporal. His brother, Stanisław, who was sharing this period of military service, and who had also become a corporal, began to cultivate a spreading moustache, and Lech, always in the shadow of his older brother, followed suit.

Lech loved the uniform. "It fascinated me, just as a kid loves to dress up like a cowboy," he says. He was popular and well thought-of. "A bit of a disciplinarian," said a fellow-conscript, "but human with it. He never harassed anyone just for the hell of it. He liked a joke, and could achieve more that way than others did by shouting. I remember him coming to the cookhouse and asking 'What's cooking?' And we all shouted back: 'Wałęsa's whiskers.'"

One of the officers was keen for him to make a career in the regular Army, reporting that he was "intelligent, keen to learn, determined. Would make a leader. Should be promoted." Had his advice been heeded, history might have been different. But Wałesa did not want to become a professional soldier. However much he had enjoyed the experience, he had had enough.

It was a tight squeeze in the cottage when Lech returned from the Army. "We couldn't all fit in," says Stanisław. "Some of us had to be farmed out on neighbours."

But they all came together for the big Church Feast Days, as they would continue to do as long as it was feasible. And for New Year. One New Year's Eve, Stanisław and Lech went to a party at a neighbour's house, and Stanisław got very drunk. Realising that his brother was incapable of walking home, Lech heaved him on to his shoulders, threw his sheepskin jacket over him, and began the long walk through the fields knee-deep in snow. But Lech was more than half-sloshed himself, and, somewhere along the road, Stanisław fell off unnoticed. Lech was quite unaware, and even when he arrived home believed he was still carrying his brother. But all he was carrying was the sheepskin jacket. In a panic, Feliksa had to organise a search-party to go back and search for Stanisław in the snow-bound fields. Many years later, Lech would claim that he had been drunk only twice in his life: once, in the Army and once, over a girl. He seems conveniently to have forgotten this other, embarrassing, occasion.

After the Army, Lech's first job was as an electrician in an agricultural co-operative in the village of Lenie. The money he earned was not enough to buy the second-hand motor-bike which he longed for. He had become an expert mechanic and was known locally as "golden hands" for his skill in mending every type of machine, particularly motor-bikes. He had a girlfriend, Jadwiga, from a neighbouring village, but, says Wojtek, the relationship was rather one-sided, since "she wanted Leszek to look at her all the time, but he preferred to sit in her parents' flat and watch TV". Girls "adored" him, claims Izabela, because he was witty and made them laugh. But he treated them all as friends and refused to think seriously about any of them.

Occasionally he wondered if he had a vocation to the priesthood. "It was the uniform again," he jokes. "Well, in fact it was more than that. I always wanted to do some good for people." So why did he not become a priest? "Because I came to the conclusion that when you're a priest you're out of touch with the way ordinary people live. I didn't want that to happen."

The better times hoped for by so many did not come, although the first few years of Gomułka-ism were the most stable that Poland had known since the war. Probably too much was expected of Gomułka. To the people he had assumed the status of Messiah; and inevitably he failed to live up to the role. What the country needed now was a rapid return to the rule of law, some bold economic reform, a recognition of the nation's cultural and religious roots, and a genuine dialogue between the regime and society.

But Gomułka's imagination was limited, and he misread the mood of the people. He was a true, old-fashioned Communist believer, who had never ceased to think that it was possible to create a Communist society in Poland and that Marxism–Leninism would finally triumph there. The "human face" of Socialism, which the Poles were hoping to see, was not part of his plan.

For obvious strategic reasons, he soft-pedalled at the beginning. As Gomułka and the Cardinal needed each other's support, sweeping concessions were made to the Church. Priests and bishops were among the thousands being released from prison; new Catholic newspapers were permitted, and five members of their editorial boards allowed to stand for election to the Sejm (Parliament); religious education temporarily began again in the schools; and the regime limited its control over church appointments to a mere right of veto. In exchange, the Church promised support, and urged Catholics to vote for the regime's candidates at the forthcoming elections. The Vatican took a decidedly cool view of such supping with the devil on the Cardinal's part.

The old unpopular Organisation of Polish Youth was dissolved. Only a few, like Lech's brother, Stanisław, regretted its passing. The Organisation's successor was no less unpopular with the majority, but had the merit of not being compulsory. More popular were the Scouts (mixed, for boys and girls), dusted off and given a new Socialist image, but with the pre-war uniform unchanged. A more relaxed attitude towards the West meant that friends and relatives on both sides of the great divide could now

108

renew contact, without fear of reprisals. Before 1956, a passport was a rarity: the majority of Poles were imprisoned within their borders. Passports (valid only for a single journey) now became possible again, even though the traveller was allowed so little dollar or sterling currency that he invariably had to find someone in the host country to finance the trip.

Travel to the West opened the Poles' eyes to the world outside. No longer was it possible to persuade them that workers in Western Europe were starving. They could see with their own eyes that most workers in the capitalist world actually had cars.

Films and books from the West began to trickle in, though no anti-Soviet, or "counter-revolutionary" works were admitted, and George Orwell and Ian Fleming were both rigorously excluded. This new influx from abroad seemed to release something in the Polish creative spirit, so that there was a new cultural flowering, with the satirical plays of Mrożek, the films of Wajda, the novels of Andrzejewski and the poems of Herbert appearing like life-giving streams in the cultural desert.

Gomułka went to Moscow almost immediately after his election and returned with a satisfactory agreement. From now on the two countries were to treat each other on a much more equal basis, each of them recognising the other's independence and national sovereignty.[1] In recognition of the cheap coal the Russians were getting from Poland and the free maintenance for Russian troops on Polish soil, Krushchev cancelled Poland's huge outstanding debt and promised to pay the troops' expenses themselves in future. Those Poles who were still in the Soviet Union and who wished to return home were to be allowed to do so.

The rumour later gained ground in Poland that at this meeting Krushchev offered to tell the truth about Katyń, and that Gomułka declined, fearing a violent reaction from the Poles. If that offer really was made, then the Polish leader missed a historic opportunity to improve the relations between the two countries. For the heavy shadow of Katyń continues to hang over those relations, and does not diminish as the years pass. There has always been a certain unnamed green square in a Warsaw cemetery, to which flowers have been brought and candles lit to commemorate those who were murdered in the dark forest near Smolensk.

Whatever Krushchev did or did not propose to Gomułka, it is fair to say that by the time Gomułka left Moscow, the relations between the two men were very cordial. Perhaps Hungary had finally convinced Gomułka that Poland's only hope was to remain firmly inside the Russian orbit. From that conviction he would never again waver.

Was it to convince his new friends of his own good faith that Gomułka so soon began to turn on his older ones? In a Party split down the middle it was up to him to hold the balance between the conservative Stalinists and the reformers. But he began almost immediately to veer towards the conservatives. It took some time for the hard truth to sink in – that whereas the reformers, led by Leszek Kołakowski, at that time a Professor of Philosophy at Warsaw University, believed they were on the threshold of change, for Gomułka the revolution was over. A relatively uneducated man, Gomułka had a deep distrust of the intellectuals who had helped him to power. He wanted now to put them in their place.

His about-turn was already obvious in January 1957 when the elections to the Sejm (Parliament) took place. The people hoped that Gomułka would curb the power of the Party and open the elections to genuinely popular candidates. A few extra names were indeed added to the usual list of Party hacks, and it was the people's electoral right to cross off the names of such candidates as they did not want. But at the last moment Gomułka took fright at so much liberty and warned on radio that if Communist names were crossed off, Poland would be swept off the maps of Europe for the foreseeable future. Shades of Hungary yet again! His appeal cut strangely little ice. He himself won handsomely, but many Party candidates came bottom of the list and one lost his seat altogether. In a Communist regime this was unheard of! Furthermore, at the risk of losing their jobs or of being punished in a variety of ways, over one million voters abstained; more than half a million crossed out at least one Party name, and three hundred thousand crossed out every name on the list.

In practice it didn't make much difference. Even with sixty-seven new non-Party members, the Sejm remained what it was – a rubber-stamp for Party policies. It was not allowed to engage in free and open debate, and had no chance of mounting a genuine opposition to the regime.[2]

Gomułka had already begun to bite the hand that had fed him. Early that year he dismissed the whole editorial board of the main Party newspaper, *Trybuna Ludu*; and in May he suppressed the chief student and intellectual paper, *Po Prostu*, which had supported him throughout the previous year. When students called a protest meeting, the police broke it up with tear gas and truncheons. Polish culture was again coming under siege.

A Party purge followed, with two hundred thousand being expelled over the next two years. These men and women were, argued Gomułka at the tenth Central Committee plenum in October 1957, far more dangerous to Poland than the Stalinists, in much the same way as tuberculosis was more dangerous than influenza. Influenza, he said, cannot be cured by contracting tuberculosis: the reformers must be expelled.[3]

When the winnowing was done, the careerists and trimmers, the guaranteed yes-men, remained in place. Gomułka, it was clear, did not want to be argued with. He was revealing himself as the dogmatic Marxist–Leninist he had always been. By the end of the 1950s he was courting his old enemies, the Stalinists. "But by then he had long since discarded the ideals of the Polish October."[4] The security police, though less powerful than they had been, were back in favour, every bit as vigilant as before and just as effective.

The rigid central planning which had been imposed on the country since 1949 simply didn't work, and it was time for a new look at the economy.[5] At last there was to be a slight nod in the direction of housing and consumer goods. At present, people were existing rather than living. In *The Ice Saints*, Rose, a visitor to Poland in the late fifties, was shocked by what she saw: "Most were dressed in little more than rags, jumble-sale clothes. There was no effort to present a façade of prosperity to the world. Each seemed to show a face and figure which said, 'Look, this is me, smashed.'"

A friend of Rose's tells her: "We were lucky to get a new flat. We had to wait many years on a list." Rose had not realised that the flat was new. Its plaster was cracked and it had already taken on the drab, unpainted look of the city.

When later on she watches one of those compulsory May Day parades which dragged on from early morning till mid-afternoon, she is struck by the grey, expressionless faces of the factory workers as they file past the huge floating faces of Lenin, Marx and Gomułka. It felt wrong, she said: "This should have been a march of protest. They should be protesting now because they were so poor, so ill-dressed, so ugly, with their swinging, work-distorted hands."[6]

An American journalist posted to Warsaw in 1958 returned home after a year, having had "a bellyful of the greyness, the dullness, the total absence of mental stimulus which is the essence of a Communist society".[7]

Yet still the people clung to their faith in Gomułka, for he

111

remained the only realistic option available. They joked that Poland, ruled by the nine-man Politburo, was in fact ruled by 100,000,000 – Gomułka and eight nothings. When they realised that the regime was not going to change, they concentrated their attention on the inadequacy of basic living conditions – on food, clothing, housing. The spring of 1957 brought strikes and threats of strikes. When electrical workers sent a delegation to tell Gomułka they would cut off the lights if they didn't get a raise, he retorted unsympathetically: "You cut off the lights, and we'll start cutting off heads."[8]

The strikes petered out, but the underlying causes remained. "Butter costs more, bread costs more, vodka costs more, clothes cost more. The only thing that's plentiful is talk." Difficulties, it was said, were the only permanent feature of Poland's economy. A new suit was a major outlay requiring months of careful budgeting.[9] Food swallowed up most of the wages, and as there was nothing in the shops to buy, the rest went on vodka. "We may not have achieved the Polish road to Socialism," said a woman wearily, "but we're well on the Polish road to alcoholism."[10]

For a brief moment in October 1956 the workers had had some hope. The workers' councils set up in 1956 were officially recognised. But workers' control could not be tolerated by the regime, and the new councils were undermined just as surely as the old ones had been. Forbidden to have links with each other, they were soon merged with the Party committees and trade union councils in individual factories. Once again they were in the hands of opportunists who owed their positions less to innate skill than to favour with the Party, and who were for the most part quite incapable of making responsible or effective decisions.

It was stalemate. But when a group of able economists put forward a feasible plan for revitalising Poland's stagnant economy, a plan which involved a measure of decentralisation and some dependence on market forces, Gomułka would not listen. He returned instead to the old policy of pursuing rapid industrial growth regardless of demand, quality, or the human cost involved. The result was even worse stagnation. "Our production" became something of a national joke:

PARTY ACTIVIST: All that matters is production. Something that will last.

WORKER: And you think what we produce will last. You must be mad.[10]

112

In the countryside, Gomułka had kept his promise to abandon forced collectivisation. But the regime was still paranoid about private farmers, and continued to give priority to the State farms and co-operatives (which never made a profit), while starving the individual farmers of supplies and technical assistance. For the most part, the peasants went on using horses, as they could not have access to tractors. They found it difficult to obtain loans for new equipment, or to get fertiliser and other essential items. Though they still managed to sell their produce on the free market, they had little incentive to enlarge their holdings or increase their production.[11] Excluded from welfare benefits and constantly harassed by local Party officials, they, like their counterparts in the factories, became well and truly alienated, while the backwardness of Polish agriculture remained an undeniable brake on the country's economic progress.

Even by the end of 1957 the truce with the Church was coming to an end.[11] The regime had gone back on a number of its promises and it had refused to broadcast the Cardinal's Christmas message (a favour which had been granted for the first time in the history of People's Poland the previous December). This refusal finally brought a sharp protest from the Church; Wyszyński threatened to ask Catholics to boycott the coming elections. Gomułka then accused him of using religion for political ends.

The Hill of Light (Jasna Góra Monastery) at Częstochowa was raided in 1959 by police looking for printing equipment; and pilgrims and police engaged in fisticuffs. In 1960, in Nowa Huta, the steel town built to the glory of New Socialist Man, the people rioted when the government reneged on its promises to allow them to build a church.

Education became a prime bone of contention. When religious instruction had been brought back into the schools in 1956, it was made optional; but as ninety-five per cent of parents asked for it, the schools reverted overnight to being religious institutions. The Party was understandably alarmed, and in 1960 they backtracked also on this, by placing the teaching of religion at the discretion of individual head teachers. RI was then dropped in eighty per cent of the schools. The Church arranged for religious instruction on its own premises after school hours. But in 1961 the Central Committee decided that not only would religion not be taught in the schools, but that out-of-school teaching should be brought under Party control.

For the Church it was the last straw. The Cardinal now went on to the offensive, urging parents to demand a constitutional guarantee of religious freedom: "If a citizen does not demand his rights, he is no longer a citizen but a slave."[12] And just before leaving for the Vatican Council in Rome in September 1963, he addressed the people of Warsaw in terms of unambiguous defiance:

> My dear children,
> Priests throughout Poland are now being subjected to penalties for teaching catechism without registering and without reporting on their teaching. In a short and very carefully worded letter which was read from the pulpits, we explained that we would not make reports on what a priest teaches the children who are sent to him by their parents. When Christ said "Go into the whole world and preach the Gospel," he was speaking to priests and bishops and not to government officials. No one may stand between Christ and his bishops and priests; no secular authority has the right to do so . . . We have to obey God, rather than man.[13]

The Cardinal proposed a nine-year programme of spiritual renewal (which he had worked out during his years of internment) for the celebration of the Polish Millennium in 1966. In the eyes of the Church this meant the thousandth anniversary of the coming of Christianity. The State saw it as an opportunity to celebrate People's Poland as the high-point of the historical process which had started a thousand years earlier.[14] And they complained with some justification that in articles and sermons the Church was attempting to undermine Marxism–Leninism.

The battle waxed fast and furious, with elements of pure farce woven into the struggle. In the run-up to the celebrations, the Church would announce its ceremonies and the State would follow suit, with its own parades or even football matches being timed for the same day and the same hour. Grażyna S. tells how, in her school, tempting special excursions were arranged for the day of the Corpus Christi procession. One year she was awarded a free ticket for an amusement park – valid for that one day only. She was only nine, and the temptation was great. But conscience won: "In the end I didn't go, and I distinctly remember that when I was singing a hymn at the end of Mass I suddenly felt happy, as if for the first time I had the feeling of being in control of my life."

With police cordons and threats of reprisals, the regime would try to force everyone into their parades, and the people would manage to escape and join those of the Church. Microphones would be mysteriously cut off when the Cardinal was about to address a crowd; and cathedral bells were half-drowned by the din of cannon-shots and low-flying aircraft. The Cardinal told the people they could do without a king or a military commander, a prime minister or any other kind of minister. "But this nation has never lived without a shepherd!" Gomułka retorted that if Wyszyński was a shepherd, he was an irresponsible one, since he was "struggling against our people's state . . . forgetting the lessons of history, [forgetting] who brought Poland to ruin and who liberated her".

In the summer of 1965, a million people converged on the Hill of Light at Częstochowa, and replicas of the Madonna were carried in procession in every town and city. When the icon itself was being taken to Warsaw it was forcibly removed by the police from the hands of a bishop and returned to Częstochowa. In a fury the people marched to Party headquarters in Warsaw – and were met by riot police armed with water cannons.

The Cardinal knew how to exploit the Communist actions. He was in the habit of travelling round the country with a framed replica of the Częstochowa Madonna. When the authorities seized the picture, he carried an empty frame instead. The effect was powerful. "The symbolism of that empty frame was stupendous," remembers a Warsaw woman. "Cardinal Wyszyński was a great opposition leader. And the Church was the only opposition party we had." Bohdan Cywiński believes that these experiences of the sixties prepared the Poles for what happened in 1980:

> People began to understand that they could gather together in large numbers for religious purposes, and no harm would come to them, no matter how many riot police surrounded them. They learned to keep calm, to carry on praying or doing whatever they had to do, and pay no attention to those who might want to stop them. It was an apprenticeship – a lesson that even under a hostile regime you can achieve something without violence.

When in 1965 Wyszyński and the Polish bishops wrote to their counterparts in West Germany, offering Christian friendship and forgiveness, they did so as a grand gesture of reconciliation to mark the 1966 Millennium. A cry of rage went up from the regime, which was furious to find the Church stepping on to the forbidden ground of foreign policy. This new move seemed to them a piece of outrageous impudence. Hatred of Germany, and fear for the permanence of Poland's western borders, were almost the only aspects of the official policy to have unqualified public support. "WE SHALL NEITHER FORGET NOR FORGIVE" proclaimed the government posters, as they sought to reinforce the Polish fear and hatred of German revanchism. If that were to disappear, so might the regime's last shreds of credibility.

Gomułka hit back. He was not going to yield an inch in the battle with the Cardinal. Wyszyński and the bishops were refused passports for travelling to Rome; a campaign of slander against the Cardinal was unleashed; the clergy were subjected to crippling taxes and difficulties were placed in the way of building new churches. Seminarians were called up into the Army, though officially they were exempt as students; Catholic writers were harassed, Catholic books axed. The Pope was refused entry to Poland for the Millennium celebrations. To underline their displeasure, the Government closed the borders for a month, and excluded foreign Church dignitaries from the festivities. As Wyszyński was to write: "Small, proud and arrogant men came and ordered that not a single mention of the Church and its work must be made at these celebrations."[15]

Gomułka had made himself look ridiculous, and at long last the people began to see him as he really was – inflexible, stubborn, humourless, puritanical, without any redeeming vision. For years they had clung to their belief that he was a Pole first and a Communist second, but now they saw that it had always been the other way round. Though he was to stay in power for another four years, he never recovered the ground he had lost when he engaged in battle with the Church. Today the Poles are inclined to sympathise with the dilemma he faced, though their sense of betrayal is still strong. Says one observer:

> I believe he was a fundamentally honest man. And so through him we learned that even an honest man – once he is in the clutches of an ideology – is helpless. Not only because he is not free to make changes, but also because he is no longer free to think. He becomes a *homo sovieticus*, a sovietised man.

[1] O. Halecki's *History of Poland*, additional chapter, "The Rise and Fall of Gomułka", by Antony Polonsky. *op. cit.*
[2] *The Polish Volcano, op. cit.*.
[3] *Poland in Perspective, op. cit.*
[4] Nicholas Bethell, *Gomułka, His Poland and His Communism, op. cit.*
[5] M. K. Dziewanowski, *Poland in the Twentieth Century, op. cit.*
[6] Frank Tuohy, *The Ice Saints*, Macmillan, 1964.
[7] A. M. Rosenthal in *New York Times* magazine, 7.8.83.
[8] Film, *Przyjaciele (Friends), op. cit.*
[9] *The Polish Volcano, op. cit.*

[10] *Idem.*
[11] *Poland in Perspective, op. cit.*
[12] *Idem.*
[13] From a collection of Cardinal Wyszyński's sermons: *A Strong Man Armed*, A. T. Jordan, London, 1966.
[14] Halecki's *History of Poland, op. cit.*
[15] George Błażyński, *Pope John Paul II*, Weidenfeld & Nicolson, 1979.

10   DIVIDED THEY FALL: The Sixties

> Of course Poles were over-optimistic. They had been led by Go-
> mułka out of hell and imagined he would lead them into paradise.
> When this did not happen they were disappointed and sometimes
> so ungrateful they forgot what he had done.
>
> Nicholas Bethell: *Gomułka*

As Gomułka turned more and more to the old guard and put the
brake on intellectual freedom, some of the radicals in the Party
did not give up. In the summer of 1964, two young reforming
Marxist scholars from Warsaw University, Jacek Kuroń and Karol
Modzelewski, published a ninety-page open letter to Gomułka,
accusing him of betraying the workers and suggesting where he
had gone wrong. Gomułka did not take kindly to such impudence
and had both young men expelled from the Party and then arrested
on charges of dishonesty and immorality. But they had voiced the
sentiments of the young, particularly the sons and daughters of
high-ranking Communists. There would have to be a reckoning.

Next it was the turn of Leszek Kołakowski. When, in a speech
to commemorate the tenth anniversary of the Polish October, he
contrasted the hopes of those days with the grim reality of the
present, he too was expelled.

Then a new and ugly factor came into play: the old anti-semitism
in a different guise. Since the war, the percentage of Jews in the
country had been around 0.1%, compared to the pre-war figure
of ten per cent. But many of these had spent the war years in
Soviet Russia as Stalin's loyal servants. Returning to Poland in
Berling's Army they had assumed positions of power and influence, and had played a major role in shaping post-war Poland.
(Large numbers of the secret police were Jewish.) Their power
had not added to their popularity either inside or outside the
Party, and those Polish Communists, who, like Gomułka, had
fought in the Communist underground in Poland during the war
(and who had been deeply mistrusted by Stalin), had long nursed
a grudge against them and envied them their lucrative jobs.[1]

The 1967 Arab–Israeli war had the vast majority of Poles cheering for the Israelis, much to the dismay of the government which, like the rest of the Warsaw Pact countries, was officially pro-Arab.[2] Gomułka broke off relations with Israel and made dark insinuations about Zionists stirring up trouble at home. This anti-Zionism was, in fact, thinly veiled anti-semitism, and over the next few months large numbers of Jewish Party officials who had expressed approval of the Israeli victories, found themselves sacked from their jobs and replaced by ambitious young Polish Communists.

Events in neighbouring Czechoslovakia took a hand. The over-throw of the Stalinist leader, Novotny, and his replacement by the more liberal Alexander Dubček, raised the temperature in Poland, where students and intellectuals were already clamouring for change – "we are waiting for our Dubček". Matters came to a head in March 1968 when the authorities banned the perform-ance of a popular nineteenth-century Polish play about Russian atrocities during the Partitions. The play, *Forefathers' Eve*, had been playing to wildly enthusiastic audiences in Warsaw and Kraków, its numerous anti-Russian lines calling forth cheers and applause. When it was taken off, students and academics marched in protest, demanding an end to censorship. The police moved in and laid about them with clubs. Many arrests were made. The discovery of a handful of Jewish students among those arrested gave Gomułka the excuse for a witch-hunt. By the end of the month, three thousand students had been arrested and hundreds injured. Scores were expelled from the universities, with a black mark against their names which would put paid for ever to their career prospects. Kuroń and Modzelewski, newly released from prison, were re-arrested and sentenced to a further three and a half years for being the "spiritual instigators" of the student revolt.

All over Europe in 1968, students had been erupting into violence. But whereas in Bonn or Paris or Rome they were demanding more autonomy, more of a say in university affairs, and an end to traditionalism, in Poland they were appealing simply for freedom of thought, for the right to hold an opinion of their own, and for the right to hold on to tradition. The Polish students did not seek power but the right to self-respect.

To a large extent, the demonstrations in the streets were merely a reflection of the internal struggle rending the Party. For this reason, the Church at first saw it as a fight between two sets of Communists, and was inclined to leave them to it. Yet the Church's attitude slowly began to change. Both Cardinals, Stefan

119

Wyszyński of Warsaw and Karol Wojtyła of Kraków, spelled out the human rights which were being flouted and condemned this new persecution of the Jews. Increasingly, the Church began to emphasise the wrongs done not only to itself but to society and to the individual. That it should come, however belatedly, to the defence of Marxist intellectuals was a straw in the wind for the future. It looked as though the old bitter antipathy between the Church and the left-wing intellectuals, so intense before the war, was about to come to an end.

For the present, however, Church support was of little use to the victims. In all, nine thousand people, Jews and non-Jews, lost their jobs, and thirty thousand were sent into exile abroad. Among them were some of the country's most able intellectuals of world stature, such as Leszek Kołakowski.

Party radicals went into shock, their hopes of establishing a Communism based on a respect for law and humanity gone, it seemed, for ever. The academics abandoned their dreams of Utopia, and Polish intellectual life entered a new post-Marxist phase. From this time on, notes Bohdan Cywiński, there was little sign of Marxist influence in science, philosophy or the social sciences.[3]

In the prevailing chaos, Gomułka seemed certain to fall. His authority was being challenged by a new group, calling themselves the Partisans, and headed by General Mieczysław Moczar. This profoundly nationalistic and anti-semitic group was intent on achieving power, and used the fact that Gomułka had a Jewish wife as a weapon against him. Gomułka was saved by the Russian invasion of Czechoslovakia, for by sending Polish troops to Prague he ensured that Brezhnev would back him for the leadership. (The Polish people's attitude to the sending of Polish troops to Czechoslovakia was generally one of unmitigated horror.) As a sign of his championship of Gomułka, Brezhnev came in person to Warsaw for that year's Party Congress and there proclaimed his famous – or infamous – doctrine that whenever a Socialist regime is "threatened from within", the Soviet Union and its allies are entitled to intervene militarily.[4]

For Poland, 1968 was a tragic year, in which she drank the dregs of moral degradation. Illusions bit the dust, the bright dreams vanished. But Gomułka seemed immune to feelings of shame. He was by now so remote from the aspirations of the people that he no longer even pretended to consider them. And so he blundered into a fatal miscalculation. For years the authorities had carefully fostered the natural division between workers and intellectuals.

As long as the three sources of potential opposition – the Church, the workers, the intellectuals – remained separate, the government could breathe freely. Real danger would only present itself if these three should unite. Seeing that the workers were largely indifferent to the demands of Party intellectuals for greater freedom of thought, Gomułka gained a false sense of security. He forgot that the workers had their own grievance – they were hungry.

Between the intellectuals and the workers the gulf still yawned, but there were unmistakable signs that the two groups had recognised and identified a common enemy and a common cause. The groping towards mutual recognition was well caught by Wajda in one of the flashback sequences in *Man of Iron*. The students Maciek and Dzidek have sought out Maciek's father, the shipyard worker and former "shock-worker", Mateusz Birkut, who had fallen foul of the Party in the intervening years, and spent many of those years in prison. They ask for the workers' help but Mateusz refuses. It's not the right time, he argues. "So they won't come out?" asks Dzidek bitterly:

Mateusz: Oh yes, they will come – when the time is right.

Dzidek: And have you any idea when that will be?

Mateusz: No lie can maintain itself for ever. But right now, stop this play-acting of yours.

Dzidek: It's not play-acting. Can't you realise, our lives are at stake?[5]

The characters in *Man of Iron* may be fictional but they are based on real people and the events and arguments are real. The students from the Gdańsk College of Technology did ask the workers for help and were refused. They could not have known that government agents had got in there before them, poisoning the workers' minds against what they described as "spoiled brats" and "hooligans". A worker in the shipyards has described how secret police agents disguised as workmen stirred up feelings against the students and even persuaded a number of workers to take violent action against "the hooligans". "Afterwards," he says, "when we discovered the truth, we had to share our shame and bitterness with someone. And that someone was a young electrician called Lech Wałęsa."

Wałęsa, showing the sharp political insight which would mark

121

him out a decade later, had not fallen for the government's line on the students. He had begged his fellow-workers not to attend an official meeting at which the students were to be publicly censored. When it was too late, the others realised that the young electrician had been right.

Wałesa's growing restlessness had finally driven him to the big city. He had had enough of the countryside with its grinding poverty. "I felt I must get out. Sometimes one knows in one's bones that one is in the wrong place, and that's how it was with me." Once, on a school outing, he had visited Gdańsk and been impressed. But it was to Gdynia that he was making tracks when one day in 1966 he had bought a single ticket on the train. By a quirk of fate, when the train stopped in Gdańsk, Lech was thirsty and got out to look for a beer. The train went off without him; and he decided not to bother waiting for the next one. "I came to Gdańsk and met my destiny," he says cheerfully. "I spent far too long drinking that beer. And in a sense I'm still drinking it."

Gdańsk – "jewel of the Baltic" – once a fine old merchant town, birthplace of Schopenhauer and of Fahrenheit. Here the meandering Vistula River collects a few last tributaries before disappearing into the Baltic Sea, turning the landscape into a little Holland, crisscrossed by rivers as still as canals. Wedged between high wooded hills and the sea, Gdańsk has had a chequered history. As Danzig, it was part of Prussia during the Nineteenth-Century Partitions and it remained a largely German town until 1918 when it became a Free City, belonging to both Poland and Germany. Hitler's determination to get it back for Germany was the nominal cause of the Second World War, though the Führer admitted it had merely been a pretext for the invasion of Poland. From the Polish Post Office, on 1st September, 1939, sixty postal workers, armed with old-fashioned rifles, held out for a whole day against the armoured might of the Wehrmacht. And then the city disappeared yet again into Germany. Danzig/Gdańsk did not survive the fury of war; almost every one of its buildings was reduced to rubble during Stalin's mad rush to the west in the winter of 1944–5. But after 1945 it was rebuilt with style, on the model of the old city. The architecture in Gdańsk is less depressing and dreary than elsewhere, and many Poles say that the Triple Township (Trójmiasto) – Gdańsk, Gdynia, Sopot – is the only urban area fit to live in.

Since the war, Gdańsk has acquired a new population. When the Germans were driven out in 1945, their place was filled by the refugees from the eastern territories seized by Soviet Russia. This huge and ever-increasing influx of new blood gave the Baltic towns a massive infusion of energy and vitality. The people of the Coast (Wybrzeże), coming more often into contact with visiting foreigners, were less stifled by bureaucracy than the citizens of inland towns like Warsaw or Katowice; they lived with a certain spontaneity and independence of spirit. This made them relatively volatile and unpredictable, and the regime, sensing a potential danger in them, watched them warily.

The vast shipyard-in-the-name-of-Lenin, Poland's industrial pride and joy, was built in the 1950s on the site of five pre-war factories. It stands, some distance from the sea, on a tributary known as the Dead Vistula; and its workforce consists of former peasants escaping from the rural areas, and older "expellees" from the eastern territories. Lech Wałęsa, who had found temporary, poorly-paid work at the State Machinery Centre in Gdańsk, began work as a ships' electrician in the yards in May 1967. He had decided to become an electro-mechanic, and had to study for this new qualification as he went along. His team-leader remembers him as a bright, eager young innocent who appeared never to have seen a ship before: "He was disciplined, never late for work. He seemed to like being part of a team and fitted in well. He was talkative, curious about people and things."

Henryk Lenarciak, a fitter in the same team, says that Lech was: ". . . a quiet boy, who didn't stand out in any way at all. Sometimes he spoke at union meetings, but never in a provocative way."[6]

"They were good years," says Lech, "perhaps the best of all. No children, no real worries. The first loves. And another thing – there, in the shipyard, I could feel I was myself at last. I began to understand that inside me was a deep, irresistible urge to go out and change things."[6]

After the cottage in Popowo, even the shared, rented hostel rooms in which he lived seemed spacious; and he revelled in the interesting new acquaintances he found there. For a time, his brother, Zygmunt, shared a room with him. They would lie on their bunks, Lech reading religious pamphlets, and Zygmunt film magazines. Girls came and went. (He was attracted to women, but lacked confidence and was easily discouraged.) One day, after a row with a girl, he went out and got roaring drunk. "It was cold and I was fed up and tired. I looked for some kind of shelter, and all I could find was a church. I went in and sat in a pew. It was warm in there, and suddenly I felt such a sense of inner peace that it was as though my whole life had taken on a new direction.

From then on I became a genuine believer, and acquired a purpose in life."

Something else changed on the day he entered the Orchidea flower shop in Gdańsk, to change some money, and saw nineteen-year-old raven-haired Danuta Gołoś. Her name was actually Miro-sława, but right from the first Lech called her Danuta. Like Lech, she had been brought up in the country, on a "middle-sized farm" in the Podlasie region of eastern Poland, where, the saying goes, there is nothing but woods, sands and carp (in Polish: *laski, piaski i karaski*). Like Lech she came from a large family – five boys and four girls. Like him, she had dreamed of escape to the city. "I wanted to get away. I wanted to taste life," she says.

It was love at first sight. He came back later that day just to see her, though neither then nor later did he buy her flowers. "He always thought words should be enough," sighs Danuta. She found him "different from other men, in the way he behaved and in his whole attitude to life", adding that he was "very persuasive". He courted her for a year, mainly at the cinema, where they went every evening, regardless of what film was being shown. There was simply nowhere else to go.

They were married on 8th November, 1969. The shipyard found them a dilapidated little room on the outskirts of Gdańsk. To help pay their half of the rent (the shipyard paid the other half) Danuta found a job in a newspaper kiosk. Until, that is to say, she found herself pregnant. "I stopped work then," she recalls. "We were terribly poor, we were hungry, we had all kinds of problems. But life was very good. I could say that it was the happiest period of my life, because Lech and I were together all the time."

Within the year, their son, Bogdan (gift of God), was born. And Poland was facing the crisis which would set the course of Lech Wałęsa's future life.

[1] *Poland in the Twentieth Century, op. cit.*
[2] Nicholas Bethell, *Gomułka, op. cit.*
[3] Bohdan Cywiński, *The Polish Experience.*
[4] *Poland in Perspective, op. cit.*
[5] *Człowiek z Marmuru,* Cztowiek z Żelaza, text by Alexsander Ścibor-Rylski, Aneks, London, 1982.
[6] *The Book of Lech Wałęsa, op. cit.*

11 WATERSHED (1970)

In order to preserve and defend the right to freedom, and so to
defend the dignity of man as an intelligent and free being, one
must commit oneself and be prepared for sacrifices . . . A man
who passively accepts the slavery imposed on him submits himself
to the yoke and in a sense ceases to be fully human. And the nation
which no longer knows how to fight for its freedom has already
fallen, since it has accepted less than its true dignity. There then
arises a need for heroic sacrifices and massive shocks to bring
about the awakening of the man who no longer fights for his
freedom as an intelligent being should; and of the nation which no
longer fulfils its obligations in the name of its most important and
sacred right – its freedom.

Cardinal Stefan Wyszyński, 1961

Prices rose, shelves emptied, queues lengthened. Drought and
bad harvests played their part. Bitterness grew and festered.
Gomułka was now unpopular with just about everyone: with the
workers because they didn't have enough to eat; with the peasants
for overpricing their equipment and making them produce all
their own grain rather than dairy produce for the home market;
with the students and intellectuals because of 1968; and with the
office workers because he was always sniping at their "bourgeois
tendencies".[1]

Hoping to recover some of his lost popularity, Gomułka
was wooing the government of West Germany, from whom he
hoped to obtain not only a guarantee of Poland's western
borders but also a massive loan. Herr Willy Brandt came to
Warsaw, and a Treaty was signed, recognising the existing
borders. It was Gomułka's only foreign policy triumph; but
it held a hidden disadvantage. Fear of the German aggression had been a kind of cement bonding the people to their
government and to the protective mantle of the Soviet Union.
Now that they need no longer fear Germany, the bonding
lost its power. The Poles grew restive. When the loan from
Germany did not materialise, and Gomułka invited them to

125

tighten their belts even further, they felt the first stirrings of uncontrollable rage.

The explosion came sooner, however, than anyone expected. On 12th December, 1970, less than two weeks before Christmas, which is traditionally the most important religious as well as family holiday in Poland, the Gomułka regime announced drastic increases in food and fuel prices, without any corresponding increase in wages and salaries. (Some members of the Politburo, including Edward Gierek, the member for Silesia, and General Wojciech Jaruzelski, who had become Minister of Defence, had tried in vain to dissuade Gomułka from this suicidal course.)

It was not the actual price rises, however, so much as the unbelievably inept timing of them, which underlined just how remote from the people Gomułka had become. For the workers, that industrial proletariat created by the Communist regime, it was the final insult. The grumblings and mutterings spilled over into an outbreak of pure rage. Unable to stand any more, they erupted on to the streets. And nowhere more violently than in the Baltic towns of Gdańsk and Gdynia.

The 16th and 17th December, 1970, are graven on to the hearts and minds of the Polish people. The memory of them remains raw and painful, as the years have gone by without healing. For Poland, December 1970 marked a definite watershed. For Lech Wałęsa too. From this time onward, he would be *"engagé"*, committed to an enduring struggle with an unjust authority.

He claims that he played a leading role in the bloody events, and that some of the responsibility for what happened must be his. Colleagues suggest that his role was a minor one, but they agree that it marked him. "It was enough to be there, to hear the shots, to clear away the corpses, to watch the terrible burials by night. It was enough – to make a man remember for the rest of his life."[2]

"I took part from the first moment to the last," Wałęsa insists. "But I was only twenty-seven. I was inexperienced and didn't know how to handle a situation like that."

On Monday 14th December, two days after the price rises had been announced, a thousand workers from the Lenin shipyard in Gdańsk surrounded the Party HQ in Gdańsk demanding that the rises be withdrawn. No one in authority would agree to discuss the matter with them; but a junior official pompously ordered them back to work. This infuriated the men. Workers from other factories had now joined the shipyard workers and together they marched on the College of Technology, to call out the students.

WATERSHED

Once again it is Wajda's *Man of Iron* which catches the undertones of the exchange. Mateusz Birkut, at the head of the crowd, shouts:

> Students, the time has come. The whole Baltic coast is saying "Enough is enough". We left you to fight alone in 1968, and perhaps we were wrong. But you must not make the same mistake as we did. Together we can do much. We want an end to repression, to violence, to lies, to needless suffering. Students, I beg of you, COME WITH US![3]

But the students, remembering their own past humiliation, stayed silent and did not come out – "neither then nor later, when the city echoed with gunfire, and when the first victims began to fall".[4]

In the early hours of Tuesday morning, as cars, buses, trucks and shops blazed against the Gdańsk skyline, a strike was proclaimed at the shipyards, and Lech Wałęsa was elected to the strike committee. Three thousand workers, with Wałęsa at their head, marched to the city, shouting "HANG GOMUŁKA, GOMUŁKA OUT!" Their destination was police headquarters, and by the time they reached there, the mood was ugly. Wałęsa, who believed in protest but hated violence, was already afraid that things were getting out of hand. Climbing on to a telephone kiosk, he appealed for calm. But the men were intent on attacking the jail and releasing the prisoners. As they stormed into the ground floor of the police building and set it on fire, Wałęsa appeared at a first-floor window, still making his appeal for calm, and begging the crowd to call off their planned attack on the prison. Not recognising him, they threw stones at first, until they recognised the familiar, rasping voice, shouting, "It's me, chaps. It's Leszek." They listened to him then, and did as he asked.

Meanwhile the authorities had proclaimed a state of emergency in the entire coastal area, and had given the security forces orders to shoot if necessary. Pitched battles between police and workers were taking place all over Gdańsk. Gomułka, caring little for the workers' misery, said angrily that it was counter-revolution organised by "anti-Socialist elements", and that it must be stopped by even more repressive measures.

The shipyard had been ringed by security police and militia, and now, as more workers left to join the demonstrations, they were fired on. The workers were stunned when they heard the firing. More shots rang out. Three were killed, eleven injured. It was a silent but bitter crowd which gathered to proclaim a sit-in at the shipyard. Throughout the coastal region, workers downed tools.

Events now assumed a terrifying momentum. Ten thousand workers attacked the Party building and set it on fire. As officials slid down ropes to safety, they were beaten up by the enraged crowd below, in no mood for mercy.

All day long the battle raged; and by nightfall, a pall of smoke hung over the city. A curfew was imposed at 6 p.m., and by then six people had been killed, three hundred injured. A Politburo official explained on radio that security troops had been forced to fire in self-defence against "hooligans and social scum".

Tanks and troops moved in overnight. Radio and telephone links with the rest of the country were cut, all flights to and from Gdańsk were cancelled. When the workers gathered at the shipyard, they were warned that the troops were empowered to use force if necessary. They responded with a set of demands: for pay increases, price freezes, tax cuts, and punishment for those responsible for ruining the economy. Deputy-Premier Kociołek went on TV in Gdańsk to say that the demands were impossible and would not be met, and to appeal for a return to work.

Wearily, many workers decided to return. But the last act of the tragedy had not yet been played. Its setting was to be Gdynia. That evening, in the Paris Commune shipyard, matters had got out of hand. The workers had seized control and were issuing ultimata to the authorities. Even as Kociołek was making his appeal, armoured tank units were moving towards the shipyards and security forces had entered the compound, to prevent the workers from sabotaging the ships and machinery. The shipbuilding industry association ordered work in the shipyards to stop forthwith. No one was to be allowed near. Kociołek knew nothing of this till later. When he realised what was happening, he tried to withdraw his appeal, and warnings were sent out to people all over the Tri-City. But the early-morning shift-workers were already en route.[5]

The thousands of workers arriving at the Gdynia railway station early next morning from the surrounding suburbs moved towards the exit, and found themselves faced by tanks. Security troops opened fire immediately, while tear-gas canisters were dropped from police helicopters circling overhead.

An hour later a crowd of five thousand was still fighting a losing battle with militia and security forces outside the now blazing railway station. As tear-gas, gunfire and smoke filled the air, and as the number of dead continued to grow, a column of workers broke from the crowd, carrying the bodies of the victims on railway carriage doors which had been wrenched off incoming trains. Official sources later admitted that thirteen were killed that day – Gdynia's "Bloody Thursday" – and seventy-four were badly injured. Popular sources suggest a much higher figure.[6] And on the same day, street fighting in Szczecin claimed at least sixteen lives.

In no cases were the workers allowed to bury their dead themselves. The anguish of families faced with a rapid identification, followed by a hasty official burial, in the presence of uniformed police and with the glare of spotlights upon them, was poignantly expressed in a little film *Pomnik (The Monument)*, which was shown in Poland only during the Solidarity era, when a monument had at last been raised to the dead of 1970. In a documentary excerpt, a weeping mother relates how a well-dressed man had come to tell her that her son was dead and must be buried within the hour. The family was allowed in to the mortuary at the cemetery to identify the body lying naked on a slab with all the others. (The bodies had all been stripped of their blood-stained clothes.) They were told to bring a fresh set of clothing and dress the corpse for burial. But in the rush they forgot the boy's boots:

> I was very upset and asked my husband to go home for the boots. But the man said no, that couldn't be allowed. He must be buried quickly, and there were others to be buried too . . . It was so tragic, we didn't have his boots. His friend said, "Don't cry. I'll give him mine." He took off his boots and put them on my son's bare feet. My daughter gave him some socks so that he could walk home in the snow . . . The priest came and blessed my son . . . We threw ourselves on the coffin, but they pushed us away. No time for that sort of thing, they said.

Grieving relatives were never able to find the graves again. When they returned to where they had buried their loved ones that night, the bodies had been removed, and all trace of the graves obliterated. It was as if they had never been.

"They've dug him up," says Anna to Maciek, when they have searched in vain for the body of Mateusz Birkut who has been killed in these events. "But why have they taken him away?" asks Maciek uncomprehendingly. "So that we shall not be able to bring flowers," she answers.

Nobody is sure how many died. The government eventually admitted to twenty-six. The people insist it was several hundred. "We tried to find out," says Lech Wałęsa, "we spoke to people, we asked questions, we searched. But they always prevented us from finding out. We were never able to complete our list. But one day we *shall* complete it."[7]

Gomułka, determined to crush this "counter-revolution" at all costs, asked General Jaruzelski whether the Polish Army could be brought in. Carefully the General replied: "The Army will do its duty." Gomułka sensed that in a struggle against Polish workers, a conscript Polish army might refuse to fight. So he turned instead to his Russian ally and asked for military help. Brezhnev refused, telling him curtly to solve his problems by political or economic means but not by force. This was a body-blow for Gomułka who by now was paranoid about the imagined counter-revolution. His frustration knew no bounds.

Within the Politburo, support was growing for his rival Edward Gierek. Forced to call an emergency meeting, Gomułka argued his case, but more and more unconvincingly. The meeting was still in session at 3 a.m. on Saturday, 19th, when Władysław Gomułka suffered a minor stroke which partially blinded him, and he was carried off to hospital in an armoured car.[8] Edward Gierek moved over and sat in the chairman's seat.

A workers' revolution had unseated Gomułka just as surely as an earlier one had brought him to power. He was given no choice but to resign and hand over power to Gierek.

Wałęsa has 1970 constantly in mind. "The biggest mistake I have ever made," he says, speaking of his decision to lead the men into Gdańsk that first day. For years he continued to feel responsible for what happened, ashamed of his own inability to prevent the crowd from becoming a mob. For the next ten years he would brood on every detail and analyse every mistake. "The killings forced me to do that," he says. "I had plenty of time later to think things through, and realise just where we had gone wrong. It was an apprenticeship, a necessary stage. After all, you don't reach the top class without passing through the lowest one."

Lech's sister, Izabela, a member of the Party and hoping to persuade her brother to join too, remonstrated with him for the part he had played. "Why must you always blow against the wind?" she raged at him, using a phrase from their childhood. "You don't understand," he said maddeningly. "But you will – some day."

[1] Bethell, *op. cit.*
[2] Jerzy Surdykowski, *Notatki Gdańskie*, Aneks, London, 1982.

[3] *Człowiek Z Żelazu*, op. cit.
[4] Ibid.
[5] Ibid.
[6] My account of the December events is taken mainly from George Błażyński's *Flashpoint Poland*, Pergamon Policy Studies, Oxford 1979.
[7] Jean Offrédo, *Lech Wałesa, Czyli Polskie Lato*, Cana, Paris, 1981.
[8] Gomułka died in 1982, without ever returning to public office.

The Wałesa quotations taken from author's own interviews with Lech Wałesa.

12 THE RISE AND RISE OF EDWARD GIEREK (1970–76)

One man lies wounded, another dying,
Blood has flowed this December dawn.
These are the rulers
Shooting down workers!
Janek Wiśniewski fell.

Workers from shipyards of Gdańsk and Gdynia,
Back to your homes now, the battle is over,
The world stood by, looking on in silence.
Janek Wiśniewski fell.

Do not weep, mothers, these deaths are not wasted,
A black-ribboned flag o'er the dockyard now flies.
For bread and for freedom
And for Poland reborn,
Janek Wiśniewski fell.

Popular song commemorating the events of December 1970.
This is the version sung by Krystyna Janda in the film *Man
of Iron*, somewhat diluted from the original in order to
pass the censor. The original, stronger version was sung
during the Festival of True Song held in Gdańsk in the
summer of 1981.

Poles had killed Poles. The workers' regime had given orders for workers to be shot in cold blood. "After December," said Anna Walentynowicz, a middle-aged crane driver at the Gdańsk shipyards, "I thought to myself, now there will be changes. After all these horrors, and all this bloodshed, it's just not possible to go back to the way we were."

The workers were in an ugly mood, unwilling to be sweet-talked into submission. Edward Gierek, the new Party Secretary, addressed the nation on television with emotion, determined to bridge the yawning chasm between Party and workers: "Comrades, citizens, fellow-countrymen, I turn to you in the name of the Party . . . I appeal to all Polish workers . . . together let us

132

learn from the painful events of the past week. I beseech you all . . ."

At this point, Wajda's film hero, Maciek Tomczyk, grieving for his murdered father, heaves a chair at the television set and smashes it. (Whereupon he is put into a straitjacket and removed to a psychiatric institute.) The attitude of the majority was less violent but no less cynical. They had been disappointed once too often. One leader, they had learned, was much like another; with each change at the top, life for the workers merely got bleaker.

But it soon began to appear that Gierek might indeed be different. Unlike most of the previous leaders, he was a genuine proletarian, son of a miner and a miner himself from the age of thirteen. He had been brought up in France, joined the Communist Party there, and been expelled for organising a miners' strike in the Pas de Calais.

So now he could legitimately claim to be on the workers' wavelength and to understand their problems. And as, unlike the penny-pinching Puritan, Gomułka, he also believed in raising living standards, he stood a reasonable chance of becoming popular.

First of all, the country had to be restored to normal. Gierek immediately pledged more housing, concessions to farmers, an increase in consumer goods and food supplies. But, while announcing a rise in pensions and child welfare benefits, he also proposed a two-year price freeze, based on the prices which had caused the December riots. This aroused the workers to renewed fury and a fresh wave of strikes (notably one at the Warski shipyards in Szczecin) hit the country in January, accompanied by demands for radical reform of the economy and punishment of those responsible for the massacres in December. The country was once again like a seething volcano. Catcalls greeted Party officials rash enough to try and speak at public meetings, and there was general disgust with the lies and evasions of the official press, which had barely acknowledged the events on the coast, referring merely to a little "sporadic activity" by "hooligans".[1]

Immediately after the riots in Gdańsk, Lech Wałęsa had his first brush with the police. Danuta has described her first experience of a house-search:

The child opened the door and said, "Mummy, there's a man here with a parcel." There was a group of them at the door. "Where's your husband?" they demanded. I shrieked at them, "Is he some kind of child that I have to keep an eye on him? I've no idea where he is." They said, "Don't shout like that." "What, can't I shout in my own

133

home? I'll shout if I want." Four of them pushed past me into the flat. They found something – some tapes recorded from Radio Free Europe, I think.

Ignoring the warning, Lech had become an active member of the Gdańsk post-strike committee, and was one of those demanding an official memorial to the dead of December. For him, this was already a Holy Grail, a quest that would preoccupy him for the next ten years. But he was prepared to be patient, having learned the hard way that to be angry was not enough: "A wall can't be demolished by butting it with your head," he was heard to remark. "We must move slowly, one step at a time. If we rush at it, the wall will still be in place, but we shall have our heads smashed in."

When Gierek came in person to soothe the workers of Szczecin and Gdańsk, Wałęsa and an older colleague, the fitter, Henryk Lenarciak, were two of the three Gdańsk delegates chosen to meet him. But in what the press described as "tough, forthright discussions", Wałęsa was a silent partner. It was Henryk Lenarciak who did the talking.

Later, Gierek spoke to the shipyard workers and made promises. Captivated by him, they listened and were won over. They complained to him about the official trade unions, about the lies told by the media and about the inefficiency of management. Gierek was sympathetic and soothing. The December events must never happen again, he agreed. "Never in my life will I shoot at Polish workers." He told them how he had worked in the mines in France and Belgium, and how he had been in trouble for organising a strike in France. It was a marvellous piece of demagoguery, and he finished by stretching out his arms in appeal. Will you help me make a fresh start? he begged. And the workers shouted with one accord, "Pomożemy", "Yes, we will help you." Lech Wałęsa would later recall with some bitterness that he shouted "Pomożemy" as loudly and trustingly as everybody else.

But as long as the price rises remained in force, the strikes (unprecedented in a Communist country) would continue. Only when, after a stormy meeting with the scandalously underpaid women textile workers in Łódź, Gierek withdrew the rises, did peace return to the factories of Poland. Within the East European Communist bloc, Polish workers had made history by forcing their government to make concessions to them. And the victory gave the workers a quite unrealistic sense of their own power.

Confident now of the workers' support, Gierek embarked on

his new policies. First of all, he established unchallenged control over the Party, by a new purge of over one hundred thousand "unreliable" members, and by the political elimination of his personal rivals. Next, he set about increasing the food supply by giving greater incentives to the private farmers. He recognised their rights of ownership to their land, reduced their taxes, admit- ted them to welfare benefits and abolished the compulsory deliver- ies to the State. By ceasing to insist on Poland producing all its own grain, and by allowing the farmers to own more livestock, by the end of 1971 Gierek was able to cut down the amount of food he imported from abroad.

But he was more interested in industry than in agriculture, a preference he would one day come to regret. Profiting from the Soviet Union's present enthusiasm for détente, Gierek set about importing modern machinery on easy credit terms from the West, for the updating of Polish industry. In theory, the plan was excellent. The goods produced in the new, high-technology fac- tories would be exported to the West in exchange for the hard currency needed to repay the debt. In practice, it did not work out as planned. The goods were certainly produced, but they were not always of high quality, nor did the West always want them. (As one writer observed, "Polish machine tools and cars will not be bought by anyone in his right mind.")[2] Nevertheless, the defects in the new system were not immediately obvious, and Gierek's optimism was infectious. Poland cultivated friendly re- lations with Europe and America, and within three years the Polish economy was one of the fastest-growing in Europe.

Living standards improved. Wages rose, while prices remained frozen. Over one million new flats were built, welfare benefits increased, and imported consumer goods began to pour into the country. Poland was transformed. Westerners who visited the country in these years saw a well-fed people, with money to spare, equipped with washing machines, television sets, transistor radios and the like. The hitherto empty streets began to fill with small cars, as Poland acquired a licence to manufacture her own brand of Fiat. Visitors from the Soviet Union looked with envy on the bulging shelves and the luxuries which never came their own way. As for the Poles, they were indulging in an orgy of travel to the more affluent West.

Gierek, it seemed, was living up to his promises. He regained the trust of the intellectuals by relaxing the censorship; and the result was a fresh flowering of creative talent. Radio and TV programmes injected more truthfulness into the reporting of political affairs. The Sejm (Parliament) was given a fraction more scope, and a few more non-Party members. And the immensely popular decision was taken to rebuild the Royal Palace in Warsaw, a move which had always been stoutly resisted by Gomułka.[3]

Even the Church came in for its share of goodwill. In his first policy speech Gierek's Prime Minister had called for co-operation between believers and unbelievers. Cardinal Wyszyński, ever pragmatic, had called for restraint and mutual tolerance. "We must forgive," he said in his 1970 Christmas homily, "because each of us bears responsibility for the mistakes of the past." Gierek gave permission (never fully implemented) for the construction of one hundred and thirty new churches, including one in the steel town of Nowa Huta, where requests for a new church had for long gone unheeded.[4] (But the government still continued its policy of demolishing those churches which the faithful were spontaneously building for themselves without permission.) Relations with the Vatican also improved, and there was much talk on both sides of *normalisation*, though it was not clear that they both meant the same thing by it.

It even seemed as though Wałęsa's desire for a monument to the riot victims would one day be fulfilled. Vague promises had been made, and on the first May Day after the riots, officials laid wreaths at selected cemeteries in honour of the dead. It seemed as though Lech's confident optimism was justified.

Gierek now began to prove that he understood what the workers wanted. Well aware that he must tread carefully for the present, he entered into consultation with small groups, discussing the country's economic and political problems with them. And although he did not go so far as to allow independent trade unions, he did allow the existing unions to hold completely free elections for the first time, and to dismiss some unwanted Party hacks from high office. In February 1971, as the result of such elections, Lech Wałęsa was elected to his section council as a work inspector.

It was exactly what he had wanted. "A job," wrote a friend, "that would let him wander round the shipyard and visit all the ships. He would be able to keep his finger on the pulse of the shipyard and know what was going on."[5]

Lech was almost euphoric, believing that at last the unions were about to become the true champions of workers' rights. "He believed that every word Gierek spoke was sacred," Izabela said later, in a newspaper interview: "Gierek was the saviour who would make the dreams of millions come true. When he promised to turn Poland into the Japan of Europe, Leszek believed he would do it."[6]

Writing with enthusiasm about the free elections, a reporter on *Voice of the Coast* referred to Lech Wałęsa as "a controversial figure":

> He is twenty-seven years old, has read books about crowd psychology, and about spontaneous action. The last months have seen him involved in unexpected and dangerous activity. It so happened that he was at the centre of the events about which everybody is talking. He did not become involved in them for fun, nor from a thirst for adventure, nor a hatred of the people who are responsible for law and order. He quite simply decided that he had nothing to lose, and for that reason became a leader of the shipyard strike.[7]

To this same reporter, Lech spoke of the need to get production moving:

> We must stop talking and get back to work. Talk will get us nowhere. I believe that the section council must stay in close touch with the people and be accountable to them. But we must ensure that nothing interferes with increased production. Even in this area, things are improving, as they are in social conditions. If people will only trust us, we in the trades unions will do what we can for them. We all want things to get better.

On the section council, Lech Wałęsa proved himself active and exceedingly stubborn, determined at all cost to get his point of view accepted: "Sometimes, when we opposed him," said Lenarciak, "he would say he'd go and tell the workers what his propositions were, and they'd be sure to agree with him."[7]

But Lech soon found that the section's activities were being limited to unimportant matters, and that the big decisions were all being taken over the heads of the workers. The unions were being expected to revert to their earlier role as a mere transmission belt for orders from the Party. This was not his idea of what a trade union was for. A year later, when new elections to the section council were held, Wałęsa did not allow his name to go forward.

Shortly afterwards, it became horrifyingly clear that the leaders of the December strike were being sacked – and blacklisted so that they would be unable to find other employment. Wałęsa was reported for having made derogatory remarks about the authorities, and came close to losing his job. On this occasion he was saved by the fact that his work was good and his team one of

137

the best in the shipyard. He escaped with a warning, and a demand that he should learn to keep his mouth shut.

Lech's parents, Feliksa and Stanisław, had for some time been making plans to emigrate to America, and Feliksa was anxious that Lech should go with them. But, whatever his problems, Lech had no desire to live in a capitalist country. As he told his mother: "I am a Pole. I shall never leave Poland. We have to try and make Poland work."

In 1972, the senior Wałęsas left Poland for Jersey City in the United States, where Feliksa's sister, Janina, had lived since before the war. It was the fulfilment of a long-cherished dream, and Feliksa was disappointed that she had been unable to persuade her favourite son to share it. As she said goodbye to her other children, it seems she told them, "Try and be more like Lech." None of them would ever see her again. Three years later, as she crossed a busy street in Jersey City, she was hit by a car and died almost instantly. Her body was brought back to Poland, and she was buried next to Bolesław, in the bleak cluttered little churchyard of Sobowo. Today, peonies, lupins and ox-eye daisies grow wild over the unmarked grave, beside which, unaccountably face downward, lie two stone tablets bearing their names.

By the middle of the decade it was only too clear that Gierek had overreached himself and the whole edifice he had built was about to collapse like a house of cards. He had experimented with too many cosmetic changes, without tackling the basic problem, which was the over-centralised, over-manned, hidebound, top-heavy structure of the Marxist–Leninist economy itself.

The external cause of collapse was the OPEC oil crisis and its knock-on effect. The increased oil prices imposed by the Arab oil sheikhs in 1973–4 sent most of Europe dizzying into recession. They finally hit Poland when Moscow, which supplied eighty per cent of Poland's oil, doubled its asking price. Poland had then to divert more of its exports to the Soviet Union in order to pay for the oil. But, as the Soviet Union paid in "transfer roubles" (about as much use as Monopoly money), the Poles then lacked the hard currency with which to continue paying for machinery from the West. Meanwhile recession and inflation in the West caused a drop in the demand for Polish exports. Unable to lay off workers in redundant industries, Gierek had to borrow more from the West, until his borrowings reached the point where what little he earned from exports had to be put to servicing the debt. When, finally, he was forced to reduce his borrowing and cut down on imports, Polish industry began to suffer a serious lack of spare parts for the machinery which kept the factories going.

Gierek's dream-bubble burst with a vengeance. As wages were still rising and food prices still frozen, there was an excessive demand for food which neither agriculture nor industry could supply. So supplies of food, especially of meat, ran short. Five years of bad weather and poor harvests had aggravated the situation, but the main problem was that, while eighty per cent of the agricultural land was owned by private farmers, they were still not given adequate incentive to produce more. It was the other twenty per cent of State-owned collectives which was allotted most of the available fertiliser, fodder and grants for machinery. To obtain low-interest bank-loans or coupons for fertiliser, private farmers had to provide the State with up to seventy per cent of what they produced – at far below market prices. Grain (now imported) was so expensive that farmers were feeding bread to their pigs, because it was cheaper than the wheat from which it was made.

In 1975, as his economic boom began to wane, so too did Gierek's façade of bonhomie. The unions were already disillusioned about the way he had betrayed them. His popularity evaporated. What is the difference between Gierek and Gomułka? went the joke. None, was the answer, but Gierek doesn't know it yet. The scales fell at last from Lech's eyes. Gierek had, in fact, never fulfilled his promise to bring those responsible for the December massacres to justice. Nor, after the first two years, had the officials continued to lay their May Day wreaths at the graveyards. All commemoration of the December events was now banned, and the promised memorial had never materialised.

On 11th February, 1976, the shipyard's section council held an extraordinary meeting, and Lech Wałesa made up his mind that he would speak at it. He warned Lenarciak, who was the retiring chairman, that he would speak his mind, regardless of consequences. "You are too soft," he said, "you ought to be more determined."[7]

Wałesa was true to his promise. "He spoke for quite a long time," said Lenarciak. "One sentence I shall always remember. It was that Gierek had misled the nation, hadn't kept any of his promises, and acted without ever asking the working class for their opinion."

The sentence was rapturously applauded, and the workers elected Wałesa as their representative to the works' Union Conference. This was a step calculated to alarm the authorities, who

139

did not want this troublemaker given the opportunity to stir up more unrest. A high-ranking director who had attended the meeting was furious with Wałęsa and with the organisation's officials for not interrupting him and throwing him out.

A few days later, a letter was sent to the directorate of the shipyard and the works council, informing them that the work contract with Citizen Wałęsa was to be terminated immediately. "This employee is difficult," the letter said. "He makes tendentious and malicious public statements about the section's managerial staff and about political and social organisations; and this creates a bad working climate within the section."

Lenarciak told his successor on the section council to do everything possible to save Wałęsa: "There is no criticism of his work and one cannot sack somebody just because they've been critical at a union meeting."

The section manager, a civil engineer, had received orders to dismiss Wałęsa, but, as he refused to sign the dismissal document, he too was sacked. Lenarciak explains:

> We were told that he'd resigned because of ill-health, but later one of the directors told us that this was not true. This man told us that if the instructions were not obeyed, the manager would not be the only one to be sacked. The new manager signed Wałesa's dismissal form the day after taking the job. He was not a bad fellow, just cowardly.

The section council would not sign the dismissal notice. It was authorised by the chairman of the works' council and countersigned "by instruction of the directorate" by the manager of the personnel department. Wałęsa was henceforth forbidden to enter the shipyard: "What's the matter with them?" he cried angrily. "I don't drink; I'm honest; I come to work on time. Why are they doing this to me?"[7]

He did not seem to realise that he had broken the first rule of survival in a Communist country – thou shalt keep thy head well down and do as thou art told.

When he appealed against the dismissal, a committee of judges decreed that criticism of the authorities at a union meeting provided quite adequate grounds for dismissing an employee from his work.

*　　*　　*

A new ice age had descended on Polish culture, the frostiest since Stalinist days. Ideological pressure was being stepped up, there was a new attempt to catch Poland's youth in the net. School timetables had been redrawn in such a way as to leave no time for out-of-school religious instruction, and not much time for the family either. In some schools, a written profession of atheism was being demanded. Wyszyński complained that this was a violation of the right to conscience guaranteed by the Polish Constitution. Matters came to a head when Gierek tried to have the Constitution itself amended, in order to enshrine the leading role of the Party and "the unshakeable fraternal ties" with the Soviet Union. As this would deny the Poles any right, at any time, to oppose the Party, everybody, workers, intellectuals and Church deeply resented the proposed changes. The bishops led the expressions of universal dismay. The age-old antipathy between the Church hierarchy and the intellectuals was visibly ending. Alarmed by such a united front, Gierek modified the offending insertions.

In the wake of the Helsinki Conference, during which the whole Eastern bloc committed itself to respect human rights and fundamental freedoms "of thought, conscience, religion and belief", the Poles had become more than ever aware of how their human dignity had been trampled on. They – and especially the young – were looking for a way of recovering their integrity. And many of them found it in the Light-Life Movement, a back-to-the-Gospel religious renewal which had been started in the 50s, but which now in the mid-70s seemed to have acquired a new life. All over Poland, young people were dedicating themselves to living the gospel of Jesus Christ, without fear. "One must be able to overcome fear in order to bear witness to and live by the light," wrote the Movement's founder, Father Blachnicki. "A person is free when he has the courage to bear witness to the truth and to live by the truth, whatever the cost in personal suffering."

The idea of living according to one's conscience without fear was immensely appealing. By 1975, fifty thousand people had joined Light-Life. This new and powerful movement within the Church was to have incalculable consequences for the future. For it signified that the young people of Poland were sorting out their priorities, and were finding that Truth came at the top of their list.[8]

Gierek did not yet know that one day he would have to reckon with the young. For the moment he had other problems on his mind. Had it not been for the economic collapse, he might just have been able to contain the intellectuals. But war on two fronts was too much. The cost of maintaining ridiculously low food prices was becoming unbearable. When the government began exporting meat, shortages at home resulted, and disillusionment became general. Already in the summer of 1974 there were strikes in Gdynia, while in spring 1975 housewives, enraged by the meat shortages and the necessity to queue, set fire to a grocery store in Warsaw.[7] The joke went the rounds: why are butchers' shops always a kilometre apart? Answer: to keep the queues in front from getting tangled.

What else could Gierek do but raise the prices? But, with memories of 1970 still fresh, he was understandably reluctant. In June 1976, however, his options ran out, and he finally summoned up the courage to announce that prices must shoot up (about seventy per cent on meat) and the rate of wage increases must slow down.

On the following day, industry virtually ground to a halt. In Warsaw and Radom there were riots. The country was uniting in rage.

[1] Neal Ascherson, *The Polish August*, Chapter 3: "Years of Disillusion", Penguin, 1981.

[2] From Tim Garton Ash's introduction to *The Polish Revolution*, Jonathan Cape, 1983.

[3] Antony Polonsky, Chapter: "Poland Under Gierek" in Halecki's *History of Poland*, *op. cit.*

[4] See present author's book, *Man From a Far Country*, Hodder & Stoughton, 1979 and 1982.

[5] *Notatki Gdańskie*, *op. cit.*

[6] *Japonia Lecha Wałesy*, interview with Izabela Młynska (née Wałesa) in Wiadomości Skierniewickie, 22.1.81.

[7] *Book of Lech Wałesa*, *op. cit.*

[8] *The Light-Life Movement in Poland*, Grażyna Sikorska, *Religion in Communist Lands*, Volume 11, number 1. Spring 1983.

13 COUNTDOWN TO CHANGE (1976–9)

Our Party, which has a long and fine-sounding name . . . reminds me of a gigantic vacuum-cleaner which sucks in everything within the compass of this ill-fated country's borders. It could also be likened to a cancer which greedily burns its way through every inch of tissue, every cell of the body politic, an infuriated cancer, a cancer in total overdrive, a cancer with a cosmic erection. Perhaps there has occurred, or is now occurring, in Europe, a degeneration in the functioning of states and in their dealings with each other, but there is no way you can imagine the nightmare that has befallen us.

Tadeusz Konwicki, *The Polish Complex*

When the fateful price rises were announced, workers at the Ursus tractor factory in Warsaw tore up the tracks of the Paris to Moscow railway line, which runs through the factory, and blockaded the line so that no trains could enter or leave Warsaw. In Radom, further to the south, workers stormed the Party HQ, and when they saw the huge quantities of food and drink stored there for the privileged few, they divided it amongst themselves and set fire to the building.

Retribution was swift and savage. The UB ran amok, arresting workers right, left and centre, regardless of whether or not they had taken part in the demonstrations. In Ursus, the arrested workers were sacked from their jobs and evicted from their hostels. In Radom, where at least seventeen men were killed, thousands were arrested and made to run the so-called "path of health" – between double lines of militia armed with batons. "They beat us senseless and smashed our bones," reports a survivor.

Within a few hours the prisons were bursting. Next day special kangaroo courts began handing down draconian sentences, making liberal use of false witnesses and manufactured evidence. Heavy fines and long prison sentences were meted out. Scores of workers were thrown out of their jobs and prevented from finding other employment, except of the badly paid, unskilled variety.

Most of the official unions made haste to condemn the "hooligans" and "anti-social elements" in their midst. But there were honourable exceptions. In Bydgoszcz, for example, Stanisław, Lech Wałęsa's brother, who had shared Lech's faith in Gierek, and who was still a loyal member of the Party, resigned as secretary of his union branch, rather than read aloud the speech which had been prepared for him, condemning the "hooligans and firebrands". As a result, he too lost his job.

To Lech, the events of June 1976 were illuminating as well as distressing. "The strike of the workers at Ursus and Radom," he said in his 1983 Nobel speech, "was a new experience, which not only strengthened my belief in the justness of the workers' demands and aspirations, but also indicated the urgent need for solidarity amongst them."

An angry crowd of workers gathered outside the shipyard management offices in Gdańsk, threatening a strike if the intolerable price rises were not withdrawn, and demanding the reinstatement of Lech Wałęsa. The Church, meanwhile, was supporting the workers, though stressing the need for calm. "It is painful," declared Cardinal Wyszyński in a sermon, "that workers should have to struggle for their basic rights under a workers' government." But nothing, he also assured them, was ever solved by violent protest. In Kraków, Poland's other Cardinal, Karol Wojtyła, begged the government to reconsider the price rises and to stop terrorising the workers. At the same time he set up a fund for the families of those arrested or out of work.

Two days later, the rises were called off. The shipyard workers therefore did not strike. Nor did they continue to insist on Wałęsa's reinstatement. On the surface, life returned to normal. But the repression continued. More and more workers were arrested. This new attempt at coercion, however, boomeranged on the government, for the net result was to drive the workers and the intellectuals together at last. On 23rd September, 1976, fourteen dissidents, among whom was Jacek Kuroń, established KOR, the Workers' Defence Committee. It was a milestone in the history of Communist Poland.

It is a long time [wrote KOR's spokesman, Jerzy Andrzejewski], since reprisals have been as brutal as these recent ones. For the first time in many years, arrests and interrogations have been accompanied by physical terror. The victims can count on no help from the trade unions – whose role has been deplorable. Society's only defence against lawlessness is solidarity and mutual support. That is why we have formed the Workers' Defence Committee.[1]

"We've done it out of shame," said Kuroń. "We were ashamed of the intellectuals' silence in 1970. We need to recover our good name."[2]

KOR brought legal aid to workers who had been at the mercy of corrupt courts; and gave financial help to their families. They collected proof of police brutality and of the crooked photographic evidence that had convicted them. For many they secured an early release. Then, so that everywhere people would understand the enormity of what had been done, they published their findings. In this way KOR effectively nipped in the bud the growing police terror, and raised the level of awareness in Poland, bringing that much nearer the hope of a real change in society.

Gierek, himself a relatively easy-going man, who was, besides, bent on preserving good relations with the West, was anxious to put a brake on police repression, while sorting out some of the more obvious disorders in Polish society. Alcoholism – always the last line of defence against misery – had passed the "biological threat" barrier; absenteeism was rife; the divorce rate was rising and the birth-rate falling. For help in this alarming situation, Gierek sought the goodwill of the Church. Reminding First Secretary Gierek that the government could only hope for good workmanship if it provided the workers with a decent way of life, and observed the human rights of all Poles, believers as well as unbelievers, the bishops nonetheless agreed to co-operate with him in this moral disaster area. They were becoming accustomed to the see-saw nature of their relationship with the present regime.

But however much it might suit Gierek to blow hot and cold with the Church, his attitude to KOR was nothing short of icy. As an illegal organisation, its members were subjected to every kind of intimidation. They lost their jobs, their apartments were ransacked, their belongings seized, and they were frequently attacked either by the police or by unknown assailants. In Kraków, a leading KOR sympathiser was Stanisław Pyjas, a final year philology student. His sudden death in deeply suspicious circumstances in May 1977 sparked off student demonstrations in Kraków, and his funeral was attended by two thousand students who walked in silent protest to the spot where his body had been found.[3] Cardinal Wojtyła gave his support to the students and asked the citizens of Kraków to see to it that they didn't get hurt.

The Pyjas affair, closely followed by the arrest of Kuroń and the young scholar, Adam Michnik,* increased public sympathy for KOR and encouraged the Church to offer qualified suppo.t to the former Marxist intellectuals they had once regarded with suspicion. St Martin's Church in Warsaw gave sanctuary to fourteen hunger-strikers protesting about the arrest of KOR members. Cardinal Wyszyński took up the cudgels on behalf of KOR, saying: "Sometimes people demand their rights too violently because they feel the noose tightening around their neck. How can a nation live when basic human rights are denied it? A nation that has no human rights is not a nation, but a collection of soulless robots."[4]

KOR itself was spurred to even greater efforts by Gierek's unblushing announcement in February 1977 that the police had not exceeded their powers after the riots of the previous June and that there was no need for an inquiry into their behaviour.[5]

After three months, Kuroń and Michnik were released in a large-scale amnesty in July, and proceeded to expand KOR's activities. Once they had believed that they could reform the Party from within, but the years had killed that hope. They proposed now to wash their hands of the Party, to let it preserve its empty façade of power, while they themselves created a genuine opposition, the foundations of a new pluralist society representing different social and political ideas.[6] Only in this way could change come about.

KOR (like the growing Light-Life Movement within the Church), had come to the conclusion that the oppressors' greatest weapon was fear. "Once you can rise above your own fear," said Kuroń, "you are a free man." Determined, therefore, to overcome fear, and to live as though they lived in a free society, KOR emphasised the need for everybody to act openly, regardless of possible consequences. In order to broaden their own scope, they changed their name to KSS-KOR (the Committee for Social Self-Defence-KOR), and backed various other audacious social initiatives and activities which were outside the control of the

---

* As a young university lecturer, aged twenty-two, involved in the 1968 academic disturbances, Adam Michnik was arrested on a trumped-up charge and sentenced to three years in prison. After his release, the doors of the university were closed to him, and he worked as an unskilled labourer in a Warsaw factory. Then the authorities decided that he was a bad influence on the workers, and he lost that job too. In 1976, at the request of Jean-Paul Sartre, he was given a passport and spent several months in France. But he returned to Poland in 1977, knowing that he would be returning to a life of personal danger. A few days later, he was arrested.

Party. One of these, the Flying University courses, reminiscent of the similar educational arrangements during the Nazi Occupation, flouted the Party taboos and provided information on a variety of long-forbidden subjects. The lectures were held in private flats and were frequently disrupted by the police, the teachers and owners of the flats all being arrested. (One story going the rounds told that after a talk entitled "Orwell's Nineteen Eighty-Four and Today's Poland" had been broken up by police, next day a new lecture was advertised with the title "Orwell's Nineteen Eighty-Three and Today's Poland"; the police left the second one alone, and it was allowed to take place unhindered.)

Censorship was as oppressive as it had ever been. Although Wadja's film, *Man of Marble*, which attacked the Stalinist terror and the moral corruption of the years which followed it, was shown in Poland in 1977, restrictions were otherwise abnormal and ludicrous. Partly because of this, there was a flourishing of independent houses which published a vast amount of underground material unacceptable to the censor. Of these, the most important were KOR's Information Bulletin and *Robotnik*, a paper for workers. "The situation was droll," comments Cywiński. "Draconian sentences were being handed out, the security police were violating every known principle of law. And yet here were writers and editors insisting on signing their own names to everything, and people flocking openly to illegal lectures."[7]

As the need to stick together became increasingly imperative, the link between workers and the intelligentsia grew. The towns of the Baltic coast, with their energetic and volatile populations, were particularly receptive to new ideas. On 29th April, 1978 ("about the time when the World Cup was being played in Argentina," he says), Lech Wałesa was one of a small group of dissidents in Gdańsk who announced the formation of the Baltic Committee for Free and Independent Trade Unions. The first of these groups had, suitably enough, been launched in Radom, for the defence of workers' economic, legal and human rights. "We got wise," said a worker, unconsciously repeating an idea of Kuroń's. "We realised you don't have to burn down Party Committee houses. We have to build our own."

So began a new more overt phase in Wałesa's long underground struggle for independent unions. "It was my first taste of genuine human solidarity," he says. "The important thing for me was that at last I belonged to a group with whose aims I could identify."

Over the next four years, Danuta complained that she rarely saw him, that his life had become an endless succession of secret meetings, underground activity and all too frequent arrests. Lech claims that in this period he was arrested "hundreds of times" for circulating leaflets, and for distributing clandestine copies of Miłosz's *Captive Mind*. "Hundreds" may well be an exaggeration, but it is true that he spent many an unpleasant forty-eight hours in a police cell. He says he did his thinking in prison and had a much-needed rest. Nowadays he looks back and marvels at Danuta's patience with him, speculating that a lesser woman would have stuck a carving-knife into him long since.

The founder of the Free Trade Union group in Gdańsk was bearded engineer Andrzej Gwiazda, a name that would become famous later on. Others were Alina Pieńkowska, a nurse in the shipyard's medical section; and Bogdan Lis, a twenty-five-year-old Party member. But the undisputed leader and spokeswoman was Anna Walentynowicz, a widow with one son. Anna, whose sacking in 1980 was the spark that set the tinder of Solidarity alight, is a remarkable woman – "pure gold" say her admirers, of whom there are many. Small, dumpy, with ugly, black-rimmed spectacles perched on her nose, she is said to have "the outward charm and gentleness of a Polish granny and the inner strength of a Polish cavalry-man". She was ten years old when the 1939 war broke out; and in the course of that war, she lost her entire family. Pain was so much a part of her life that she could not bear to see anyone making others suffer, and her whole life had been a conscious struggle to defend the weak. Lacking education – she went to school for only four years before the war – she had learned only what she had picked up in lectures for illiterates and in courses on welding at the Gdańsk shipyards where she had worked as a crane-driver since 1966. Tough though she looked, she knew she had cancer, and in 1965 she had been given only five years to live.

Until 1968 Anna worked for the official trade unions. When disillusionment finally set in, she was sacked, ostensibly for "attacking the work of a union collective", but in reality for exposing the corruption rife in the union. The workers protested at her dismissal, and she was re-instated, though not in her old crane-driving job. Then came December 1970 – "that shriek of agony, that blind terror which sent people rushing onto the streets. I thought to myself: the five years have passed and I'm still alive. If God has given me life, there must be something he wants me to do. And I wondered what it might be."[8]

She knew she could not fight alone, so she contented herself with small acts of kindness – heating hot milk and soup during

148

the work-break and serving it to her fellow-workers, to save them the long journey to a distant canteen. When she was told to stop, she tried instead to brighten their lives by planting flowers outside the workshop entrance: "The manager came and asked me if I wanted to be sacked again. 'I don't want anything except to see flowers growing,' I said. But he wouldn't listen and I didn't get my garden."

Shortly afterwards, in 1971, when she had protested about the withdrawal of promised bonuses, she was again given her cards.

"In 1978," she said, "I first heard about free trade unions. I didn't know what they were, but I thought that if we had real unions we should not be so helpless in the face of licensed evil. So I began to look for people who would explain them to me."[9]

She found KOR, and began to share the good news with her fellow-workers. And that's when her troubles started: "The workers were forbidden to talk to me, and the department head made sure that I went straight from the gate to the cloakroom, and from there to wherever I was working. Any step outside the area allotted to me would mean dismissal."

Harassment did not deter her. The Free Trade Union group of which Anna was co-founder did its best to convince people that if only they would act together, their strength would be a match for the security police. The conspirators met in small groups, always in a different place and at a different time, sometimes on a wild seashore, sometimes deep in a forest. Whenever they held larger meetings – to hear Flying University lectures on modern history, work-law, the need for society to organise itself – they were infiltrated by police agents.

When the group decided to produce its own newspaper, *Solidarity* was one of the titles considered. But they settled for *Worker of the Coast*, to link it to the nationally produced KOR magazine, *Worker (Robotnik)*.[10] The first issue (August) contained a statement of aims:

> We do not have political aims; we do not wish to impose on our members, collaborators or sympathisers any precise political and social views, we do not aim to take over power. We realise, however, that we will be accused of indulging in political activity. The range of matters considered in our country to be political is very wide and encompasses almost everything except excursions to pick mushrooms.

In the September issue, *Worker* published a thousand-word Charter of Workers' Rights. It was signed by sixty-five activists, among them Wałęsa, Walentynowicz and Gwiazda. They called on workers to "throw off all feelings of apathy; stop passively accepting restrictions on our rights and the erosion of our living standards". And they concluded, somewhat prophetically: "Only independent trade unions, with the backing of the workers they represent, stand a chance of providing an effective challenge to the authorities. They alone can become a power with which the authorities will be obliged to negotiate on an equal footing."

Lech had the reputation of a loner in these years. He would sit at the back of the meetings, soaking up the discussions, learning. When each member of the group was asked to produce a blueprint for his or her ideal society, Lech produced an exhaustive list. When he reached point twenty-four, "the director should treat his employees better", the others laughed at his naïvety. None of them saw him as a possible future leader. He was merely the group's postman.[11] (He was also the goalkeeper when they played football. "That's how he always saw himself," said a colleague. "The perfect anchor-man.")

Since May 1976, he had been working in the transport section of the ZREMB building company. Here, at a time when there was a catastrophic shortage of spare parts for almost any machine, Wałęsa made his name as a first-class mechanic who could work wonders with clapped-out cars. He was popular, and his boss turned a blind eye to his more doubtful activities. "Just do your job well and I shan't bother about all the rest," he told Lech.[4]

When he brought clandestine leaflets, posters and copies of *Worker of the Coast* to work, they were snatched up immediately. Others he scattered in the streets, in trains, buses, churches, or distributed to other factories. In the middle of December he put up posters reminding people of the coming anniversary. When a workmate who had angrily torn down such a poster later broke his leg, Lech assured him that the accident was God's punishment for tearing down Truth!

He was frequently taken away by the police. The first time, they treated him as a poor innocent, too naïve to realise he was being used by men cleverer than himself. But when they realised he had actually written some of the leaflets himself, they changed their tune. The UB followed him everywhere. Once after a funeral a friend invited him to his flat for coffee. Lech refused. "I'm being watched," he explained. "If I go to your place they'll come and turn it upside down later." At work his personal dossier was carefully scrutinised by the police.

As a delegate to the Party-dominated "factory Parliament" he once again showed an undesirable outspokenness, and complained moreover that elections to the post of president and secretary were rigged. "Gentlemen," he asked during the election, "what have I come here for? To take part in an election, or just to applaud? What sort of election is it when the result has been decided beforehand?"

After showing his hand like that, it was only a matter of time before they sacked him. All that was needed was a pretext. In the end they fell back on making him redundant, though they did also charge him with "moonlighting", since he repaired his own and other people's old "bangers" on the works premises. (Hardly an impressive charge, since almost everybody did it.)

As from 31st December, the management told the works council in November 1978, it intended to dispense with the services of Citizen Wałęsa. Lech's section-manager spoke up for him, praising his extraordinary skill as a craftsman, the initiative he showed in solving difficult and complicated problems: "Besides he's never drunk, never late for work. He's a disciplined, conscientious worker who has a gift for creating a good atmosphere around him."

The manager's opinion was unwelcome and he was demoted to a store-room job with a considerable drop in wages. The works council could not oppose a dismissal which was supposedly on account of redundancy, so they signed the necessary documents. Only when Wałęsa had appealed against the decision, on the grounds that he was a breadwinner with a wife and four children to support, were they able to ask the directorate to reinstate him. The directors agreed to take him back but only as a sort of general dogsbody in another section. Wałęsa said he had no intention of becoming an errand boy and refused the job. On 29th December, he was sacked again.

Lech's workmates were furious about the way he had been treated, and there were mutterings about a strike. Wałęsa would not hear of it. "Don't make trouble," he advised, "you'll only get yourselves the sack. You've got children too, don't expose yourself to the risk. We're not strong enough yet. But the time will come when we shall be stronger than they are, and that's when we shall act."[12]

"Some of us cried when he went," remembers a fellow-worker. But many, perhaps the majority, still thought Lech was mad for provoking the authorities so often. Years of pressure had resulted in an ostrich psychology which preferred to keep its head down and hope not to be noticed. "My workmates," Lech wrote later, "were full of repressed hatred of the system, but they believed they were powerless. The fact that I was repeatedly thrown out of work was seen by most of them as a confirmation of their own greater realism. There was this deadening conviction that there was no point in doing anything, since nothing could ever be changed."[13]

[1] *Poland in Perspective, op. cit.*

[2] John Taylor, *Five Months with Solidarity*, Wildwood House, 1981.

[3] *Dissent in Poland 1976–1977*: reports and documents presented by the Association of Polish Students and Graduates in Exile, London.

[4] Błażyński, George, *Flashpoint Poland*, Pergamon Policy Studies, Oxford 1979.

[5] *Poland in Perspective, op. cit.*

[6] Antony Polonsky in Halecki's *History of Poland, op. cit.*

[7] Bohdan Cywiński, notes on *The Polish Experience*.

[8] Jean Offrédo, *Lech Wałesa Czyli Polskie Lato, op. cit.*

[9] Ibid.

[10] *Book of Lech Wałesa, op. cit.*

[11] Ibid.

[12] Ibid.

[13] *Uncensored Poland*, News Bulletin published by the Information Centre For Polish Affairs, London, Number 19/83, 30th September, 1983.

14   SCATTERING THE GRAINS (1979–80)

By 1979, then, there was already the embryo of that tacit alliance of workers, intelligentsia and Church, unprecedented in Polish history, unique in the Soviet bloc, unseen in the West, which was to grow into Solidarity.

Tim Garton Ash, *The Polish Revolution*

That December, for the first time, an illegal ceremony was held outside gate number two at the shipyard, at the spot where the workers had been killed. It was organised by the Young Poland Movement, one of the independent Human Rights groups which had sprung up in the wake of the Helsinki Agreement. Lech Wałęsa, who had placed flowers at the spot every year, spoke to a crowd of about four thousand and vowed: "Next year there will be more of us."

He spoke more truly than he knew. The following year, 1979, there were seven thousand. And part of the reason lay in the electric shock which had galvanised Poland into life when, in October 1978, Cardinal Karol Wojtyła of Kraków had been elected Pope. It was one of those times, like the outbreak of war or the death of President Kennedy, when everyone claims to remember exactly where he was when the announcement was made. Not since the defeat of the Bolsheviks in 1920 had the Polish people known such heart-warming national pride. The winter that followed was freezing and there was no coal; production in the factories was paralysed; queues were longer than ever for less and less; hospitals were closing for lack of drugs and medicines; pharmacies put up "closed for repair" signs; and several cities were without light, heat and water. But everything was somehow bearable because there was a Polish Pope. Hope had been reborn along with self-respect. Perhaps a new society was possible after all. KOR's attempts to make society realise its potential, the frequent flouting of the censorship, the growing demands for free trade unions were all straws in the wind. Suddenly the Poles began to believe that they were not, after all, "abandoned by man and by God", and that a major political change had now become not only possible but inevitable. In the words of Anna Walentynowicz: "When he became Pope, every Pole held his head a bit higher. We were no longer just a nation of alcoholics and work-shy labourers."

In June, Pope John Paul II returned to his homeland in triumph. He had wanted to come in May, to celebrate the 900th anniversary of the martyrdom of St Stanisław, a bishop of his former Kraków diocese, but this was found politically unacceptable. (The bishop, slain in the eleventh century by the king's stooges, was a symbol of human dignity oppressed by the authorities.) So the visit was delayed, and it was on the feast of Pentecost that John Paul arrived to kiss the soil of Poland. Gierek and the Party had hovered between delight and dismay at the time of his election, but had finally settled for a cautious chauvinistic pride in this "son of the Polish nation, which is building the greatness and prosperity of its Socialist fatherland with the unity and co-operation of all its citizens".

They doubtless hoped that the visit of this particular son to his Socialist fatherland might encourage and enhance this unity and co-operation.

Even the weather rejoiced. It was a blazing hot summer's day when he arrived, to be greeted like a king, with garlands, flowers and song. Any of the grey faceless Politburo men would have given his eye-teeth for such a demonstration of love and allegiance. Who could doubt that John Paul was the real leader of Poland? For two weeks the Poles acted out the fantasy that their actual leaders did not exist.

The sight of Warsaw's Victory Square dominated by a huge oak cross draped with a red stole was miracle enough. On that square a quarter of a million people waited for John Paul. The atmosphere was one of carnival. The very fact that so many had arrived in this place without being compelled to go there was in itself memorable. And when the Pope, standing by an altar built on that very Square which had so often witnessed their humiliation, spoke to them of man's need for Christ, they cried out: WE WANT GOD, again and again over the roaring applause that seemed as though it would never end.

On Pentecost Sunday, the students came on foot from miles around. Everywhere he went, the young made it plain that their loyalty was his. Be proud of your Polish inheritance, he told them. Add to it, hand it on to future generations! Do not be afraid of the difficulties. Be afraid only of indifference and cowardice:

"From the difficult experience we call Poland, a better future can emerge. But only if you yourselves are honourable, free in spirit and strong in conviction."

In Silesia, miners, the darlings of the regime, defying a government ban, turned out in their thousands, wearing their traditional dress. The regime knew the baffling humiliation of a quarter of a million miners singing: "Christ has conquered, Christ is king, Christ commands our lives" at full throttle. The media did their best to play down the visit, to give it a minor place in the evening TV bulletins, to limit the film shots to close-ups of old ladies or brass bands. But nobody was fooled, not in Warsaw, not in Częstochowa, not in Gniezno, not in Kraków, not anywhere. John Paul spoke to the whole of Poland, giving voice to truths that had too long been silenced, convincing the people that social renewal was possible only at the price of their own moral renewal. He was inviting them to change their lives, and it was as though he had opened a locked door, letting in the light. Adam Michnik, listening on radio, said: "When he asked believers never to deny Christ, I felt he was talking directly to me, an unbeliever."

Michnik, like many other intellectuals, had long realised that since 1945 the Church had been the most consistent defender of human rights and freedoms in Poland.[1] Consequently, the Polish left had abandoned its outdated stereotype of a reactionary, right-wing and anti-semitic Church.

It was like the first Pentecost, they said, when the Holy Spirit came down on the followers of Jesus. "The Spirit will come upon you and change the face of this land," John Paul promised, adding, in Kraków, "the future of Poland will depend on how many people are mature enough to dare to be non-conformists!" Everybody heard, everybody was repeating his words. "It was a strengthening of the whole nation and everyone was aware of it," said a man from Poznań. "People wanted to start again, to become authentic human beings. It was an incomparable spiritual experience."

Significantly, throughout the whole visit, perfect order was kept by volunteer stewards, and there was no violence. A voluntary ban on alcohol had been observed. There was a sense of national unity and solidarity such as had not been experienced since the years of Nazi occupation.

The writer and former Communist, Kazimierz Brandys, had come to believe that the Poles cared only about their own material well-being. But the Pope's visit made him realise that:

. . . as soon as there was but half a chance of regaining an authentic human existence, all the cars, refrigerators and television sets would be tossed onto the barricades. Yesterday somebody said to me: "This is not an outbreak of religious feeling. This is a manifestation of patriotism, a national uprising without a shot being fired. He has come to lift us out of the mud."[2]

A new concept of the nation – as a community – was being born. John Paul "scattered the grains", reflected Bohdan Cywiński, explaining how harvesters used traditionally to make a festive wreath of the grains and take it along to the big house where a celebration would take place. From now on, said Cywiński, people like Lech Wałęsa felt that they were carrying the Pope's wreath, and they lost whatever fear they had had.

Lech had been working since May 1979 with "Elektromontaż", an engineering firm which produced electrical equipment. A senior employee of the firm described him as "the best automobile electrician bar none", and he was much liked. But he was a marked man, and security police shadowed him from the moment he arrived. If he went to repair equipment at a building site, the UB would be on the scene as soon as he had left it, asking what he'd been doing, to whom had he talked and about what. In spite, or perhaps because of this harassment, he won many sympathisers to the cause of free trade unions, both in the works and on the building sites. He brought in leaflets and got discussions going, and he persuaded many to join the organising committee. But when someone asked him whether he had any hopes for the immediate future, he replied: "I'm convinced that one day there will be independent trades unions in Poland. But not in my lifetime."

As the December 1979 anniversary drew near, surveillance was stepped up. One car with police markings was now permanently parked outside the works, and three days before the anniversary a second car joined it: "We were afraid they would arrest Leszek," said Florian Wiśniewski, a fellow-worker, "but we were determined that he was going to be at the wreath-laying ceremony at Number Two gate of the shipyard where his colleagues were shot in 1970. It was unthinkable that he shouldn't be there. So we arranged to smuggle him out in a container truck as soon as the police entered the compound."[3]

The workers kept a round-the-clock watch on everyone entering and leaving. When a group of officials arrived on the day before the anniversary, and went straight to the office, Lech was promptly smuggled out, but in a "Nysa" car, not a container. Too many people had known about the container, and it was all too probable that the information had leaked out.

Next day, Wałęsa did not come to work. He was in hiding. It was the 16th December, and that evening, outside the Lenin shipyard, seven thousand men and women gathered to honour their dishonoured dead. Wałęsa was one step nearer the fulfilment of his vow that one day a monument would be erected in that place. "This obsession with the martyred dead, so much a part of the national psychology," a British journalist was to write, "was the source of his driving anger and his obstinacy. This young electrician is best understood, when all has been said, as Antigone."[4]

In front of that crowd of mourners, Wałęsa was at his best, and many people noticed him for the first time that day. He spoke to them about his own experience of that terrible December, his feelings of responsibility for what had happened. He told them how deeply he had trusted Edward Gierek, and how that trust had been betrayed. And he appealed for them to come forward: "Only an organised and independent society can make itself heard," he said. "I beg you to organise yourselves in independent groups for your own self-defence. Help each other."

And finally he issued an appeal that was also a challenge, that: "next year on the tenth anniversary, each of you must bring a stone or brick to this spot. We shall cement them into place and we shall build a monument."[5]

Almost immediately after this event, the "Elektromontaż" works council was informed that there were to be redundancies. According to Florian Wiśniewski:

> Fourteen people were on the list, all but two of them members of the Free Trade Unions. The idea of redundancies was ridiculous. We were so short-handed that on one building-site we had had to borrow workers from elsewhere. The chairman of the council was under the management's thumb, but the majority would not agree to the dismissals.[3]

To strengthen their case against Wałęsa – "the company's most outstanding electrician" – the management officially reprimanded him for "absence from work" on the day of the ceremony. He appealed to the council. At the meeting which was to hear the appeal, the director and First Secretary of the works' Party branch turned up – an obvious attempt to scare the council members into submission. The members, however, decided that if Wałęsa had stayed away on the day in question, it was because of the police pressure within the factory; and they voted to quash the reprimand. It was a brave gesture, but the dismissals were not revoked. Angrily, the men set up a committee to defend their mates who had been sacked; but though a delegation went to plead with the management, it achieved nothing and the dismissals were put into immediate effect.

Inevitably the workers had lost their battle with authority. But they were determined at least to show their solidarity with the victims. From then on, they held a collection every pay day for their support.[3]

One of the Free Trades Union activists who was dismissed along with Wałęsa was a teenage boy, Jan Szczepański, who lived near him, on the Stogi estate. Not long afterwards, the boy disappeared without trace; and later his mutilated body was found in a canal. His feet had been cut off, his fingernails pulled out. Lech Wałęsa was one of hundreds from Stogi who planned to attend the boy's funeral. But on the night before, police trucks surrounded the estate. A neighbour of the Wałęsas takes up the story:

> At first we thought it was a raid on the amber-collectors who were digging up the coastal forests and doing a lot of damage. The police were all round our apartment block. In the early morning, there were cars standing outside, and I could see two UB at the bottom of the staircase. I guessed they were waiting for Wałęsa, so I rushed down to his flat to warn him not to go out. He was getting ready, and there was an enormous wreath in the passage. I told him the police were there, but he said he had to go to the funeral, no matter what. As he left the building, the UB rushed him and tried to get the wreath, but he held on to it. Then another lot rushed out, and there was a scuffle. They tore the wreath out of his hands and pushed him into one of the cars.[3]

It was probably then that his local fame began. Stogi was a clannish district, where neighbours helped each other and shared each other's problems. Before this, Lech had been remarkable chiefly as the chap who put holy pictures in his window on feast days and who regularly every Sunday led his clutch of children to church. Now they saw him in a different light. As Lech was detained more and more often by the police, they developed a system of warning signals for him. Once Lech and his family (five children now) barricaded themselves into the one-and-a-half roomed apartment, to prevent the police from entering.[6] He opened the window and shouted to the policemen through a loud-hailer, while neighbours poured hot water from the windows and threw slippers, buckwheat kasza and anything handy at them. The police withdrew, and next day Lech hung out a huge banner thanking the neighbours for their support.

The Young Poland Movement which had organised the December ceremony had also re-awakened public interest in the 3rd May Constitution of 1791 – the first written constitution in Europe, and inspired by the principles of the Enlightenment and the French Revolution. Before the war, 3rd May had been Poland's National Day, but the Communists had abandoned it in favour of 22nd July, which marked the 1945 Communist takeover. Young Poland planned to revive the earlier tradition, and had issued a leaflet containing the text of the 3rd May Constitution. Wałęsa stuck a copy on the window of his clapped-out old car, and before long found himself under arrest and minus a driving-licence.

Quite clearly he was unafraid. Perhaps also he had decided that he had nothing to lose, being already out of work and hungry. With a family of five to support (and a sixth on the way) he had appealed for help to the Committee for Social Self-Defence – KOR (KSS-KOR). "Kuroń gave me bread," he was to say later. Through KOR, Kuroń also gave him a legal adviser, Jacek Taylor, who found his new client more than he had bargained for: "He had his own ideas about how I ought to defend him," recalls Taylor. "With other clients I could persuade them where their own reasoning was at fault. But not Lech. I could never explain anything to him. There was I, with all my legal experience, confronted by this simple worker – and completely baffled by him."

Lech kept Taylor busy, rescuing him from police clutches. Once they arrested him in the middle of Gdańsk as he was pushing his baby daughter Magda in the pram, brazenly sticking up posters as he went. They bundled him, the baby and the pram into a car, then drove back to Stogi to deposit pram and baby before taking him off to cool his heels overnight in a cell.

*　　*　　*

By the late 1970s the economy had skeetered right out of control, like a runaway train on the wrong track. Industrial and agricultural production were plummeting – "only prices, alcoholism and foreign debts were rising in a spectacular manner".[6] Poland was almost bankrupt, the Western banks had run out of patience, no one but Russia was buying Polish exports. Food supplies dwindled. When stale bread was delivered in November to Kazimierz

Brandys's local co-op because the bakery had run out of electricity to make fresh, there were grumblings in the queue. Whereupon the driver who'd made the delivery said, "You'll be kissing the ground for bread like this when winter comes."[2]

Everyone was tired and frustrated with the degrading living conditions. The young had to wait ten or fifteen years for a three-room flat in which the bath was usually out of order because of a lack of spare parts; women rose before dawn to catch a tram into town and be in the meat queue by 6 a.m. (Some of the queues began at 2 a.m.) They would wait for two, three, four hours and then be fobbed off with rubbish. Shortages were such that when anything at all was available – candles, soap, toothpaste, toilet paper, razor blades, shaving-cream – "You rush to buy as much as you can, because heaven knows when you'll get it again." Before the war, went a current joke, you could go into a butcher's shop and find meat. Today the sign outside the shop says *Meat*, but you go in and find only the butcher.

Another joke concerned the man who went into a shop and asked for a long list of foodstuffs which were as scarce as gold-dust. He was quite mad, everyone agreed. "But what a memory," they added admiringly.

Yet for those who had money, there were few scarcities. A Polish Fiat (for which normally there was a four-year wait and cash to be laid down at the beginning of the waiting period) was available for dollars. A plumber could be paid in nylons, veal was on sale in the extremely expensive "commercial" stores. In these stores, opened by Gierek after the food riots in 1976, the better cuts of meat could be found, at three times the usual price. And for those lucky enough to have dollars (the majority were not in this category), there were the hard-currency Pewex stores where Western goods could be bought. Likewise in the PKO shops Polish products were on sale – for dollars only. "We now have three classes in our classless society," said a Polish taxi-driver. "Those who have dollars, those who have złoty, and those who have neither." The black market was a way of life – the good life – in Poland, for those who could afford it.

The privileged ones, those in the *nomenklatura*, "the bosses" – that new class called into being by the demands of the Communist state, valued for their ability to say "Yes" to the Party, holding all the best jobs and well-protected by the police – were insulated from the reality which afflicted everybody else. They were known as "the owners of People's Poland", and they were deeply resented. Shortages were not for them or for their children, who

160

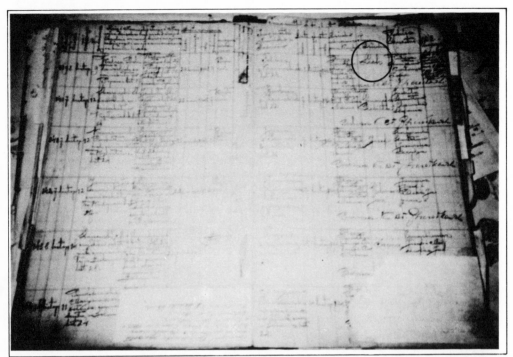

Lech Wałęsa's birth entry in the register of the church in Mochowo – 29th September, 1943.

Lech (third from left) was the fourth of seven children, born into grinding poverty: "We were rich in the things that mattered."

The little house (left) in Popowo where Wałęsa was brought up.

Chalin: the school Wałęsa attended for eight years.

Danuta Wałęsa at home in 1982.

Marriage: 8th November, 1969.

Defiance in a Warsaw churchyard outside St Stanisław Kostka Church where Jerzy Popiełuszko is buried.

Dreams and determination: the vision can become reality.

Occupation strike in the Lenin shipyard and a new leader is born: Lech Wałęsa addresses the crowds.

Bread for the strikers: the nation expresses its overwhelming support.

Confession on site.

31st August, 1981, euphoria and relief as the agreement is signed guaranteeing independent
self-governing trade unions.

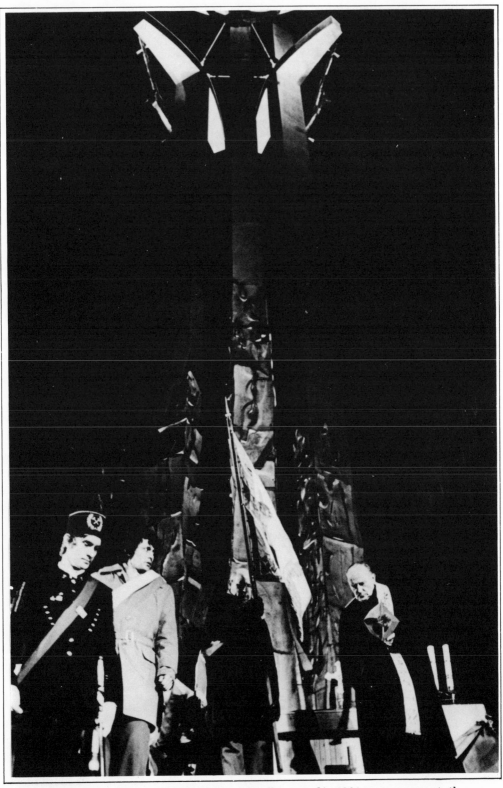

Cardinal Wyszyński at the Gdańsk monument, finally erected in 1981 to commemorate the tragedy of 1970.

Western Europe rallies to provide food and supplies for the Poles, struggling to survive the winter of 1981 in a shattered economy.

The nation unites in dedicated support for Solidarity.

"War": 13th December, 1981, the tanks move in overnight as the authorities declare martial law.

The realist.

Father Jerzy Popiełuszko, murdered in
October 1984.

Encouragement from Father Henryk Jankowski.

Lech Wałęsa with Pope John Paul II in Rome, early in 1981.

V for Victory!

Stamps from the underground.

Mary Craig with Lech Wałęsa at his home in May 1984.

The whole family in 1981. There have been two additions to the family since, both girls.

inherited their parents' privileges. Corruption was rife among them. In this Polish People's Republic, Edward Gierek's friend, TV and radio boss, Maciej Szczepański, was a walking legend by reason of his extravagant lifestyle. He cruised round Warsaw in a huge BMW (he was said to have eight cars), and crossed Poland in his private plane. He had a luxury flat, a sheep farm, a mountain retreat stocked with valuable antique furniture and plentifully supplied with call-girls, and enough ready cash to present Gierek with 5,000 dollars' worth of gifts on his sixty-fifth birthday. He had a yacht and a private cinema complete with nine hundred pornographic films. All that, plus a Swiss bank account. Szczepański was unique, but the corruption was general. "When I grow up," wrote a schoolgirl in a report on children's ambitions organised by the newspaper, *Polityka*, "I want to join the police and have a Rolls Royce." And a schoolboy contributed: "I shall be in the militia and have a house and a Mercedes."

Ideology, and whatever idealism had accompanied it, was absolutely dead. But the regime had to go on using the jargon for the sake of holding on to power. They clung to the rule-book, to the Marxist–Leninist theory, which enabled them to keep the reins in their hands. But it could only express itself as a lie. As everything got worse, so did the government hasten to assert that everything was for the best in the best of all possible worlds. Words like "crisis" or "strike" were taboo. The "propaganda of success" was mandatory. The television evening news was derisorily known as "the prosperity hour", and a TV series which set out to show that life in People's Poland was markedly superior to life in the capitalist West met with the contempt it deserved. Newspapers were still trumpeting of achievements even as the walls were caving in.

The joyous euphoria of the Pope's visit had vanished, but the memory of the pentecostal spirit it had aroused lingered on. It was kept alive not only by the Church but by the efforts of KOR, the Young Poland Movement, the Flying University and other dissident groups. There was a general acknowledgment of the disastrous gulf between society at large and the Party. A questionnaire printed and distributed by the private (KOR) publishing house, Nowa, revealed that the public no longer believed anything their masters told them, not even the bad news. There was an overwhelming contempt for the Party structures which claimed to represent the people, and an overwhelming demand for honesty and openness after years of living with official lies and "doublespeak".

Leszek Kołakowski, exiled to the West, claimed that this mendacity had not come about by accident. It was the very essence of
the Communist system:

> Mendacity is the immortal soul of Communism. They cannot get rid
> of it. The gap between reality and the façade is so enormous that the
> lie has become a sort of normal and natural way of life . . . Because
> Communism lives on inevitably impossible promises; because its
> legitimacy is based upon expectations which necessarily will not be
> fulfilled . . . In order to keep this legitimacy principle alive, they have
> to keep the mendacious façade, without which they'd fall apart. It is
> perhaps the most oppressive part of life under Communism. Not
> terror, not exploitation, but the all-pervading lie, felt by every-
> body, known to everybody. It is something which makes life intoler-
> able . . .[7]

Whether the government allowed the word "crisis" or not, crisis
was confronting them. There was a general feeling that the coming
storm would be the biggest yet. Kuroń knew that it was not the
dissidents who would provoke it. Only the workers, if they were
united and determined enough, would have the power to do so.

In February 1980, Gierek admitted to the Party Congress that
the economic situation was out of hand. He tried a change of
Prime Minister. The new man, Babiuch, went on TV in early July
and told the workers that things were going to get even worse.
He did not, in so many words, announce that prices would go
up, but it amounted to the same thing when he said that all
better-quality meat would be diverted from the state shops (cheap
but empty-shelved) to the "commercial" shops (expensive but
full).

If the government hoped that the people would be too much
absorbed in their summer holiday plans to notice, they could not
have been more wrong. And it would be from Gdańsk that the
knell would sound for Edward Gierek as it had for his predecessor,
Gomułka.

In that city, feelings were already running high. The Young
Poland Movement had organised another rally to mark the anniversary of 3rd May, and two of its members had been arrested as
they addressed the crowds. A summary court had sentenced them
to three months' imprisonment each. (Others, including Lech
Wałęsa, who had been distributing leaflets, were detained for
forty-eight hours.) Throughout May, daily prayer services were
held for the release of the two men. In July, a higher court quashed
the sentence and the two were released. But June had already

brought a different kind of trouble, when, as the result of an explosion in the Lenin shipyards, eight people died and sixty were injured. There was deep anger among the shipyard workers, and Anna Walentynowicz, who had never ceased to campaign for better safety precautions, stepped up her demands for protective clothing and for less dangerous methods of operation. On 9th July, after thirty years at the Gdańsk shipyards, she was fired, on the grounds of being "too often wilfully absent from work". In her own words:

The clerk who dismissed me said: "Anna, it's terrible what they're doing. I had to take two pills before I could bring myself to give you your cards." I replied: "Then why have you done it?" "They'll sack me if I don't do as they ask," she said, "and then someone else would come in and do it." "And what if the next person wouldn't do it either? And the next? And then the next? They couldn't sack you all, could they? . . ."[8]

The action was still off-stage, but a new and infinitely more dangerous stage of the Polish Revolution was in the making.

[1] Adam Michnik, *Kościół, Lewica, Dialog*. Instytut Literacki, Paris, 1977.
[2] Kazimierz Brandys, *A Warsaw Diary 1978 – 1981*, Chatto & Windus, 1984.
[3] *Book of Lech Wałesa, op. cit.*, Chapter 1.
[4] From Neal Ascherson's introduction to the above.
[5] *Notatki Gdańskie, op. cit.*
[6] *Poland in Perspective, op. cit.*
[7] Leszek Kołakowski, *The Eagle and the Small Birds – The Eclipse of Ideology*.
[8] Jean Offrédo, *Lech Wałesa Czyli Polskie Lato, op. cit.*

PART TWO

SOLIDARITY – AND AFTER
1980–1985

15 THE CROSS, THE EAGLE AND THE STATUE OF LENIN (AUGUST 1980)

Give over telling us you're sorry,
What guilt for past mistakes you carry;
Look in our faces, weary slaves,
Grey and exhausted like our lives.

Give over calling us the foe
Of all society, of our brother;
Just count our numbers, and you'll know
How strongly we can help each other.

Give over making us eat lies
With lowered heads and tight-shut eyes,
And for our culture, wait before
One vast, monopolistic store.

Stop prising us apart with wedges
Of conduct marks and privileges,
Suppressing facts that do not fit,
And stewing history down to shit.

Put back our words to what they mean.
Words which are empty and obscene,
So we can live with dignity
And work in solidarity.

Give over telling us you're sorry,
What guilt for past mistakes you carry,
Look at our mothers and our wives,
Grey and exhausted, like our lives.

The Twenty Second Demand: anonymous verses circulating during the strike at Gdańsk in August 1980. From a collection of young strikers' poems, published unofficially.[1]

"It was bad enough that there was next to nothing in the shops. But to raise the *price* of nothing took the people over the top."[2]

Ordinary life had become a struggle for mere survival, and Polish women foraged, as animals did, for food for their young.

The first strikes broke out in Warsaw, and the government dealt with them one at a time, forbidding the official media to refer to them. This attempt to keep the workers isolated and ignorant was rudely shattered by KOR who again began monitoring the strikes and telling the world about them. Accordingly, the Polish people heard what was happening by courtesy of Radio Free Europe and the BBC Polish Language Service. Then the whole country seemed to erupt in a rash of strikes, the most serious being that of the Lublin railway-workers who disrupted the lines to the Soviet Union, along which much-needed Polish food supplies were being siphoned off for the 1980 Moscow Olympics. None of this, however, discouraged Edward Gierek from setting off for his annual pilgrimage-cum-holiday in the Soviet Union on 8th August.

Successful revolutions, Lenin once said, are made when popular discontent coincides with a loss of self-confidence within the ruling regime. That collision was at hand. It is fascinating to speculate at what precise moment the routine rumblings about the high cost of food became something qualitatively different: a struggle for the nation's soul with a corrupt and discredited regime. What occurred was spontaneous combustion, an irresistible bush-fire which enveloped everyone in its benign flames. The silent majority, who had for so long been coerced into clapping, cheering and voting to order like so many sheep, found their voice at last. All over the country, Poles were declaring themselves ready to stand up and be counted. Not just for the sake of bread, but for freedom and justice.

The main fire was ignited in Gdańsk, where as yet there had been no strike. And the match that set the tinder alight was Anna Walentynowicz, the crane-driver granny, the "Mother Courage of the Shipyards".[3]

At a gathering of "oppositionists" in Gdańsk on 9th August, the possibility of a strike over the reinstatement of Anna Walentynowicz and Lech Wałęsa was discussed. Wałęsa was present. "See that little chap over there in the corner," someone explained, "that's Wałęsa." "Wałęsa?" said someone else. "Oh yes, isn't he the little guy who sings the national anthem at the top of his voice and out of tune?"[4] He was also the guy who, on the night of 1st August, had been arrested for delivering pro-strike leaflets, just as Danuta was about to give birth to their sixth child, Anna. Danuta had screamed in protest, loud enough to waken the whole block, but the police took Lech away in spite of her. Anna was born at 3 a.m., and Lech was allowed home at 10 a.m. He was not a man to bear grudges, but the humiliation of that night went deep.

Just before dawn on 14th, the Free Trades Unions group smuggled a pile of posters into the shipyard, demanding the reinstatement of Anna Walentynowicz and a thousand złoty rise. The early shift-workers were doubtful at first, but gradually they became more determined to fight. A crowd gathered, work came to a halt. A few wild spirits suggested taking to the streets, but memories of the 1970 carnage were still raw among the older workers, and wiser counsels prevailed.

Nevertheless, a dangerous situation was in the making. The director of the shipyard climbed on to a bulldozer truck and promised that if the men returned to work, something could be arranged. They were wavering, unsure of what they really wanted. And then a stocky little man, with quick, darting eyes, in a jacket far too big for him, climbed on to the bulldozer's roof and towered above the director. "Remember me?" he shouted. "I gave ten years to this shipyard; but you sacked me four years ago. I'm here to tell you we don't believe your lies any more."

Indeed, the director remembered. That flat, foxy face, that flowing moustache that looked as if it had been stuck on, the Charlie Chaplin walk. It was Lech Wałęsa who stood there, tense with the accumulated anger of a decade, and already declaring an occupation-strike by the workers. Minutes earlier he had been helped over the twelve-foot high perimeter fence, in order to be "in the right place, with the right ideas, at the right time".[5]

Why had Wałęsa chosen to act as he did? Because, as he would later tell a French journalist,[6] he had a score to settle. His arrest at the moment of Anna's birth rankled, though his bitterness was directed less against the men who had arrested him than against the system which forced them to act with such heartless insensitivity: "They were only carrying out someone else's stupid orders. It was not their fault but the system's. So when I heard there was trouble at the shipyard, I knew I had to go there and start changing things. So that my children don't go on being humiliated; so that they may have access to the truth."

Some of the men who clustered round that bulldozer had no idea who Wałęsa was. But a great many of them remembered him from his shipyard days and knew that fast-talking and truculent though he might be, he was a fundamentally decent man who had already suffered much for his genuine devotion to the workers' interests. They knew he was to be trusted, and so, if he declared an occupation-strike, they would go along with it. Lech, for his part, had taken the lesson of 1970 to heart. No more marches for him, no more street demonstrations, no more attacks on Party buildings, no more shouting of anti-Soviet slogans. Such activities played right into the government's hands and provoked bloody reprisals. Far better to stay in the place of work and cease production.

Immediately he set about forming a strike committee and arranging for negotiations with management to begin. Although he seemed perfectly relaxed and affable, once the discussions began he revealed a steely determination. On his instructions, the director's car was sent to bring Anna Walentynowicz in style to the shipyard. When Anna arrived and was given a bunch of flowers, and saw the banners demanding her reinstatement, she had difficulty in holding back the tears.

Wałęsa gave the director a list of five demands: the reinstatement of Anna and himself; a pay rise; an increase in the family allowance; a promise of immunity for strikers; and a monument to the victims of December 1970, forty metres high. In vain did the startled director protest that the area chosen by Wałęsa for his monument was already earmarked for a new hospital, a supermarket and a car park. In vain did he suggest that perhaps a plaque . . . A monument, insisted Wałęsa. And the director reluctantly caved in.

Thoroughly alarmed by events in the shipyard, the government (in the continued absence of Gierek) cut the telephone links between Gdańsk and the outside world. (When challenged about this, one government spokesman blamed the lack of contact on a storm which had disrupted the lines from Warsaw!) But by Saturday, the strike was already running out of steam, as the director was flatly refusing to negotiate on any other issue than the pay increase. He offered a raise, and threw in the reinstatement of Anna and Lech as a bonus. The question of the monument had already been agreed. Lacking Wałęsa's wider vision, and against his advice, a majority on the strike committee was ready to take what was on offer. It was all over bar the shouting. About half the striking workers had already left the shipyard, and the relieved director was actually announcing the end of the strike over the works radio when, all of a sudden, the whole picture changed.

What happened was this: following the shipyard workers' example and relying on their powerful support, a number of other

170

concerns like Gdańsk Transport, the Gdynia shipyard and several other enterprises large and small, had also withdrawn their labour. They sent delegates to the Lenin shipyard to see how things were going. When they saw that the strike was fizzling out, their dismay knew no bounds. Transport workers seized the microphone outside the conference hall and protested that they had been betrayed. The woman leader of the tramdrivers, Henryka Krzywonos, cried out: "If you abandon us now, we are lost. Buses can't face tanks."

Wałęsa, leaving the conference hall, was barracked by an angry crowd of workers. In a moment, he sized up the situation and made a lightning decision. "What do you mean?" he asked. "We *are* striking, aren't we?" Promptly commandeering an electric trolley, he drove round the shipyard, shouting through a loud-hailer to drown the voice of the director telling the workers to leave the place forthwith. Fewer than one thousand workers were still there; most of them did as Lech asked, and stayed put. Some of those who were already leaving ignored Lech's appeal, but some turned round and went back in.

Had the moment of confrontation arrived? Would the tanks roll, the security forces move on to the attack? For the men in the shipyard, it was an anxious time. But their numbers began to grow almost immediately, as soon as it became known that though the old strike was over, a new, inter-factory solidarity strike was beginning, with about twenty factories from the Gdańsk area taking part. Significantly, among the strikers at this early stage there was also a small group of non-manual workers from the Young Poland Movement.

Dropping those cautious spirits who had been ready to give in without a struggle, the new strike committee embraced men and women who were concerned with more than the satisfaction of immediate needs. With Andrzej Gwiazda and his wife, Joanna; Anna Walentynowicz; Bogdan Lis and Lech Wałęsa on board, it was hardly surprising when the strike committee scrapped the old list of five demands and replaced it by a new set of twenty-one. It was significant that, though these certainly included the wage rises and demands for a shorter working week common to strikers everywhere, those particular issues did not have top priority. Like a gallant David arming his puny sling for the unequal struggle with Goliath, the committee set forth its ideals, stating in its manifesto: "The workers are not fighting merely for a pittance for themselves, but for justice for the entire nation. We have to oppose the authorities' attempts to break up the unity of our

171

strike movement. We must live up to the words, Man Is Born Free."

Independent trades unions; the right to strike with impunity; freedom of speech and a curb on censorship; access of all denominations to the mass media; reinstatement of workers who had been sacked for taking part in earlier strikes; the release of political prisoners; and a ban on all measures directed against freedom of conscience. These were the issues, the freedoms taken for granted in the West, which had pride of place in the Gdańsk workers' list. They demanded also an overhaul of the economy, and a guarantee that in future managers would be selected for their skills and not for their readiness to toe the Party line.

Taken as a whole, the demands reflected the nation's overwhelming frustration over food shortages, poor medical care, long waiting-lists for houses, cars, fridges; and with the scandalous inequalities which flourished in this supposedly classless society. They were the fruit of all the broken promises of the past, and the disillusionment of a generation whose legitimate hopes had been consistently thwarted. The workers were demanding not just more bread, but an end to the humiliating lies and half-truths with which they had always been fobbed off. "Better the bitter truth than a sugar-coated lie," one of them said. "Sweets are for children. We are adults."

On Sunday 17th August, Father Henryk Jankowski, from the nearby church of St Brigid's, celebrated Mass for about seven thousand workers on a makeshift altar erected by the workers themselves just inside Number Two Gate. "The workers took on the government," said the BBC's Tim Sebastian, "and claimed God on their side."[2] Father Jankowski, tall, ruddy-complexioned, "with a strong voice and the carriage of a retired colonel",[7] would become a familiar figure to the strikers and to Wałęsa, whom he had only recently met. It was Father Jankowski who gave Lech the lapel badge of the Virgin of Częstochowa, which he wore throughout the strike and continues to wear to this day, though he has long forgotten who gave it to him. Lech, in his turn, asked the priest to look after his family, if anything should happen to him.

As the strikers knelt with bowed heads at Mass, many of them must have felt the fear which the priest later acknowledged: "I had seen what happened in 1970, and I was scared. So sure was I that they'd start shooting, I had a New Testament in my hip pocket as I said Mass. We were commemorating the 1920 Miracle of the Vistula that day – and at the end of it, when we were all still alive, I felt we'd lived through the 1980 Miracle of the Baltic."

It was, however, with no visible sign of fear that Father Jankowski blessed a rough wooden cross made by the workers. And with a growing sense that he had been born for this hour, Lech Wałęsa took the cross on his shoulders and, placing it on the spot intended for the Monument, cemented it into place. That night a sheet of paper decorated with a ribbon in the Polish colours and a picture of the Virgin Mary was nailed to the cross. On it was inscribed a new version of some lines by Byron:

> For Freedom's battle once begun,
> Bequeath'd by bleeding Sire to Son,
> Though baffled oft is ever won.

Now, however, to underline that there was to be no more shedding of blood, the word "bleeding" had been omitted. For years, the regime had imposed its will by violence and fear. But violence and fear did not figure in the programme of the Gdańsk strikers.[8]

The numbers inside the shipyard gates had grown to two thousand. As the director made a last, hopeless attempt to insist over the radio that the strike was over, he must have realised that, on the contrary, with that Mass and that cross, it was entering a new and even more dangerous phase.

It was now that, as if by magic, the whole of society swung its weight behind the strikers, as though they were carrying the hopes and fears of the entire nation. "People came from the city," remembers Wałęsa, "by bicycle or on foot; they baked and cooked and carried food and cigarettes. As the news spread, horse carts began arriving at the docks, loaded with potatoes, cabbages, cheese and apples. There was even a cart-load of pigs! . . . Taxis cruised round, offering transport to anyone who was bringing food to the strikers."[9]

"We were all friends. We were together at last," was how many people described the prevailing atmosphere.

Communication with families was only through the railings by the gates. As food was passed in, a team of women prepared it in a hastily improvised strike kitchen. The self-discipline over food and drink was impressive. The workers too had learned from 1970, and would not dissipate their strength in drunkenness. Right from the start the strike committee banned alcohol, and the ban was rigorously adhered to throughout the whole Baltic region – as foreign journalists discovered to their cost. Pickets checked baskets of food for hidden bottles, and emptied their alcoholic contents over the ground. Given Poland's dire reputation for alcoholism, this was something of a miracle in itself. There was a powerful feeling of "We are in our own house and we must behave ourselves." The feeling extended even to swearing and dirty stories. One man who used the Polish equivalent of a four-letter word remembers how "unclean" he suddenly felt!

A song of the moment spoke of:

> those days full of hope,
> filled with talk and heated argument,
> of the nights we hardly slept
> and our hearts that beat so strongly;
> of those who suddenly felt that at last
> they had really come home.

The gates were ablaze with colour, festooned with red, white and gold flowers, bedecked with pictures of the Pope and of the Virgin Mary. Symbols such as the Polish flag – the use of which was allowed only on official occasions – and the Polish eagle made a dramatic reappearance. (At first, it was the crowned "royal" eagle of pre-war Poland, but later, to show that they had no political intentions, the workers sawed the crown off!) Posters and banners appeared all over the shipyard, carrying excerpts from the poetry and song of Poland's heroic past. A number of them bore the words of a song popular during the 1830 November Uprising: "Farewell, my lass, our country calls me from your side." The sun shone and voices over the loudspeaker system reinforced the carnival atmosphere with their non-stop requests: "Will Mr Tadeusz C. please come to Gate Three where his family's waiting. Mr Wojciech G., your sister is at Gate Two. Please don't keep your families waiting, gentlemen. Mietek K., your mother is at Gate Two with your tablets."

And so on. Strikers slept where they could – on the grass, on stone floors, on air-beds, on table-tops, or stretched out on sheets of polystyrene. The fine dry weather made it as much an adventure as a test of endurance.

As each group of new arrivals from other factories came to join in, they were clapped and cheered. By Tuesday, two hundred and fifty factories and firms were taking part, and as their delegates deliberated at long tables groaning under bottles of pop, mugs of tea, flowers and tape-recorders, they stood the debris on the base of the lifesize statue of Lenin, sharing its pre-eminence now with a large crucifix and the Polish flag.

174

Each evening the delegates returned to their own workplaces with a cassette of the day's discussions. But first, there was Mass at five o'clock. Lech Wałęsa, round his neck a rosary given him by an old woman at the gate, was always there, singing lustily along with the choir of strikers. It gave him strength, he said. "I fear nothing and nobody, only God." At moments of great tension throughout the strike period, he would draw aside to pray. Nor was he alone in this profound religious feeling. With time on their hands, many of the strikers were recalling the ethical and moral values in which they had been reared, and which they had largely abandoned. Father Jankowski worked overtime, hearing confessions.

Lech Wałęsa was the hero of the hour. It was a collective leadership, not a one-man show; but it was his finger that felt the pulse of the strikers. He responded to them with a rare awareness, showing an intuitive grasp of their feelings and needs. The chemistry between the strikers and this emerging "tribune of the people" was like an electric impulse. Not for nothing, said a reporter, was Wałęsa a first-class electrician "who senses currents and can master powerful forces".

Each evening, as he was hoisted on top of the gates to give a run-down of the day's debates, several thousand people chanted LESZ-EK! or WAŁ-ĘS-A! Spontaneous, unconventional, profoundly charismatic, speaking a language they could understand, cracking slightly off-key jokes, he aroused the affection and trust of them all. He was friendly, he was funny, he was a bit of a card. When spirits were low, he tried to raise them, with a mixture of rapid comedian's patter and the harmless vulgarity of the street urchin. "My wife will be furious when she finds out what I've been up to," he clowned. "I already have six children. I guess I'll have to give her a seventh."

When he was sure he had them, there in the hollow of his hand, he would smooth down his thick hair and pat that grotesque moustache; up would shoot both arms, fists tightly clenched in joyous greeting. As he left them, his fingers would spread into the "V" sign.[10]

It was all a far cry from the grey, colourless officialdom to which they were accustomed. He was everything the grey men were not. "I am not your master, I am your servant," he would proclaim. And as he was no demagogue, but palpably one of themselves, they took his word for it. His colleagues within the presidium (the "cabinet" of fifteen which had been chosen to negotiate with whatever team the government might send along) might complain that he was moody, truculent and morose. But out there he was in his true element.

Five hundred firms were represented in the shipyard now. Gierek (who had finally returned from his visit to the Crimea) broadcast once again on TV his shopworn mix of confession, sympathy, and exhortation. Strikes don't solve anything, go back to work – for Poland's sake. The familiar cliches evoked hollow laughter. No one this time felt like shouting "POMOŻEMY". "I think I've seen this before," says a studio electrician in Tom Stoppard's *Squaring the Circle.* "Typical bloody August," agrees his companion ". . . Nothing but repeats."[11]

At about the same time, the chief leader-writer of the Party's *Tribune of the People* issued a dire warning to the Gdańsk strikers: *The Soviet Union is running out of patience. There is a limit which no one must exceed.*

The message was clear: go back to work, or the Soviet Union will intervene directly. It was a lamentable admission that Socialism in Poland could be justified to the workers only in terms of a Soviet military threat. The Polish Party, the "power", had forfeited the people's respect and lost its power even to arouse their fear. One third of the workers were under the age of twenty-five and better-equipped than their predecessors to ask awkward questions and demand answers. They had not lived through the Nazi Occupation nor experienced the Stalinist Terror. They were well-educated, under-employed, disillusioned and alienated. They saw the system for what it was – a hollow sham, dependent for its very existence on lies. The desire for truth exploded. "We've had enough of years of lies," said the workers. "Now we want to clean up the mess."[12]

They did not hate Gierek, but they hated the system which bred him and his like. And the brash little electrician from Gdańsk spoke for all of them when he cried out to an unresponsive TV screen: "But what has any of that to do with us? We have our list of demands, and we shall wait for the government to come to us and discuss them."

---

[1] Quoted by Neal Ascherson, in *The Polish August, op. cit.*
[2] Tim Sebastian, *BBC TV, A Year in Poland,* 21.7.81.
[3] Tim Garton Ash, *The Polish Revolution: Solidarność,* Chapter 1: "Inside the Lenin Shipyard" Jonathan Cape, 1983, Coronet, 1985.
[4] A. Pawlak and M. Terlecki, *Każdy Z Was Jest Wałęsa, op. cit.*
[5] Denis Macshane, *Solidarity: Poland's Independent Trade Union,* Spokesman Press, 1981.

6 Jean Offrédo, *Lech Wałesa Czyli Polskie Lato*, *op. cit.*
7 Jerzy Surdykowski, *Notàtki Gdańskie*, *op. cit.*
8 Walter Brolewicz, *My Brother, Lech Wałesa*, Robson, 1984.
9 *The Book of Lech Wałesa*, Chapter 5 *op. cit.*
10 *The Book of Lech Wałesa*, Chapter 3 *op. cit.*
11 Tom Stoppard, *Solidarność: Squaring the Circle*. Faber & Faber, 1984.
12 *Robotnicy 80*, film from Polish Film School, 1980.

16 THE FAMILY WE CALL POLAND (1980–81)

Żeby Polska była Polska
So that Poland may be Poland

Refrain of the theme song of Solidarity

And the mountain *did* go to Mohammed: on Saturday 23rd August, 1980, Edward Gierek, after a couple of half-hearted attempts, sent a really competent negotiator, Mieczysław Jagielski, a Deputy Prime Minister responsible for economic affairs.

It was high time. Other industrial cities had followed where Gdańsk had led and set up inter-factory committees of their own. There was one in Szczecin, another in Elblag. And smaller strikes were continuing to break out in the rest of the country.

One of the KOR advisers in Gdańsk had started up a strike bulletin and called it *Solidarity*, after the word which was constantly on Lech Wałęsa's lips. The first issue of twenty thousand copies sold out immediately. In 1970 the intellectuals had failed to support the workers; in 1976 they came in time to pick up the pieces. But in 1980, they were there right from the start.

Since telephone links with Warsaw were still cut, it was Radio Free Europe which informed the strikers that a group of distinguished academics had addressed an Appeal to the authorities, supporting the strikers' claims and urging the authorities to avoid bloodshed. Late on Friday 22nd, two of the signatories, Tadeusz Mazowiecki, editor of the liberal Catholic weekly, *LINK*, and the mediaevalist professor, Bronisław Geremek, came in person to Gdańsk and gave Lech Wałęsa a copy of the Appeal. "Thank you," said Wałęsa bluntly, "but actions are better than words." "What sort of actions?" asked Mazowiecki, somewhat surprised by this reception. "Well, for a start," replied Wałęsa, "we need experts to help us deal with the government negotiators. We are only workers, after all."

Mazowiecki needed no further invitation. Next day he returned to Gdańsk with a six-man group of advisers, which included Geremek, and the bearded historian, Bohdan Cywiński. "When I arrived," says the latter, "I saw this little man with the moustache, but I'd no idea he was the boss. Yet it soon became clear that what *he* said was what counted." "How long do you intend to stay?" asked Wałęsa. "Till the end, no matter how it turns out," Mazowiecki replied. The answer pleased Lech, and, although some members of the strike committee were unwilling to admit the intellectuals into what was a workers' strike, he successfully overrode them.

It was the advisers' job to check the small print on any document and make sure that the workers were not being tricked. On the other hand, they also had to present the workers' demands in a way that the government team would accept. It was a difficult task, and a round-the-clock marathon, with Wałęsa, as Cywiński recalls, a relentless taskmaster:

> Round about four in the morning, Wałęsa would push back his chair and say, "Right, we can snatch some sleep now till eight, and that will give the experts time to sort something out." Then he would hand us enough work for forty-eight hours. He never actually consulted us. He would listen, yes. But he'd always decide for himself. He never asked *whether* we should do this or that, but *how* it was to be done, and what the consequences were likely to be. And he would trust the judgment of the workers outside. When we came up with a decision, he'd go off to the main gate and tell them about it, then, as often as not, come back and say, "Sorry, they didn't like it." Then we'd have to start all over again.

On Saturday evening, Deputy Prime Minister Jagielski and his team arrived by coach. As the coach tried to edge its way into the shipyard, it was surrounded by a crowd of angry workers, who drummed on the windows and shouted "Get out and walk" and "On your knees". Wałęsa, who had come to meet the government delegation, calmed the crowd and persuaded them to let Jagielski and his men pass through. Twenty thousand pairs of hostile eyes followed them as they strode disdainfully past, to the glass-walled room at the back of the conference building where the talks were to be held. It was a bit like a fish-tank in a zoo, with hordes of workers, newspaper men, observers, photographers, peering through the glass wall. Every gesture and facial expression was visible to those outside the fish-bowl; every word was relayed by loudspeaker to the crowds outside.

> Seated on low easy chairs, the two sides faced each other over a bowl of red and white flowers on a formica-topped coffee table. Jagielski, dapper and trim-suited; Wałęsa scruffy in his usual baggy jacket and trousers. Wałęsa had, in fact, offered to stand down from the talks, in

179

case his reputation as a fighter should impede progress. But his colleagues had insisted that he remain.

In the rest of Poland, people who had heard about what was happening only through Radio Free Europe were beginning to wonder who this man was. Experience had taught them he might well be a Party stooge, put there to stir things up. Only when the official media began to attack him and insinuate all kinds of terrible things about him, were they reassured that he must be an honest man. The media, in fact, gave little information, referring only to "sporadic interruptions of work", or "certain breaks in production"; admissions still outweighed by the confident assertions that, under the wise guidance of the Party, Poland was "marching towards a better future".

> Yet, how it really was at that time we all know [wrote Lech Wałęsa later]. Millions of people were shedding the invisible veneer of the lie and breaking the equally invisible barrier of fear. It was repeated loudly and thousands of times. Strike! Strike! Strike! – a taboo word, a word they tried to suppress all too unsuccessfully.[1]

After a polite welcome from Wałęsa, the talks began. Without preamble, Jagielski said: "These strikes must stop"; and Wałęsa, puffing imperturbably on his pipe, replied: "They should have been stopped ages ago, but we were waiting for you. So where do you stand on our twenty-one claims?" When Jagielski answered with an expansive: "Allow me to begin by making a few general points," Wałęsa cut him short. "No, I want a solid answer, point by point." To the people outside, listening over the loudspeakers, this was a moment of pure joy. At long last they had a spokesman who would not content himself with evasive answers and the familiar meaningless slogans. Wałęsa's ability to nail Jagielski down to each consecutive point and force him to give coherent answers was one of his most distinctive and important contributions to the success of the August strike.

Nevertheless, the talks did not get off to a promising start, since Wałęsa was insisting on the release of certain KOR activists (including Kuron and Michnik), who had been arrested since the strike began; and Jagielski refused to be drawn. Before returning to Warsaw that night, he had rejected most of the workers' twenty-one demands.

Next day, yet another Central Committee reshuffle produced a new Prime Minister, the virtually unknown Mr Pińkowski. In the upheaval, Gierek held on as First Secretary, but only by a whisker.

Monday and Tuesday (25th and 26th August) produced much the same stalemate. Jagielski refused even to discuss the matter of free trades unions. Outside, the hours of waiting seemed endless. The strikers took to writing and reciting verse, pinning their own compositions to trees and lamp-posts for all to read. They scoured the Polish classics for suitable quotations, and perhaps most popular of all were the verses which concluded Słowacki's *Hymn of the Confederates*:[2]

> Never shall we league with kings,
> Never bow our heads to force . . .

Then on Wednesday, things began to move, in more senses than one. The government rocked on its heels, when the miners of Silesia and the steelworkers of Nowa Huta not only came out on strike but set up their own inter-factory committees complete with demands. Cardinal Wyszyński chose this moment to appeal for caution and to warn that prolonged strikes could only harm the nation. Delighted with this timely intervention, the evening TV news carried carefully edited highlights of the sermon. But this was one of the times when even such devout Catholics as Lech Wałęsa felt free to disregard the Cardinal's advice.

In any case, the Cardinal's unwelcome caution was more than offset next day by a very explicit statement from the Bishops' Council, spelling out "the inalienable rights of the nation: the right to freedom of worship, to a decent existence, to truth, to daily bread, to a true knowledge of the nation's history".[3] It was a veritable litany of human rights, a gauntlet thrown down by the Church on behalf of the workers.

By Thursday 28th August, Jagielski was conceding some ground – on the liberty of the press and the right to strike. But he was still unhappy to talk about the free trades unions, an unhappiness which reflected that of his masters in Warsaw, and, still more, that of *their* masters in Moscow. The Russian bear was, in fact, positively growling with alarm.

The government was anxious at least to preserve the fable of "the leading role of the Party", which they understandably felt to be at risk. Here was a ludicrous situation: a People's Democracy, with the people on the far side of the barricades. The Politburo was agitated: some wanted an end to the strike by any means at all; others called for a "state of emergency" and for troops to be sent in to the Baltic ports. The official mass media again warned, Cassandra-like, that the situation was like that in the eighteenth century, just before Russia, Prussia and Austria moved in for the carve-up . . . Everyone understood: Prussia and Austria were not part of the present scenario. But Russia . . .![4]

According to one source,[5] the Politburo voted eight to five for military action, but the security and military chiefs would not sanction it, as they were unable to guarantee the loyalty of the troops. "I will not send my army against four hundred fortresses," the Defence Minister, General Wojciech Jaruzelski, is alleged to have said.

Jagielski did not return to the shipyard on the Friday, and the workers were afraid that he would not come back at all. Perhaps they had lost. Perhaps the security forces would move in: there were rumours of paratroopers getting ready to land in the shipyard. Memories of 1970 were never far from their minds. But their solidarity held firm. "We held on to the phrase, 'it is better to die standing than to live on our knees'," said Anna Walentynowicz. Amid the prevailing tension and the need for strong nerves, Lech Wałęsa was superb. He managed to convey some of his own calm to the crowd. "He grew in stature from one hour to the next," said Cywiński.

When tensions threatened to boil over, or spirits were low, he would start up the National Anthem – "Poland is not yet dead, so long as we are still alive" – in full throttle and completely off-key; and the religious hymn, which was almost another national anthem, "God, who protects Poland".

Wałęsa's magnetism never failed:

It is pure, Polish magic [wrote a British journalist].[6] You know the magician has turned it on, deliberately, almost cynically. Yet as he sings he is transformed: no longer is he the feisty little electrician in ill-fitting trousers, the sharp talker with many human weaknesses; no longer does his authority derive merely from his patter and repartee; now he stands up straight, head thrown back, arms to his side, strangely rigid and pink in the face, like a wooden figure by one of the naïve sculptors from the Land of Dobrzyń where he was born.

Lech Wałęsa had true charisma. In fact his growing authority was deriving increasingly not just from his gift for oratory, but from the fact that he used words honestly, and gave them a truthfulness that years of double-speak had taken from them. Wałęsa, speaking the truth, even though his Polish was rough and ungrammatical, was offering the moral leadership for which Poland hungered.

On Saturday Jagielski came back, in jovial mood. The air had been cleared in Warsaw; a settlement was now possible. Possible, but not yet in sight. The workers had asked for immunity not only for strikers but also for their "supporters". Jagielski knew well that this meant the KOR people. In his avuncular way, he tried to drive a wedge. The "supporters" were irrelevant, he suggested. What were men like Kuroń and Michnik to such as them? An outraged Andrzej Gwiazda stood his ground, demanding either a fair trial or a release. "Are we to be defined as a police state or as a democracy?" he asked. "We do not want to live in a land forced into unity by police batons." Jagielski looked pained, but Gwiazda, Wałęsa and others continued to assert that they had a moral obligation towards those who had helped the workers in the troubles of 1976–7.

Jagielski tried to move on to safer ground, but Wałęsa pursued him like an angry terrier. If the activists were not released, he threatened, there could well be another strike after this one. Jagielski agreed to see what he could do. He was, in any case, preparing to fly back to Warsaw to consult the Central Committee. "It's Saturday," he remarked, "a lucky day." "It's Our Lady's Day," said Lech Wałęsa. "That's right," agreed the disciple of Lenin. "Our Lady's Day, when my parents always used to start the harvest." The strikers cheered ironically. Then, with a reminder from Wałęsa to "stop arresting those KOR people", he went on his way.

Next day there would be a signing. That much seemed sure. Wałęsa was carried shoulder-high to the main gate, and the workers sang the obligatory *Sto Lat* – may he live a hundred years. They were excited, scenting victory. Wałęsa chatted in a relaxed way.

The atmosphere [recorded Bolesław Fac],[7] was more like that at a picnic than a mass rally. He was at ease. He had the crowd's attention, the sense of oneness with it, the sense of being able to prevail upon it by using exactly the right words. In a place and at a time when anyone else might have felt uneasy, he was consumed with joy. 'And now we'll all go home, take a bath and go to bed. But first let's sing the National Anthem for this country of ours. Oh – and one more thing. Let's sing a hymn to God too, because now we can't go any further without God.'

Film-maker Andrzej Wajda had arrived the previous evening, in search of a sequel for *Man of Marble*. He more than half-expected that the action had run its course and that the workers would settle for what they could get. But the atmosphere in the shipyard changed his mind: "peace, calm, something holy, sublime, extraordinary. I feel I'm witnessing a fragment of history. As a rule, history passes us by, but here I can feel it, see it, touch it."[8]

As for Wałęsa, here, felt Wajda, was the very embodiment of the literary character beloved of the Poles, Sieńkiewicz's Little Knight, "with his moustache, his sense of humour, sometimes even his melancholy; his calm in a crisis; his patriotism. A great soul in a little body."

Wałęsa's first words were: "Mr Wajda, this may be the last chance for our country," and Wajda instantly understood that the strike was more important than he had realised:

> I understood then that this matter could not be considered in the way I had thought of it before; that it must be considered in the context of our national existence, not of the victory of the Gdańsk shipyard over provincial and central authority. I suddenly realised that Wałęsa had in himself a much greater sense of historic responsibility, historic importance, than I had. I was impressed by this. No matter what happens to him in future, no matter how the voters assess him, the fact will remain that at a time when nobody had yet thought this was an event of world importance, it was he who gave it that status and imparted it to all those whom he met.[8]

Wajda was in no doubt that he had found the subject for his next film. The *Man of Iron*, suitably disguised, would be Lech Wałęsa. The background would be the true history of those days.

Everyone was dashing around, signing one another's leaflets by way of souvenir and wearing stickers with the new *Solidarity* logo, with its thick red jumbly letters resembling a group of marchers with the Polish flag. "I wanted the marchers to appear to be supporting each other," said the designer, who conceived the idea on top of a crowded tram, "so that they cannot be broken up or forced away from each other."

Yet at the eleventh hour, this precious unity was threatened. The experts had worked out a face-saving formula about the Party's "leading role" *vis-à-vis* the free trades unions. But a girl now burst into the conference room and accused the presidium of betraying the workers and selling them out.[9] Uproar followed this outburst, as tension snapped and the delegates began shouting at each other. Wałęsa seized a microphone. "Listen, all of you," he shouted over the din. "We're going to have our own building, with a large sign over the door, saying IN-DE-PEND-ENT, SELF-GO-VER-NING TRADES UNIONS.''

The words, which in Polish have more resonance, rolled off his tongue, and the delegates stopped to savour them. He had calmed them down, even if he had not stilled their doubts. The crucial question was asked – and answered – at the end of the day, by the serious-minded Gwiazda: "Will the new unions be totally free and independent? No written agreement can ensure that. Our only guarantee is ourselves. We know that hundreds of thousands, millions of people think like us. There we have our guarantee . . . We know that the word Solidarity will survive.''

As the two teams faced each other for the last time on Sunday, 31st August, Jagielski announced that the KOR detainees were to be freed, and Wałęsa stroked his moustache with satisfaction. He began a prepared speech, in which he spoke of "a success for both sides"; then he jettisoned it in favour of a spontaneous response to this historic moment when, as he saw it – for he was a fighter who loved to make peace – former enemies had been turned into partners:

Kochani [he said] – beloved friends. Tomorrow, 1st September, we return to work. We know what this date means to all of us. We remember 1939 and think of Poland, our motherland . . . the shared concerns of the family we call Poland. You have trusted me so far, so I beg you to trust me now. We have got all we could in the present situation. The rest we will get in time, because we now have the most important thing of all . . . our IN-DEP-END-ENT, SELF-GOV-ERN-ING TRADES UNIONS. That is our guarantee for the future. We have fought, not for ourselves nor for our own interests, but for the entire country. We have fought for all of you. And now I declare this strike to be over.

"Right to the very end," wrote a Gdańsk docker in his diary,[10] "we were afraid there would be some kind of police provocation . . . And then at last we heard Wałęsa's rough, staccato voice, so different from the smooth, monotonous, woolly speeches of the people in authority. That's why, for all its ugliness, that voice sounds beautiful.''

The ecstatic applause in the hall was matched by the cheers – and the tears – of those who waited outside. Everyone rose for the National Anthem, and then the two delegations proceeded to the hall for the signing ceremony. On paper, at least, all the workers' demands had been agreed. There in the hall, flanked by Lenin, the Cross and the Polish eagle, Jagielski repeated that there were "no winners and no losers". "We have settled," he said, "as one Pole with another."

He signed,[11] and Wałęsa followed suit, wielding a giant plastic ballpoint pen, tasselled and decorated with a picture of the Pope – a souvenir of the Papal visit in 1979. Then he went outside, to be hurled into the air again and again by the crowd. LESZ-EK, LESZ-EK, they chanted. He gave them the familiar impudent two-fisted salute, shaking both fists like a victorious prize-fighter. Smiling, relaxed, enjoying himself hugely. "Better this way than a long-drawn-out struggle," he said. "But the next stage will be harder, and I'm a bit afraid of it. We'll make mistakes, and there will be those who try to lead us astray. But we'll not let them."

Telling them that Mass was to be broadcast on the state radio from now on, and that the KOR prisoners were to be released, he came at last to the issue closest to his own heart:

One thing more, even if I do sound like a dictator. I have always felt responsible for the blood that was shed in December 1970. It was partly due to my own incompetent leadership. So I want us to meet here on 16th December always, at this same place. I shall be here, even if I have to crawl on hands and knees. Remember that. And I shall always tell you the truth in this holy place. I shall tell you whether things are going well or badly for us.

He pointed with his hands to the spot where now stood the great wooden cross.

---

[1] From Lech Wałęsa's *Afterword* to Józef Tischner, *The Spirit of Solidarity*, Harper & Row, 1982.

[2] Juliusz Słowacki was a nineteenth-century Polish Romantic poet.

[3] Tim Garton Ash, *The Polish Revolution: Solidarność*, Chapter: "Inside The Lenin Shipyard: Day 15".

[4] Jean Offrédo, *Lech Wałęsa Czyli Polskie Lato*, Cana, Paris 1981.

[5] O. Halecki: *History of Poland*, chapter by Antony Polonsky, "From Kania To Jaruzelski". *op.cit.*

[6] Tim Garton Ash, as above, "Day 14".

[7] *The Book of Lech Wałęsa, op. cit.* Chapter 2, by Bolesław Fac.

[8] As note 7, Chapter 10, interview with Andrzej Wajda.

[9] Tim Garton Ash, as above, "Day 17".

[10] *The Book*, as above, Chapter 9 – extracts from memoirs.

[11] It is typical of the way Communist regimes operate that within a year Jagielski had been demoted and consigned to political oblivion.

17 "OURS IS A MORAL REVOLUTION"

For good or for ill, it was there – in that mass which had learned to be silent and not only to be silent, but to repeat the prescribed slogans – that knowledge was preserved of what was just and what was unjust. It was they – one day in the distant future, when they had become the real owners of the smelting works, of the mines, and of the factories – who would protect with their hands the uncertain light, and without any illusions that they were discovering absolute truth.

> Czesław Miłosz: *The Seizure of Power, 1955*

At last the Polish revolution had reached a more hopeful stage. During those days between the signing of the Gdańsk Agreements and the ones signed in Szczecin and with the Silesian miners at Jastrzębie,* the Polish workers were on top – and if what they had had in mind was power, they could have seized it. But their revolution was not about power, any more than it was about hatred of one class for another. The Poles' chief complaint against their rulers was that they had divided the nation against itself. They wanted to reunite society, to break down the barriers which divided Pole from Pole. The demands made by the shipyard workers and miners (the highest-paid of all workers) in August

---

* It appears to have escaped the attention of most of the writers and analysts of Polish affairs that the most comprehensive of all the Agreements signed during the Solidarity period was that negotiated by the students at Łódź on 19th February, 1981. This Agreement covered such sensitive areas as the banning of the activities of security services within university precincts; students' military training; university budgets and student grants; repression against the activists of the democratic opposition; the teaching of history; the independence of the judiciary from the State; the issuing of passports; the abolition of the *nomenklatura* system; the celebration of the anniversaries commemorating historical events of great significance for the Polish nation; the release of the contents of the Polish-American, Polish-French and other cultural Accords; and the abuses committed by militia and security service functionaries.

This Agreement was the basis of the subsequent law on Higher Education which revolutionised the academic world. The Law was finally repealed in 1985, after a long battle with the academics and students.

1980 gave the lie to Lenin's claim that the working classes could not raise their sights higher than their own immediate wants. Their demands were, as Wałęsa had said, not for themselves but for the nation. For lower-paid workers, for exploited women workers, for pensioners, for the sick. They had no ambitions to overthrow the government, but to make it responsive to the needs of the nation, and answerable for its own larger lunacies.

A massive charge of energy was released by the sudden explosion of hope, and the floodwaters reached even the Party. Five days after the Agreements, Gierek was swept away, with a heart-attack which merely brought forward his inevitable departure from the political scene. Stanisław Kania, a middle-of-the-road *apparatchik*, replaced him as First Secretary, and the "errors and distortions" of the Gierek era were, as was customary, blamed for the shambles Gierek had left behind. Kania made the expected carrot-and-stick broadcast on television. But this time no one was listening.

It seemed, though, that the Party too wanted to put its house in order. Within its ranks there was a noisy clamour for social reform and a more conciliatory attitude towards the workers they had so conspicuously lost. Kania adopted the workers' word *Odnowa* – renewal – and embarked on the gradual removal of many prominent figures who had long been feathering their nest at public expense.

And as the new union, INDEPENDENT AND SELF-GOVERNING, as its banners proudly proclaimed, set up shop in the Hotel Morski, a dingy Gdańsk hotel for shipyard workers and itinerant seamen, some nine hundred thousand Party members joined it. So great was the rush that Kania began to hope that the Party could place itself at the head of the new movement. But first a wedge would have to be driven between the workers and the "wreckers" and "anti-socialist elements" who were presently acting as their advisers.

Alas for Kania's hopes. When, on 17th September, a group of delegates from all the major industrial centres met in the Hotel Morski, Jacek Kuroń was there too, newly released from prison and promptly made official adviser to the new union, *Solidarity*, made up of workers grouped horizontally region by region. A provisional National Co-ordinating Commission was set up and to nobody's surprise Lech Wałęsa became its chairman. Already the new union had three million members.

As if at a hidden signal, similar self-governing unions sprang into being all over the country, taking the place of the old

188

discredited factory branch unions. But the latter did not give way easily, and the new young unionists frequently had a bitter struggle to obtain recognition, not to mention the premises, telephones and cars they needed.

Organising and controlling these loosely knit new groups was a major headache. They came to Gdańsk for advice and reassurance, and to learn about the democratic principles they were so keen to put into practice. They marvelled that things had progressed so far in Gdańsk. Back home, they said, it was "like being behind barbed wire". One delegate from Częstochowa said that people there were paralysed with fright. "They think they are breaking the law. And the press is silent on the matter." "If you don't defend us, they'll flatten us," they told Lech Wałęsa, streaming into his office, where they usually found him sprawled in an armchair, dressed in an open-necked shirt and jeans. On the wall he had hung a large crucifix, but he knew very well that not everyone shared his enthusiasm for religion. "Religion," he said, "is my peace and my strength. I'll just say a short prayer, and that way I'll avoid a coronary. But I don't push God down anybody's throat. I don't want the unions to be churchy, just Polish."

Wałęsa had hoped to go on working at the shipyards, at least part-time, even if it meant going there by taxi. All his old employers were falling over themselves trying to get him back. But the hope was unrealistic. The union needed him to be available. When workers from other regions came, it was Lech they demanded to see. Maria, a girl who worked as a helper there, says that his door was always open, and that nobody else would do: "Right from the beginning, they wanted only him. They came to see him if they'd lost their jobs, or if they were having trouble with their marriages. And they wanted instant answers. No one gave him time to think. He was haunted by people who expected him to work miracles."

In those early days, gratitude spilled over him in cascades. The letters that poured in by the sackload ascribed every virtue to him: courage, integrity, dignity, honesty, compassion, heroism, sincerity and moral rectitude. Though a few were critical to the point of loathing, and one man expressed his intention of shooting him at the first opportunity, the majority saw him as the embodiment of all human values. They wanted him to be a saint, so they made him one. And since they had no king, they made him a king too. At a meeting of Polish writers in Warsaw, a speaker commented on the phenomenon: "When we Poles find ourselves without a king, we immediately begin to look for one. After Poniatowski[1] there was Józef Piłsudski. And now Wałęsa."

The rise from unemployed electrician to unquestioned leader of Poland and a world figure had been truly spectacular. Lech, never a modest man, was flattered by the admiration. He enjoyed being a symbol. But when this meant sitting in an office, he hated it, dreading the loss of spontaneity. He was only truly at home on a factory floor, addressing the workers in his execrable Polish, pouring out crude slang, making grammatical mistakes by the score, contradicting himself constantly, but holding his audiences spellbound by the vibrancy and truthfulness of his speech. "If you want to see what he's really like," said a friend, "go and watch him among people whose hands are as dirty as his own. That's where he's most himself."

Some of those who heard him found him too coarse, a mountebank playing to the gallery, a soapbox orator, a buffoon. A group of students in Kraków, when they heard him for the first time, wondered how such an ill-spoken lout had achieved so much; but when they heard him again they were already under his spell. He was a man of the people, a people's tribune rather than a politician. And he took care, whenever possible, to reassure the government that Solidarity had no political ambitions and should not be seen as a challenge to the "leading role of the Party" or to the system of alliances within the Soviet bloc. Solidarity, in fact, saw its role as that of a permanent loyal opposition, and was content to let the Party be seen to govern, even if only in name. In 1980 most Poles were realistic enough to understand that they could not hope to become independent either of the Party or of Soviet Russia. When an admirer compared the non-violent Wałęsa to Gandhi, Lech replied with a sigh, "Well, his geopolitical situation was simpler than ours."

The whole of society was bursting out of its straitjacket. Private farmers were organising themselves into unions; writers, journalists, teachers, students were in the vanguard of those revising their existing statutes in the search for a new honesty and freedom. As the Gdańsk manifesto had asserted, they were acting out the belief that Man Is Born Free. For the first time in thirty-five years, people began to speak freely, and to stop leading a double life.

The sheer joy and exuberance of those early weeks was described by a young woman assistant in the Warsaw (Mazowsze) branch of Solidarity, led by the charismatic young Zbigniew Bujak, and claiming one million members:

190

Hundreds and hundreds of people dropped in every day, with every kind of problem, not just how to set up a factory cell, but divorce problems, housing problems, drink problems. It was chaotic, but it was wonderful, the absolute spontaneity of it all, the fantastic enthusiasm. It was like a huge love affair. We all believed in the same things, we believed desperately. And we were all very young. Older people supported us, but they couldn't cope with the sheer physical hard work, all hours of the day or night. Of course, we had the feeling of making history: we knew that, right from the start.

A volcanic eruption; an earthquake; a dam-burst; something out of the Gospels; Easter; Pentecost. The comparisons were all made, and they all attempted to express the inexpressible, the huge surge of joy and hope, that now the bad times were over, that Solidarity was the new salvation and Lech Wałęsa its Messiah. In October, in the Gdańsk market square, Wałęsa had solemnly sworn the famous oath of Kościuszko before the 1794 Uprising: "I will never abandon my country; I will serve it till the day I die." He believed that he had been chosen for this task; and his vanity was decidedly not all personal.

Solidarity was already working out plans for a better future. Its university members had set up a working-party on how to get the country back on its feet, with *ad hoc* teams discussing work safety and health safeguards; and with a flourishing publicity and counselling department. Could it have worked? Perhaps it could, if the Party had had any intention of keeping the promises it had made. "You don't understand," says a Party boss in Wajda's *Man of Iron*, "no one wins against us." And the journalist, Winkel, in the same film, reflects that though the workers had succeeded in banning alcohol during the Baltic strikes, they would find it harder to bring in the democracy they wanted. "After all, drunks don't have their own army, police and prisons; but the Party has all three," he said prophetically.

The Party's first act of sublime bad faith came in October, when the judge at Warsaw's Provincial Court refused to register Solidarity as a union, without the insertion of a clause recognising the Party's leading role and the system of alliances. Wałęsa and the Solidarity delegates were stunned at this revelation that the judges were still mouthpieces of the Party; and that the Party appeared to be backing out of its promises. The court's action destroyed any belief they might have had in the goodwill of the authorities. It not only increased their resentment but also made it harder for Wałęsa to get his conciliatory line accepted within the union. From this time forward, a new radicalisation of Solidarity was in prospect.

Although Wałęsa was standing firm on the registration issue, he was already considered by many to be too cautious, too ready to seek a compromise; the other union leaders watched him warily. Passions were running high, and a nationwide strike was threatened for 12th November, if Solidarity was not registered by then. The country prepared itself mentally for a showdown.

It was the Party which offered an olive branch: they invited a Solidarity delegation to come to Warsaw for talks. Interpreting this as a sign of weakness, Solidarity immediately raised the stakes, demanding not only to keep their statutes unchanged, but reviving four issues from the summer accords on which no progress had been made. These were: access to the mass media; immediate pay rises; an increased flow of goods to the shops; and an end to the oppression of KOR and other oppositionists. As for an independent union for the peasant farmers, which Solidarity was also demanding, it was unthinkable. Peasants, as private producers, were not eligible to form a trade union at all, let alone a self-governing one. On all these issues, therefore, the government stayed reproachfully silent. But they promised action on the statutes. Unwilling to trust them, Solidarity continued its plans for a strike. And to make an already tense situation even tenser, on 2nd November, All Souls' Day, a large crowd in Warsaw held an open air public service for the victims of Katyń.

The Supreme Court found a compromise solution regarding the statutes; and the tension eased. Wałęsa diplomatically said once again that there were no winners and no losers, but Solidarity on the whole believed it had won a victory. The strike was called off and the nation switched over to a celebratory mood. Wałęsa was guest of honour at a special festival of song and poetry at the Warsaw Opera House. DON'T BE AFRAID; THE NATION IS WITH YOU, said one of the many waving banners. And the nation heard for the first time the song which would become the theme song of Solidarity, the haunting *Żeby Polska była Polska* – so that Poland may be Poland. Or, as some preferred to sing, "so that Poland may be Polish". In the Polish language, it was only a question of adding or removing a final accent.

"My wish," echoed Wałęsa, in a speech later that week, "is that Poland may be Poland; that hope may be real hope, and that all men may be brothers." But hope was already dented, and mistrust of the government's good faith was universal. As the demands for change everywhere came up against a brick wall, the workers began taking matters into their own hands and using the only method that had proved to be effective. After the registration crisis was over, Wałęsa suggested that there was no further need for these wildcat strikes; but they did not cease. In fact the crisis seemed to have triggered more of them, as workers sought to remedy their own specific grievances and rid themselves of their own corrupt and over-privileged officials.

Wałęsa and the other Solidarity leaders found themselves darting from one place to another, putting out the fires of discontent. "No one can deal with the unexpected twenty-four hours a day," grumbled Lech. But that was precisely what they did. Lech travelled the country in a little white Polski Fiat (with an ex-shipyard worker as his bodyguard and driver), catching up on sleep as he went, or listening to rock concerts on Radio Free Europe. His sense of mission was urgent. Face to face with the workers, his magic usually worked, as he tried to calm their growing thirst for revenge and retribution: "Let us forgive one another. Everyone is guilty to some extent. If there was something to take, we took it. It was the rules that were wrong. No one gives up his comfortable armchair without a fight."

And again: "We can't put all the corrupt officials in prison. After all, who would pay for their keep?"

He warned against the dangers of individuals, punch-drunk with freedom, carrying on their personal vendettas against corrupt managers and union leaders. His political antennae told him that this business of settling scores, however understandable, could easily get out of hand and lead to that most dreaded of all evils, civil war. "Let us be human and everything will be all right," he insisted. He believed in reconciliation wherever possible: "I am a believer, which is why I forgive blindly. I can be having a real go at someone, and then all at once I see standing opposite me another human being. Perhaps he acted as he did unwittingly? Maybe my arguments were wrong? I don't believe in other people's badness, only in my own inability to convince them."

Many of the disputes could have been solved by patience and diplomacy. But the workers had run out of patience, and they were low on trust. Wałęsa would later regret that Solidarity did not set out at the beginning to "educate the people". "We should have explained things to them," he said, "and brought them up to a certain common level of agreement." The failure to do this would cost Solidarity – and the whole nation – dear.

The next major crisis followed hard on the heels of the previous one, and while the forest fires were still raging. Solidarity's Warsaw office had got hold of a document from the Public Prosecutor's Office, which outlined tactics for the elimination of "illegal anti-Socialist activity". They were stung by this further illustration of Party bad faith. When police broke into the Solidarity office on the evening of 19th November and arrested Jan Narożniak, a young mathematician helping in the printing section, Solidarity's anger was intense. Zbigniew Bujak, the young Warsaw chairman, threatened a regional strike unless Narożniak was released immediately. For good measure, he threw in five other demands, including one for the investigation of police brutality in 1970 and 1976, and for an overall investigation into the activities of the police and security services. Not only the government was shocked by such demands, which struck at the very roots of the sacred security apparatus on which the Party rested. The more moderate Solidarity leaders like Wałęsa were also shocked. The advisers were shocked. And most importantly, the Soviet Union was shocked.

Alarmed not only by this frontal onslaught on Marxism–Leninism, but also by the possibility of a rail strike which would endanger its routes into East Germany where it had twenty armed divisions, the Soviet Union moved to surround Poland to the north and east. A poignant notice appeared in the window of a Warsaw travel agency: VISIT THE SOVIET UNION BEFORE THE SOVIET UNION VISITS YOU.

It was a cliff-hanger. With only eight hours to go till the strike, and with twenty Warsaw factories already striking, Jan Narożniak was released. But the Warsaw workers refused to call off their action until an assurance was given them, on television, that the investigation into police behaviour would take place. (Though why they should have believed any such assurance on TV is a mystery.)

A cooling-off period was badly needed. Although the strikes had been called off, the Soviet threat remained. It became known that at a December 1980 summit meeting in Moscow, the Warsaw Pact comrades had promised in their final communiqué that the Polish people could rely on their "fraternal solidarity and support" – a nasty threat that was scarcely even veiled. And though the Polish Church was making conciliatory noises towards the authorities (far too conciliatory for some), the belief gained ground – and later became certainty – that Karol Wojtyła had sent a letter to Brezhnev, assuring him that Poland "will help itself" and would manage its own affairs. This letter, which assured Brezhnev of the Church's willingness to continue as mediator, was of crucial importance.

"OURS IS A MORAL REVOLUTION"

Few people are in a position to know whether the Russians really intended to invade just then, or to what extent these were signals of their desperation. However, all the evidence available would strongly suggest that the threat was more than just an empty one; and it was taken seriously by both the Pope and Wyszyński on the one hand and by the Polish regime on the other. The Pope's intervention seems to have been crucial in avoiding a very major international conflict in the centre of Europe.[2]

The threat from the fraternal comrade to the east, whether real or imagined, had a sobering effect on all sections of Polish society. Subsequently, a joint government/Church commission in December agreed that unity was a top priority, "regardless of differences in world outlook or political views". The Polish bishops appealed to the people to work for the process of renewal and for the "rebuilding of mutual trust".

With Russian warships in all probability only forty miles away on the other side of the Bay of Gdańsk, a new spirit of reconciliation was in evidence on 16th December, as senior members of the government and the armed forces stood in driving icy sleet, with foreign diplomats, bishops, clergy and one hundred and fifty thousand ordinary Poles, to unveil the long-awaited memorial to those who had died in December 1970. On this tenth anniversary, it seemed as if the ghosts of December were at last reconciling the nation. In a three-hour ceremony specially devised by Andrzej Wajda, who was filming a sequence for *Man of Iron*, one of Poland's leading actors read out a roll-call of the twenty-eight officially admitted dead, and paid tribute to "those whose names we do not know". As each name was called, the crowd solemnly intoned, "He is with us still."

Lech Wałesa, who had for many years worked towards this moment, had begged the people beforehand to welcome every guest, no matter how unpopular. Then he made the worst speech of his career (he was never good with scripted material; a critic remarked that he read aloud like a schoolboy stumbling over a lesson), lit a long oxy-acetylene torch, and a huge flame flared up. It illuminated the spectacular, forty-metres high monument – "we wanted it big," said a worker, "they'll have a job knocking *that* down" – with three steel crosses from each of which hung a black anchor, traditional symbol of hope, and the wartime symbol of Fighting Poland. "The crosses," explained Anna Walentynowicz, "represent the three workers' rebellions of '56, '70 and '76, the three crucified and unfulfilled hopes . . . The monument is tall, because it is a cry to heaven of the people's bitterness."

195

Beneath the three crosses was an eternal flame to symbolise life, and some emotive lines from the pen of Poland's greatest living poet, Czesław Miłosz, who had that year won the Nobel Prize for Literature:

> You, who wronged a simple man,
> Bursting into laughter at the crime,
> And kept a crowd of fools around you,
> Mixing good and evil to blur the line.
> Though everyone bowed down before you,
> Saying Virtue and Wisdom lit your way,
> Striking gold medals in your honour
> – And glad to have survived another day,
> Do not feel safe. The poet remembers.
> You can slay him, but another is always born . . .
> The words are written down, the deed, the date.
> You would have done better with a winter's dawn,
> A rope, and a branch bent down beneath your weight.

In Wajda's film, Maciek kneels at the spot where his father had been shot by the security forces. "I'm sorry I didn't believe you," he whispered. "But then you didn't believe me either. Now, every one of us in Poland has witnessed the truth for himself, and *nothing* can take that from us."

"For having seen that truth," commented Wajda, "I am indebted to this man with a moustache, whom I did not know before, whose existence I had not even suspected, and who expresses the desires and longings of millions of people."[3]

To which Miłosz added: "What I feel for Lech Wałęsa and the shipyard workers can be expressed in one word – gratitude."[4]

---

[1] King Stanisław August (Stanisław II), the last king of Poland.
[2] Bogdan Szajkowski, *Next to God . . . Poland: Politics and Religion in Contemporary Poland*. Frances Pinter Publishers. Chapter 3: "The Triumph of Solidarity".
[3] From *The Book of Lech Wałęsa*.
[4] From *The Book of Lech Wałęsa*.

For a fuller account of events in this and the following three chapters, see:
Neal Ascherson, *The Polish August*, op. cit.
Tim Garton Ash, *The Polish Revolution*, op. cit.
Kevin Ruane, *The Polish Challenge*, BBC Publications, 1982.
Bogdan Szajkowski, *Next to God . . . Poland* (see note 2 above)

18　A BASKETFUL OF ANTS

You think you have passed all danger . . . but now careful deliber-
ation is needed, so that, having escaped one evil, we may avoid
another. There is a terrible road before us yet, and God knows
what may happen to us.
　　　The "Little Knight" in Sieńkiewicz's *With Fire and Sword*

Fears of immediate Soviet invasion passed – and with them passed
December's fragile unity. The government's continuing refusal to
honour the Agreements reached in the summer, brought renewed
industrial action in January. Wałęsa, for the first time in his life,
was out of the country. Having acquired a passport, he had gone
to Rome, "as a son to his father", to see the Pope.

When he returned, greeted at the airport with flowers, like a
conquering hero, he was plunged straightway into the strike being
waged in Bielsko Biała for the dismissal of no fewer than twenty
corrupt local government officials. It was a strike that lasted twelve
days and almost brought the region's industry to a standstill. Not
all Wałęsa's pleading could prevail against it, and only the personal
intervention of Cardinal Wyszyński finally brought it to an end.

"The Church is with the workers," the Cardinal assured them.
But he was unhappy about all the strikes that were taking place,
and was having talks with the Party leader, Stanisław Kania in
an effort to defuse the dangerous situation. In return for his
mediation, however, he hoped the government would agree to
register the new peasant union, Rural Solidarity. In March, the
Polish bishops reaffirmed their support for the farmers' organisation:

The eyes of all honest citizens are on the Polish countryside with
sympathy and trust. We are full of respect and admiration for the
work of the farmers, who with such determination defend their land
and their rights. Our farmers must have the same rights as other
workers to form trade unions that would serve their interests and at
the same time promote the economic development of the entire

197

country . . . The Church will continue to support the efforts of the Polish farmer in his patriotic and social service to the nation.[1]

While the argument was still going on, and strikes and stoppages were taking place on behalf of Rural Solidarity, a new crisis blew up over Saturday working and the five-day week which Gierek had promised ten years earlier but never delivered. Struggling with an economic crisis which already threatened to drown it, the government would not concede more than alternate free Saturdays. This did not satisfy Solidarity, although Lech Wałęsa pointed out that in its present parlous state, the country could not afford a shorter working week. His more radical colleagues in the National Commission overrode him and called on union members to stay at home on working Saturdays. After a series of warning strikes had taken place in ten selected cities, the authorities hurriedly agreed that there could be three free Saturdays a month, and in addition that Solidarity might in time be allowed access to the media and have a newspaper of its own. On the issue of Rural Solidarity, however, they refused to budge. This annoyed the Cardinal and provoked an angry protest.

In such a volatile situation, too much pressure was being put on Solidarity. It was being asked for too much and too soon. Everything had to be played by ear, and the union leaders had little experience of democratic procedure. As the authorities were clearly not going to keep their promises unless forced to, the union was constantly having to fight on ground it had already won. It was hardly surprising that they could not agree on the tactics, and that there were frequent squabbles.

Lech Wałęsa had his detractors within Solidarity. Since August he and Danuta, with the union's approval, had moved out of their cramped two-room lodgings (so small that when the six children[2] were put to bed on inflatable mattresses on the floor, the door wouldn't open) and into a larger six-roomed flat-cum-office in the classier Zaspa area of Gdańsk. Inevitably the move aroused envy in some quarters, and there were a few who cut Danuta dead in the street. Others hinted darkly that the flat had been a bribe from the government, although the truth was that in September the government *had* tried a much glossier bribe on Lech, offering him a well-furnished villa in Warsaw if he would take charge of the Central Council of Trades Unions.[3]

The rumours persisted. Lech was being corrupted, they said; he was putting on airs on account of all the publicity, the autograph-hunters, the awards, the doctorates, the Man Of The

Year titles,[4] the films, songs and articles which had him as hero. He had put on weight, they observed, acquired more clothes, taken to wearing a collar and tie at meetings. And, though cigarettes were scarce, he seemed to have an endless supply of them. Power had gone to his head. When a *Who's Who* of Solidarity officials was published and included pictures of Lech's (indispensable) secretary and of his (equally indispensable) body-guard, disapproval reached an aggrieved peak. "Next time they'll have a picture of his dog," someone commented sourly. It had not passed unnoticed that he arrived late for meetings, often appeared to go to sleep in them, or sat there pulling grotesque faces for the benefit of the photographers. His restless impatience with other people's long-windedness was all too obvious, and was taken as a sign of incipient megalomania.

To Wałesa it seemed different. "You've become public pro-perty, haven't you?" a journalist asked him. "You mean a slave, don't you?" he countered wearily. "I haven't got a life. I'm not living at all."[5] He complained of poor health, and of not having much time left (he was always convinced he would die young). He couldn't relax, he felt trapped by his status as star, unable to ogle a pretty girl without everybody noticing. Nor was he under any illusions about his present status. Those who cheered him today might well be stoning him tomorrow. As he told Italian journalist, Oriana Fallaci, in an interview:[6]

If the worst happens, all the rage of the people will fall on me. The same people who applauded me, erected altars to me, will trample me underfoot. They will even forget that I acted in good faith. If I had any sense, and if I were more selfish, I'd cut off my moustache right now and go and find a job in some shipyard or other. But I can't do it, because there's too much danger ahead. I must stay where I am and try to transform this movement somehow into an organisation.

To keep his feet firmly on the ground, he started each day with Mass – "to defend myself against the power that corrupts, to remind myself to be careful . . . God may not need me, but I need God as my support."

He was a lonely man, with no close friends (except possibly his bodyguard, Henryk Mazul). "I've always been alone and I probably always will be," he said in an interview,[7] adding that he had never in his life been happy. There was a strong streak of tragedy in his make-up, and those who cared to look could see a deep sadness in his eyes.

When Kania brought in General Wojciech Jaruzelski as his new

Prime Minister on 11th February, Wałęsa was pleased. "I like soldiers," he told a French journalist,[8] "I respect him. He's a good Pole." Jaruzelski, slim, ramrod-stiff, his face inscrutable behind heavy dark glasses, was a bit of an enigma. Undoubtedly a loyal Party servant, but one who came from a respectable family with a small amount of land somewhere in eastern Poland. He had spent two years in a lycée run by Marian Fathers. Sending the boy to a private school must have been a considerable drain on his parents' financial resources, and the only way they could pay their son's fees was in sacks of potatoes. His education had been interrupted by the start of the Second World War and the subsequent death of his parents in somewhat mysterious circumstances in the Soviet Union. Although he then went on to the Officers' College in the USSR, most observers, even those most hostile to him, would agree that he was not entirely trusted by the Russian leaders. This may have accounted for the popular view that Jaruzelski was perhaps a Wallenrod, a Polish patriot in disguise.* At all events, the people were willing to give him a chance.

Solidarity's National Commission appealed for an end to the plethora of strikes, and it made its own top-heavy structure more flexible by electing an executive – the presidium – empowered to act for the union in an emergency. General Jaruzelski asked for a ninety-day moratorium on strikes, to give the government a chance to tackle the economic crisis. Solidarity agreed. An air of faint optimism prevailed. Or maybe it was a feeling that a last chance had been offered.

Ninety days, Jaruzelski had asked for. It was neither his fault nor Solidarity's that in the event he was given no more than ten.

At the XXVIth Congress of the Soviet Communist Party held in Moscow immediately after Jaruzelski's accession, the Warsaw Pact Allies fraternally threatened not to abandon Poland in her hour of need. Immediately after the Congress, the Polish delegation had been ordered by the Soviet Central Committee "to remove the peril hanging over the Socialist achievements of the Polish people".[9]

Next morning Jacek Kuroń was arrested again, and Adam

---

* A character in a verse-novel by Mickiewicz. Carried off from Lithuania as a child by the Teutonic Knights, he becomes Grand Master of the Order. But all the time he is planning the Knights' destruction, to avenge the wrongs of his people. It is easy to see the parallels with the early story of Jaruzelski, who was also carried off by the Russians from Lithuania as a boy. But there the similarities seem to end.

Michnik narrowly avoided a similar fate. By 7th March, when Solidarity's National Commission met again, delegates all contributed harrowing tales of union workers harried by the police. Members of Rural Solidarity were being set upon and intimidated; tear-gas had been loosed on a Warsaw shop where the assistants all wore Solidarity armbands; and the chairman of a Solidarity branch in southern Poland had been found hanged after twenty-four hours in police custody.[10] Eighty-six-year-old Antoni Pajdak, a respected pre-war Socialist and Resistance leader, a founder member of KOR, was attacked by an "unknown assailant" (a euphemism for "secret policeman") and left with a broken hip.

The facts added up to a near-certainty that certain people were determined to prevent a rapprochement between Solidarity and the government. Frustrated hardliners within the Party hated the concessions which had been made to Solidarity and saw their whole way of life threatened by Kania's policy of "Renewal". In a more democratic and less corrupt Poland, they would lose their jobs and the privileges that went with them. So it was in their interests to see that nothing changed; and to provoke a confrontation with Solidarity that might plunge the country into crisis and force the Soviet Union to intervene. One such group (approved by the Russians as "a healthy force" in Polish politics), was the anti-student, anti-Zionist, extremely nationalistic Grunwald Patriotic Union, which was busy spreading rumours that KOR was made up of Jewish intellectuals.

On 14th March, Wałęsa was talking to Solidarity leaders in Radom, asking them to put an end to wildcat strikes and give the government a chance to govern: "With strikes," he said, "we shall simply destroy ourselves. We must all stand together at present. We must . . . behave in such a way that future generations will not curse us. Let's learn to sit down at the same table with government representatives. Let's talk to them."

On that very day, in the western town of Bydgoszcz, a group of Rural Solidarity farmers, with the support of Jan Rulewski, the aggressive and reckless local Solidarity leader, began a sit-in against the authorities' refusal to sanction their union. On Thursday 19th March, while discussions were taking place, two hundred militia and plain-clothes police burst in and ejected the men by force, driving them into the courtyard outside where they were forced to run the "path of health" through police truncheons. Twenty-seven were injured. Three, including Rulewski, were taken to hospital. One of these, the sixty-seven-year-old peasant leader, had suspected brain damage as well as battered ribs.

Wałęsa, rushing to the scene, immediately suspected that this was the work of the hardliners, and stated that the affair was "an obvious provocation against the government of General Jaruzelski". Press and television (always hardline strongholds) at first launched into a fury of invective and innuendo, blaming everything on Solidarity. But as public fury mounted, with angry crowds shouting M-O- (i.e. militia), GE-STA-PO, and outsize portraits of the injured victims being carried through the streets, they changed their tune to one of muted regret.

Solidarity's National Commission called an emergency session for 23rd March and wanted to order an all-out strike without further ado. Professor Geremek warned that this might bring the country to the edge of civil war; and Wałęsa added that it was politically unwise to put all one's cards on the table straight away. He was in favour of a four-hour warning strike to be followed by a general strike if the guilty ones were not brought to justice. (Wałęsa's tactics were those of a poker player. He believed in high stakes, but not so high as to place victory out of reach.) The battle was stormy and went on till three in the morning. Finally, using the technique which would become known as "the Wałęsa effect", he stood up, took off his jacket and strode out, having given the delegates eight hours in which to consider what he had said, and threatening to resign if he didn't get his way.[11] They agreed to hold the warning strike, but they would not forgive him for such undemocratic behaviour.

In the days that followed, moderate elements on both sides desperately sought a solution. Jaruzelski had appointed Mieczysław Rakowski, editor of the respected weekly *Polityka* newspaper and a long-time advocate of reform as Deputy Prime Minister with responsibility for unions. Wałęsa and his team held talks with Rakowski against renewed backstage rumblings from the Warsaw Pact, who had extended their spring manoeuvres, thus re-awakening Western fears that invasion was imminent.

Rakowski accused Solidarity of waging "a holy war against people's power", and suggested that the union was trying to cut its own throat and invite Soviet intervention at the same time. But Wałęsa reminded him that the situation was not of Solidarity's making: "On so many occasions in the past," he said, "in 1956, 1970, 1976, we had situations like this one. In 1980, events would have gone the same way if we'd followed your reasoning. We cannot allow the militia to beat us up."

These first talks got nowhere, and the four-hour warning strike took place. Despite numerous attempts at intimidation, it was the biggest disruption of work ever seen in the Soviet empire. Support for it was absolutely solid, even among the Party members of Solidarity, who had been expressly forbidden by Kania to take part. Solidarity then prepared for a count-down to the General Strike that they believed must follow. Mobilising their ten million members, they set telephones and telexes humming with instructions and contingency plans, which were immediately rushed into print and distributed to the various factory commissions all over the country. The young radicals in the union approached the coming showdown as though it were the decisive battle between the forces of heaven and hell. They were confident of victory, and they had the nation behind them.

I don't know what the Warsaw Rising was like [said a girl from the Warsaw Solidarity office], but it must have been something like that. We dossed down on sleeping-bags on the office floor since there was no possibility of getting home. Scouts came in with flowers for us, old men with ration cards for sausages, old ladies with cold drinks, jam and blankets. The whole country was like a coiled spring, we were ready for "them" to do their worst. The spirit was incredible, and the people were one hundred and twenty per cent behind us.

Lech Wałęsa was in the eye of the approaching storm. He was aware of the nation's euphoria, but his own political instincts warned him that to go ahead with the strike meant to plunge the country into civil war. Cardinal Wyszyński and the General had held crisis talks and agreed that the crisis must be speedily defused.

Wałęsa and the National Commission were summoned to the Cardinal's residence, and solemnly warned of their responsibilities by Wyszyński: "Is it right to fulfil the demands of the moment, however just, at the cost of endangering our freedom, our territorial integrity? Is it not better to achieve only some of those demands, and for the rest say: 'Gentlemen, we shall return to this matter later'?"

Rakowski warned that they were on the brink of the abyss, and the advisers all urged restraint. As always, Wałęsa listend to them all, and made up his own mind. (Nobody could have accused him of underestimating his own worth. He claimed that his superiority over the advisers was "that of a decathlon athlete over mere runners"!)

Meanwhile, at a meeting of the Party's Central Committee, a letter from journalist Stefan Bratkowski was read, warning that forces in the Party were working against renewal and that "our hardliners stand for no programme except that of confrontation and disinformation''.

Rakowski and Wałęsa reached an agreement, the former promising that those responsible for the Bydgoszcz outrage would be punished, and that a parliamentary committee would examine the question of Rural Solidarity. It was not much, and there were no guarantees, but it was all that was on offer. Wałęsa confronted the Solidarity presidium with the package deal – there was no time to summon the full Commission – and, with one hour to go, the strike was called off. But even then the agreement was reached only after a direct intervention by Cardinal Wyszyński. It had been spelled out to him that unless the strike was called off, a ''state of emergency'' would be declared on 31st March. As proof of the regime's total seriousness, he had been shown a poster with the proclamation already printed on it. So it was Wyszyński who had begged Wałęsa to call off the strike.

There were sighs of relief in the West, but within Solidarity itself there was grief and despair. Not everyone understood the reasons behind Wałęsa's decision:

It was the beginning of the end [a girl from Warsaw said sadly], a breaking of the spirit. For three days after that betrayal, I felt physically ill, so depressed I wanted to die. It was such a terrible mistake. I don't think it would actually have come to a strike, the authorities would have backed down. The Russians? They wouldn't have come. It would have meant too bloody a struggle. They knew we'd fight to the death.

It was the old Polish cavalry-versus-tanks romanticism, and it was strong among the young people of Solidarity.

Inevitably, Lech was accused of selling-out, of acting like a prima donna, of being paranoid about Russian tanks, of behaving like a mediaeval king. This last was hurled at him by Karol Modzelewski, who indignantly resigned as Solidarity's press officer. Rulewski and his wounded companions wrote from a hospital bed in Bydgoszcz that ''Wałęsa has bungled. We can compromise over supplies of onions, but never over spilt blood.'' Anna Walentynowicz, who had pleaded for the strike to go ahead, lost her job as the Lenin shipyard's delegate to the National Commission. Henceforth, she and Wałęsa would always be on opposing sides. Gwiazda too warned Wałęsa of the dangers of autocratic leadership. Lech's tendency to decide things for himself offended Gwiazda's passionate concern for democracy. Wałęsa defended himself vigorously, claiming that the result was an achievement:

> Three times I made a storm, three times I whipped things up. But I won't allow things to come to a confrontation. The point is not to smash your head open in one day, but to win, step by step, without offending anyone, not a single person. The world is surprised at us for walking a straight line, and as long as I'm here, that's how we're going to walk, step by step and cautiously.[12]

That Solidarity's precious unity might be lost was Wałęsa's chief dread. If that happened, everything would fall apart: "We are like a basket of ants," he said colourfully. "If the ants stay in the basket, they stay together. But tip them out on the ground, and then look what happens."

But the Bydgoszcz incident, and the subsequent Warsaw Agreement, cast a long shadow over the day when the ants would leave the basket and invite their own destruction. Yet, though Wałęsa had cold reason and commonsense on his side, in one sense the Solidarity Young Turks were right: never again would the country be in such a high state of preparedness, and never again would it be so united. If the government had declared a state of emergency then, in March, it would have met with a great deal of determined resistance. As it was, Solidarity knew that from this time forward their strike weapon had overnight lost much of its power.

For many Wałęsa had lost his cutting edge. Yet it was Rulewski, of all people, who said that he was indispensable. Poland, he said:[13] "has a psychological need for a leader who will allow us to go to bed peacefully in the knowledge that there's someone we trust standing guard over us. For half a century we have had no such man. But now we have Wałęsa, and whatever else we do, we have to stick with him."

> I know [said Lech], that this moment needs a chap like me, a chap who can make sensible decisions and solve problems in a cautious, moderate way. I am not a fool. I am well aware that too many injustices have accumulated over thirty-six years and things cannot change overnight. It takes patience, and it takes wisdom. The rage that people would like to explode like a bomb must be controlled. And I know how to control rage because I know how to argue. I know how far we can go with our demands. I know in what country we live, and what our realities are.[14]

In the annual May Day parade, Kania, Jaruzelski and President Jabłoński actually led the workers in procession, instead of taking the salute from a balcony on high. Two days later, they celebrated the one hundred and ninetieth anniversary of the 3rd May Constitution, the old Polish national day which the Young Poland Movement had revived; and Jabłoński spoke of the need for "a right attitude to our national past".

Thanks mainly to the restraining influence of the Church, April and May were relatively quiet. Lech Wałęsa went off to Japan, where he was given star treatment, his popularity remaining undimmed even when he told the Japanese trade unionists that they had become more like functionaries than true activists. In Poland there were only sporadic incidents, like the one in Otwock outside Warsaw, where a crowd of drunks tried to burn down a police station with the police in it! The situation was saved by Adam Michnik who leaped to his feet, shouting: "Listen to me. I'm what is known as an anti-Socialist element." (They did burn the police station down next day, but by that time it was empty, and the policemen came and thanked Michnik for saving their lives. A situation not without a certain irony, considering that, for the police, arresting Michnik was almost a habit!)

The promised talks about Rural Solidarity really did take place, and the union was actually registered on 12th May. The new atmosphere of mutual goodwill was reinforced by the appearance in April of the new *Solidarity Weekly*, edited in Warsaw by Wałęsa's friend and adviser, Tadeusz Mazowiecki; and by a small ration of radio and TV time bestowed on them early in May.

In his first interview for the new weekly, Lech Wałęsa suggested that before social renewal could take place, people should examine their own personal consciences and start a renewal in their own lives.

There was indeed an increasingly serious attempt to speak and print the Truth – a novelty in a Communist Party-ruled State. School text-books were in the process of being reprinted to give a more realistic and truthful account of history; and the hunger for Truth was such that uncensored publications were snapped up as fast as they were produced. When a public sale of *samizdat* (i.e. underground) literature – the first of its kind for thirty-five years – was staged at Warsaw's College of Technology, all the books were sold out within a couple of hours. Satisfying this ravenous hunger for Truth was one of Solidarity's most tangible achievements.

There was also a thirst for real information as opposed to the disinformation so long ladled out by the Party. The thirst affected the whole of society, and ever since August even the official journalists had started to be more truthful. The queues for weeklies such as Rakowski's *Polityka* were almost as long as those for meat. Only those whose lives had been clouded for so long by lies could appreciate the rare beauty of the new dispensation.

It was all deeply worrying for Kania and Jaruzelski, caught between the old guard and the reformers. The Party had lost one hundred and sixty thousand members since the previous July, and two thirds of those who remained had joined Solidarity and were flouting Party orders. The rank and file members were in open revolt, deluging the leaders with complaints about the hardliners and their provocative tactics. These reformers pushed Kania into holding an emergency Party congress in July, to discuss radical reform. They were already beginning to set up a new kind of party organised on horizontal lines, region by region, and controlled from the base. Lenin, who had insisted on a vertical control line from top to bottom, would have turned in his grave. And it was indeed this grievous heresy of "horizontalism" which alarmed the Soviets more than almost anything that Solidarity might do. The Polish Communist Party seemed all set to become a Social Democratic Party in the Western mould, and this the Soviet Union would not tolerate.

It was widely suspected that the Soviets had been behind the establishment of "Grunwald", with its anti-semitic, anti-intellectual prejudice. And in May 1981, they were surely behind the new ultra-conservative Katowice Forum, which produced a manifesto of which Stalin would certainly have been proud, and roundly condemned Kania for "revisionism" and "counter-revolution".

If hopes had been roused by the registration of Rural Solidarity on 12th May, they were brutally dashed on the following days by news of the assassination attempt on John Paul II in Rome. The death of Cardinal Wyszyński from cancer followed soon after, and with the passing of that "voice of moderation and conciliation", the Poles felt truly bereaved. Hundreds of thousands lined the streets for the funeral procession. Flags stood at half-mast, theatres and cinemas closed, radio and TV programmes reflected the sombre public mood. For the funeral service in Victory Square, a quarter of a million mourners stood before an altar dominated by a cross twelve metres high. And at the Cathedral where the body came to rest, the Cardinal's last will and testament was read, in which he expressed gratitude for the grace which had enabled him to bear witness to truth as a political prisoner; and in which he freely forgave all those who had slandered him.

In view of the people's immense grief, the regime had little option but to join in the general mourning for the Primate. Without precedent in the Communist world, the head of the Roman Catholic Church in Poland was publicly proclaimed "a great statesman, a man of great moral authority recognised by the nation".[15]

But the provocateurs were no respecters of grief, and the incidents continued to multiply. When the Soviet ambassador complained that Soviet war memorials were being daubed with white paint, few doubted that the pro-Soviet hardliners were themselves responsible. Lech Wałęsa, protesting Solidarity's innocence, went out with a bucket of hot water to scrub one of these memorials clean.

On 5th June, Brezhnev made it clear in a letter to the Polish Central Committee that Kania and Jaruzelski had lost control and should be replaced. The hardliners triumphantly called on Kania to resign. But the rest of the Central Committee indignantly closed ranks in the face of this crass interference from outside, and they confirmed Kania in office.

Nevertheless, Brezhnev's letter, with its thinly veiled hints that what had happened to Czechoslovakia on the eve of just such an Extraordinary Party Congress in 1968, could happen in Poland in 1981, caused no little consternation, and rather dampened the Politburo's ardour for internal reform. Their self-confidence took a further knock when the magazine *Kultura* published the results of a nationwide poll to find out which institutions in the country were the most respected. The Church came first, followed by Solidarity, then the Army. The Party came near the bottom of the list, lower even than the police!

Solidarity was being careful not to stir things up during the run-up to this momentous Party congress. Wałęsa told Solidarity meetings all over the country that the union should resist the temptation to play politics. "There has already been too much confrontation," he said. At a ceremony in Poznań, which commemorated the twenty-fifth anniversary of the workers' riots "for bread and freedom", in which sixty people had been killed, he made a further plea for national unity:

We used to be called troublemakers and vandals and other names that were an affront to our dignity. Today . . . our path lies in solidarity, the solidarity of the world of labour, the solidarity of honest people against those who are dishonest, who try to keep our mouths shut . . . If we do not want to have any more monuments like this, we must not allow ourselves to be divided or to be set against one another . . . The world of labour is not counter-revolutionary, it is for honesty and truth . . . Let us remember that victory is already within our grasp, provided we do not allow ourselves to be divided.[16]

When the Extraordinary Congress met on, of all days, 14th July, Bastille Day, it was hung over by the Party's own anxieties about unity. And though it was extraordinary in more senses than one, being composed of two thousand freely elected delegates, voting by secret ballot for an agenda chosen by themselves, there was one unforeseen result. Caution led the delegates to avoid *both* extremes, so that although most of the old Central Committee and seven out of eleven Politburo members lost their seats, the men who took their places were middle-of-the-roaders, evenly balanced between conservatives and reformers, it is true, but cautious on the subject of change. Kania was re-elected as First Secretary, and the Soviets sent him a telegram of congratulation. The Party hierarchy which he inherited was collectively something of a eunuch, incapable of filling the political vacuum which now yawned dangerously wide.

[1] Bogdan Szajkowski, *op. cit.* Chapter 3.

[2] The sixth child, a girl, was born just before the August strike.

[3] *The Book of Lech Wałesa.*

[4] Wałesa was voted Man Of The Year in West Germany, Denmark and other countries. Elsewhere, he was second only to the Pope.

[5] *The Book*, interview with Marzena and Tadeusz Woźniak.

[6] Interview with Oriana Fallaci, reprinted in *Sunday Times*, 22.3.81.

[7] *The Book*, interview with Marzena and Tadeusz Woźniak.

[8] Bernard Guetta, *Le Monde*, 21.3.81.

[9] Tim Garton Ash, *op. cit.* Chapter, "The Ides of March".

[10] Tim Garton Ash, *op. cit.* Chapter, "The Ides of March".

[11] *The Book*, interview with Marzena and Tadeusz Woźniak.

[12] Halina Mirowska, *Lechu, op. cit.*

[13] Dobbs, Karol, Trevisan, *Poland: Solidarity: Wałesa*, Pergamon Press, 1981.

[14] Interview with Oriana Fallaci, reprinted in *Sunday Times*, 22.3.81.

[15] Bogdan Szajkowski, *op. cit.* Chapter 3.

[16] Kevin Ruane, *The Polish Challenge*, BBC, 1982.

19 "CONSCIENCE PLANTS FORESTS"

> It is hard to think of any previous revolution in which ethical
> categories and moral goals have played such a large part; not only
> in the theory but also in the practice of the revolutionaries; not
> only at the outset but throughout the Revolution . . . Moreover,
> it is an indisputable fact that in sixteen months this revolution
> killed nobody . . . This extraordinary record of non-violence, this
> majestic self-restraint in the face of many provocations, dis-
> tinguishes the Polish revolution from previous revolutions.
>
> Tim Garton Ash: *The Polish Revolution*

"I rack my brains to understand," wrote Kazimierz Brandys,
returning to Poland in July, after a brief absence abroad,[1] "how
things have come to be stripped so bare, and what people are
living on here. Pure spirit? In the course of seven months, goods
have almost disappeared and there is talk of hunger. But the
crowds . . . inundate the streets, gather in churches to sing 'We
Want God' and 'Let Poland Be Poland' and wear ironic badges
pinned to their summer shirts – CCR – Creeping Counter-
Revolutionary. These are the same crowds about whom six years
ago I wrote that they lacked faith, for they were under the sway
of material desire and indifferent to the ideas of freedom and
justice."

As Father Józef Tischner pointed out, the words most frequently appearing now on posters were those which had for
years been lost in the stagnant mud of "newspeak" – words
like Freedom, Truth, Equality, Dignity, and Homeland. Human
dignity was coming into its own: "Our present defiance," said
Tischner, "is not an ordinary mutiny. Rather it is a voice, great
and piercing, calling the people to fidelity."[2]

In Solidarity opinion polls, demands for truth in the media and
in schools came second only to demands for freedom. Being able
to speak the truth, without fear of the secret police, was not only
a great relief but meant that they could hold their heads higher.
An American professor spoke of "an entire country without
alienation". Through Solidarity, hope and a sense of purpose had

210

been reborn. Even the famous Polish jokes had disappeared: they had represented the impotence of a gagged nation and the Poles had other ways of expressing their feelings now. It was striking that the number of suicides and the sales of alcohol both fell dramatically.

Archbishop Józef Glemp who, in July, succeeded Cardinal Wyszyński as Primate, signalled his intention of following where his predecessor had led, "looking at the changing times and listening to what is happening in the nation". He pleaded, as Wyszyński had, for charity and mutual understanding to prevail, for an end to hatred and thoughts of revenge. In churches all over the country, altars of reconciliation were being set up, and every day thousands went to pray for the unity of their country. The churches were fuller than they had ever been. "The conscience plants forests," said Józef Tischner. "Solidarity is a huge forest planted by awakened consciences."

The people had great need of this interior nourishment, for there was precious little of the material kind. That summer the economic situation had gone from bad to worse. The reasons were the usual ones, plus a huge fall in coal exports due to the end of Saturday work and, inevitably, the wage-increases given to the workers. There was now the classic case of too much money chasing too few goods. Under pressure from the Western bankers, who had run out of patience with the Poles, the government now took the commonsense but unpopular step of raising food-prices by over one hundred per cent. As Brandys had remarked, the shelves were almost bare. Many staple foods, among them the humble potato, had disappeared altogether. There was strict rationing of meat, sausage, butter, sugar, rice, oats, flour and buckwheat kasha; but the ration cards were often worthless, since the food was unavailable. There were no cigarettes, matches, petrol, or even vodka.

Hopelessly, Barbara D., a dietician in a big general hospital, confessed that it was impossible to do her job properly: "How can you plan a diet when there is nothing to plan it on? Patients in hospitals have to rely on whatever food their families can scrape together for them."

In many cases, mothers and fathers went hungry in order to give their children what little food there was.

As hunger grew, anger mounted. People were exhausted by the shortages and the endless queues. (On the whole the queues were remarkably good-natured, but quarrels did break out, and fist-fights often took place.) In order to take the potentially violent

211

edge off this anger, local Solidarity groups tried to channel it into relatively harmless hunger marches through the streets of the most afflicted towns. Children carrying I AM HUNGRY, MOTHER banners, housewives holding up empty shopping-bags and saucepans paraded peacefully through the streets.

In the textile town of Łódź, where two hundred and fifty thousand women worked a three-shift system, the women's plight was especially tragic. Most of them had families to look after, and for most it was a question of working all day and then spending the night in a queue, or joining such a queue immediately after coming off the night-shift. Tim Garton Ash has movingly described the drudgery of their lives:

> Young women with complexions ruined by the sweat-shop air, dressed in dirty torn cotton dresses (on their wages they could not afford new ones: washing-powder and thread were unobtainable), told how they joined the butcher's queue in the evening of one day, on the chance (just the chance) that they might get some meat at two o'clock the next afternoon.[3]

Solidarity had appealed for better conditions for these women. On a film released at that time they spoke of hands lacerated by flax, the choking dust, the varicose veins, the exhaustion: "Nothing is done for us here," the women said. "The management wants everything but gives nothing. Look how dirty we are. All we get is two lumps of soap a month like paupers. But take a look at their offices – and just see the luxuries they have."[4]

Only a drastic overhaul of the economy, or a massive and unlikely influx of aid from outside, could have had any effect on this tragic mess. The Solidarity leadership was in a dilemma. They had always imposed a discipline on themselves and deliberately refrained from politics. Their revolution had been a self-limiting one, which did not aim at taking power. But now there was a government which seemed unable even to pretend to govern, while the country slid rapidly downwards towards total disaster. The union leaders stood at a crossroads. With the country looking to them for a lead, and with their own credibility at risk if they did not give one, they took a momentous decision to enlarge the scope of their revolution, and to step into the yawning political vacuum.

At the end of July, they offered to support the necessary price rises and to persuade the people to accept the need for sacrifices, in exchange for information about available food supplies, and access to government stores in order to check how food was being distributed. (It was still widely believed that the privileged few were not going short.) In addition they asked for workers' self-government in the factories, in order to improve production by removing useless and incompetent managers. (Preparations for this had been going ahead in many factories. It must be remembered that most workers were well-educated, and that many of them were well-qualified to take the managerial posts which were currently available only for Party trusties.)

What Solidarity had in mind was a genuine new partnership with the government, a positive programme of regeneration which could save Poland even at this eleventh hour.

For a brief moment, it all seemed possible, and the government offered negotiations. But the partnership got off to a bad start. When the Solidarity delegation arrived in Warsaw for talks, it was to find the whole city brought to a virtual standstill by a transport strike. Rakowski greeted them with a stream of denunciation, and dismissed their proposals as a mere bid for political power. In return, he put forward an impossible list of conditions which would have reduced Solidarity to the state of impotence enjoyed by the old "transmission-belt" official unions.

It is only fair to recognise that in all probability the government, and the Soviet Union, were frightened by the new direction that Solidarity was taking and could not fail to believe that the union's ultimate aim was the overthrow of the Communist regime. This conviction increased the alarm and despondency in an already demoralised Party, and strengthened the hands of those who wanted nothing better than to provoke discord and upheaval. But they were wrong about Solidarity's motives. Though many of the union's rank and file wanted nothing better than to be rid of both the government and the Soviet Union, the majority of their leaders were more clear-sighted:

> Certainly we were setting off in a more political direction [said a member of Warsaw Solidarity], but that didn't mean we wanted to set up political parties and overthrow the regime. The truth is that *everything* in Poland is political. If you want to buy a worker a pair of protective rubber gloves, you have to change the whole system in order to be able to do it.

As the summer wore on, a great many Poles were hungover by a sense of doom. The assassination attempt on the Pope in May, the death of Wyszyński which followed almost immediately, had tragically robbed them of the very two people who had shepherded them through their most difficult and dangerous times, and who had never been more needed than now. Of the three Ws, there remained only Wałęsa, and on him they had to focus all their remaining hopes.

Interviewed on Polish Television, Lech repeated that Solidarity was not seeking power, but "since the government has lost public confidence, it has automatically thrust that confidence and the solution of problems on to us". In an interview for a Western magazine, he added:

> The Party mustn't be allowed to collapse. I don't want that. I'll help the Party once it starts to discredit itself or collapse. There are no other realities here. We cannot overthrow the Party, we cannot take power away from it. We have to preserve it and at the same time tame it and let it eat with us, so that it will come to relish what we create.[5]

But the Party backed away now from the prospect of "eating" with Solidarity. Frightened by the union's new programmes for reform, and by the hunger marches, the government hit back through the media it so powerfully controlled. All the stops were pulled out, as programme after programme accused Solidarity of being the architect of all the nation's ills, responsible alike for rising prices and falling food-stocks. A torrent of disinformation poured out, and Solidarity was given no chance to present its side of the story. Though it had its own newspaper, distribution was slow compared with that of the government papers; and it had almost negligible access to the media.

The Bishops issued a statement to the effect that renewal was bound to be difficult, but that the people were willing to bear hardship if it could be seen to be in a good cause. They insisted that the mass media should serve the general good and that everyone had the right to access to them. Then they pleaded again for mutual tolerance. "Let none of us shake his fist. Let each of us abandon hatred." At Częstochowa, Archbishop Glemp appealed for a month of peace, and said that neither side had a monopoly of virtue: "Tensions and emotions are rising while poverty knocks at the door. Meanwhile the two contestants tell poverty to wait until one of them wins and can drive it away. Let us look at ourselves truthfully. We shall then see our own sins . . . and this will allow us to see the good done by the other side."[6]

Poverty was indeed at the door. "Thirty-six years and still nothing to buy," complained a man in the street.

"I stood in line twenty minutes for bread," noted Brandys in

August, "and succeeded in buying half of the last loaf. The stores are empty, not a single piece of cake, not a single apple to be bought."

Kania warned that if the street demonstrations continued, it could "only be a matter of time" before an explosion occurred. For the moment, people were still blaming the government exclusively. But, in the face of an increasingly hysterical TV campaign against Solidarity, guaranteed to confuse and instil fear, how much longer would they continue to do so?

[1] Brandys, *Warsaw Diary*, *op. cit.*

[2] Józef Tischner, *The Spirit of Solidarity*, *op. cit.*

[3] Tim Garton Ash, *The Polish Revolution*, *op. cit.*

[4] Feature film in *Life on the Shelf*, shown on BBC, 1981.

[5] Interview in *Playboy*, October 1981.

[6] Kevin Ruane, *The Polish Challenge*, BBC, Chapter 12, "The Question of Power".

20 THE TIME OF ROOTING

Friends, to-day is ours
and to-morrow cannot be known.
But let us live to-day as though the century were ours.
Let us create the foundations of peace in this our country.

And if anyone sets our house of friendship on fire,
Then each of us must be ready to defend it.
For it is better to die on our feet
Than to be forced to live on our knees.

Friends – let us be united, for we all have a common aim.

Rough translation of a poem by
Tadeusz Mazowiecki, May 1981

For Solidarity, it was no longer a question of what to do, but how to do it. The desire "to save ourselves by our own efforts", was uppermost in the minds of the delegates to the First Solidarity Congress as they assembled in early September in the Oliwa sports stadium in Gdańsk. It was now twelve months since the summer Agreements had been signed, and the government had carried out scarcely any of its promises.

Was it a coincidence that as the Congress opened in Gdańsk, on the other side of the Gulf of Gdańsk the Soviet Union began a new set of naval manoeuvres? Cardinal Glemp prayed in the Oliwa Cathedral for peace, and Józef Tischner, whose influence on Solidarity both then and later was immense, expressed the feelings of everyone present in his opening sermon: "Nothing like this has ever happened before in this land . . . We all feel it . . . this is a historic place, this is a historic anniversary; something is being built. Here is Poland."

The majority of those present shared Father Tischner's view that Solidarity was not so much a trades union as a way of life deeply rooted in Poland's age-old struggle for freedom. Its true meaning lay in its championship of basic human values: the restoration of truth, the struggle against exploitation, the sacredness of the land, and the importance of satisfying and meaningful work. As regards this last, said Tischner[1]: "Polish work is sick. The volume of work is great, like the Vistula River; but, like the Vistula, it is polluted . . . Let the water in the Polish Vistula become clean and independent – like the water in the Five Lakes in the Tatra Mountains."

It was historic, it was exciting; and the delegates were determined to make it work. There were, of course, differences of opinion amongst them, differences which, in a free country, would have been expressed in membership of different political parties. But they were united in their determination to behave democratically, a new and uncharted experience for them.

Everyone had the right to intervene at any time; and at elections the urns were turned upside down so that everybody could see there had been no cheating. Much of the discussion was about the nature of democracy: should they, for example, choose for themselves a system which would give the regions and their leaders control, or one that would consolidate the power of the already powerful "king" – Wałęsa?

Wałęsa was fairly clear on the matter. He wanted democracy and was prepared to fight for it. But not if it was interpreted as a free-for-all; not now, not when they were in so much danger, and hadn't learned how to cope with democratic freedoms. Look at their meetings, he argued. Speakers droned on endlessly, and nobody seemed to understand that there had to be limits to what was allowed. What Poland needed more than anything else was for Solidarity to be united, not fragmented into dozens of dissident factions, all arguing with each other about democratic procedures. "I have a vision," he had once said,[2] "and I'm capable of putting a lot of things right. I can bring about the kind of Poland we'd all like to see . . . But to do that I'd have to stop dissipating my energy in unnecessary and stupid in-fighting."

Didn't they understand that they faced a power which had the police and the army under its control, and that if they did not present a solid front to that challenge, they were lost? "That's why I am a dictator here," he said stubbornly.

But Solidarity had had enough of dictators, and they had begun to resent this one. Lech was too cautious, too eager to go on talking to the government, too ready to see the good in the other side, and, worst of all, too ready to strike a deal on his own initiative. There was growing pressure from below, from the ten million members, to throw off restraint; and their present sense

217

of mission made them believe in their own power to change things, to make an imperfect world perfect again. They lacked Wałęsa's political vision, the long-sightedness that could foresee what lay ahead. They were youthful (or not so youthful) idealists, he a realist with a strong sense of what was possible and what was not.

Lech Wałęsa, who claimed that in this one year he had aged ten, found himself frequently opposed by Andrzej Gwiazda. It was said that they loathed each other. Like many others, Gwiazda disliked Wałęsa's penchant for acting on experience and instinct, on a poker player's hunch. Wałęsa was a wheeler-dealer, always demanding more at the outset than he knew he could get, quite ready to yield a point here and there, in order to secure his ultimate objective:

> I am a radical but not a suicidal one. I am a man who has to win, because he does not know how to lose. At the same time, if I know that I can't win today because I don't have a good enough hand, I ask for a re-shuffling and then check whether I have got a better hand. I never give up. I'm a radical, I say it again, but I don't walk into a stone wall with my eyes shut. I'd be a fool. There are some such fools, but I'm not one of them.[3]

This sounds like the bravado of an increasingly desperate man. But at the same time, Lech knew when to stop, and would never compromise on the really important issues. Gwiazda, the bearded engineer, more intellectual than Lech, was a political babe-in-arms compared to him. He shunned gamesmanship, disliked taking risks and believed that any compromise at all was immoral. His was an all-or-nothing, cards on the table, take it or leave it approach, which seemed to Wałęsa the height of political unwisdom. "Gwiazda is like a character out of Dostoievsky," says Bohdan Cywiński. "He tends to see things in terms of a cosmic struggle between good and evil, all blacks and whites."

Inevitably, to such as Andrzej Gwiazda, Wałęsa's cocky pragmatism was offensive. And Lech's infuriating technique of bulldozing his own decisions through maddened him most of all: "Andrzej was passionate about democracy, he would insist on everyone having his say," Cywiński adds. "Yet, for all his crude pushiness, Lech was actually the better diplomat. The fact that he was so often proved right didn't make Andrzej like him any better!"

Janusz Onyszkiewicz, Solidarity's new press officer, put the same criticism more gracefully though no less forcefully than

Gwiazda: "Lech is a surfer who rides the waves," he said. "It was his de Gaulle complex that maddened us – his conviction that he and he alone *was* Solidarity, that he alone knew what was best for everyone, best for Poland."

The first part of the Congress ended with a hair-raising exhibition of the sort of "walking into a stone wall with one's eyes shut" that Wałęsa had so deplored. As the government Bill on Workers' Rights continued to insist on State control over hiring and firing (while conceding that workers might be "consulted" about appointments), Karol Modzelewski now proposed that a national referendum should vote on the matter. This provocative idea was carried enthusiastically, and was followed by an even more hot-headed, short but explicit *Message To The Workers Of Eastern Europe*, in which an emotional appeal to join the workers' struggle was addressed to the whole Communist world, including "all the nations of the Soviet Union". A further *Letter To Poles* (i.e. the émigré groups scattered throughout the world) began with the stirring but impolitic words: "Here on the Vistula, a new Poland is being born", and referred to "the homeland and its independence".

A seismic shudder ran through the Soviet leadership, and in the West there were head-shakings and dark murmurs that "Poles are beginning to behave like Poles again". Was Solidarity inciting the Communist world to revolt? Was this the start of World War Three?

Congress, in fact, was surprised by the international fuss. As regards the two *Letters*, they had simply been carried away by their own rhetoric. But about the referendum they were in deadly earnest.

In the fortnight that separated the two parts of the Congress, Lech Wałęsa scarcely slept. Proving that he was indeed a "democratic dictator", he set himself to undo the harm that had already been done. He could foresee only too well the chaos that would result from the holding of a referendum, but he lacked time and patience to explain the possibilities to his more volatile colleagues. Instead, he went direct to Rakowski, persuaded him to change the wording of the proposed Workers' Self-Government Bill, and persuaded an unusually small presidium of four to accept the government's new proposals. (The firebrand Jan Rulewski was one of the four, and he voted against the compromise.) Unfortunately, the government backed away from its agreement the very next day, and went back to its original insistence on the right to hire and fire. At this point, the Sejm refused to "rubber-

219

stamp" the Bill, and forced the government to accept a near-approximation to the Solidarity demands.

It had turned out well, but the Congress delegates were furious with Wałęsa for his high-handed effrontery, and a motion was passed reprimanding him and the two others who had voted his way. Rulewski was praised for refusing to give in to him.

Lech was worn out by all the diplomatic activity. A picture of him taken at the Conference shows him stretched out on two chairs, asleep. Many people were beginning to wonder which would get him first, the government or exhaustion. He was afraid that the movement was falling apart. His own earlier warning, "Our most vicious enemy is ourselves . . . we threaten our existence when we fight each other", seemed to have gone unheard.

Another ordeal awaited him: three candidates – Gwiazda, Rulewski and Marian Jurczyk from Szczecin – were opposing him in the elections for Chairman, and he would have to plead his own cause. Asked what he would do if he failed to be re-elected, he said wearily: "I really don't want power. I'd like to be by myself by some lake, fishing. I'd like to be able to get up, look out of the window, see it's a nice day, go to the station and buy a ticket. Only, damn it, I've no money."

When the elections began on 1st October, he was tense and nervous, ill at ease and in poor speaking form. Each of the four candidates had to make a speech outlining his programmes, and then subject himself to a barrage of questions from the floor. In the first round, the other three were applauded, Wałęsa hardly at all. In the second round he rallied somewhat. Asked what he would regard as the most urgent need of Solidarity, Poland and the world, he replied feelingly that he would like most of all to see peace: "Let us leave our arguments, let us stay together, victory is possible for us. But we really underestimate our enemy. He is strong. Economically, he is weak, but politically he is strong. And let us at least face the fact that he also thinks."[4]

They were still there at midnight, by which time the candidates were supposed to be asking each other questions. Lech said he was too tired to ask any: "Today, ladies and gentlemen, I have answered five hundred questions. Five TV teams have been round since this morning, whether I liked it or not. If I'd sent them away, they'd start saying I'm growing horns. That's why I'm asking no questions. I'm tired of questions."

Perhaps, he added with a flash of his old good humour, turning to the audience with his fists up, they might like to settle the matter with a fight. "Anyone got a pair of boxing-gloves?"

Lech won, but gained only fifty-five per cent of the votes. In spite of the narrowness of the margin, however, there was never any possibility of his losing. As a Warsaw delegate said later:

Lech has always been our leader and always will be. He's the symbol that keeps the movement together. No one really doubts that, even when they criticise him. But at the Congress, people felt he was getting too sure of himself, and a lot of people voted against him, just to teach him a lesson. Nobody wanted him not to be leader. In a country where lies and censorship still held sway, we had to have a name which stood for honesty and truth. We had to have someone whom everyone knew could be trusted.

When voting later took place for election to the presidium, Lech "moved heaven and earth" to stop Gwiazda and Rulewski being chosen, because he would have found it impossible to work with them. They were dropped. One of his successful nominees, press officer Janusz Onyszkiewicz, was under no illusions about the difficulties that lay ahead. "We are," he said, "like a water-skier who is being pulled by a very powerful boat. Obviously we can zig-zag in order to stay on our feet. But whatever happens, we must not drop the rope. If we do that, we shall sink."

The key question, Father Tischner had said at the beginning of the second part of the Congress, was: "Can we transform our Polish hope into reality? The trees of hope have many flowers, and on those trees flowers bloom easily. The crucial problem is, however, rooting. Now the time of rooting has come."[5]

In spite of all the noisy bickering, the programme which the Solidarity Congress finally produced was a serious attempt at such rooting. It was a masterly blueprint for the sort of society most people in Poland wanted.

What we had in mind [the preamble stated], was not only bread, butter and sausage, but also justice, democracy, truth, legality, human dignity, freedom of convictions and the repair of the republic. All elementary values had been too mistreated to believe that anything could improve without their rebirth. Thus the economic protest had simultaneously to be a social protest, and the social protest had to be simultaneously a moral protest.[6]

There was no demand to leave the Soviet bloc, to overthrow the system, dislodge the Party or to privatise the means of production. Those planks of the "geo-political reality" were left untouched. What they asked was that Poland should become a pluralist society, with free elections, a representative parliament and a

221

judiciary that was not bent. They made a strong case for workers' control of industry, and for the decentralisation which alone could save the economy. They asked that economic power should not continue to be concentrated in the hands of the Party alone, that "social ownership of the means of production" should mean ownership by groups and individuals and not only by the State.

The programme showed a mature, statesmanlike vision of how to overcome the crises afflicting not only Poland but the whole world: Solidarity's answer lay in sound economic reform accompanied by greater freedom to participate in public life. If their plan owed more to the example of self-management in Yugoslavia, or of liberal Western democracies, than to any wild utopian dream, it was because the Poles had had their fill of what ninety-year-old Professor Lipiński, a respected veteran Socialist, called "this Socialism of rotten economy, this Socialism of prisoners, censorship and police".

The very word socialism, as used in the Soviet bloc, had been discredited, and the accusing phrase "anti-Socialist forces" had no real meaning. "There are forces," said Lipiński, "who demand freedom, who demand conditions of normal life for the Polish nation. And those are *not* anti-Socialist forces."

It was Father Tischner who shed light on this semantic dilemma. Socialism, he said, "is about creating the right conditions in which human brotherhood can come about, and therefore involves a constant struggle against exploitation. But there are two ways of being Socialist and the difference is crucial."[7]

There is "open" Socialism and "closed" Socialism, he explained. Both types identify the main source of exploitation as private ownership of the means of production and resolve therefore to do away with it. To the "closed" Socialist mind, this is the end of the matter: if there is no private ownership, exploitation cannot exist. The "open" Socialist, on the other hand, sees that things are not so simple as that: one form of exploitation may have disappeared, only to be replaced by others. For the "closed" Socialist, a strike is an impossibility, since one cannot strike against oneself. But his "open" colleague would argue that it does not do the workers much good if they are co-owners of a coal-mine, but cannot own a bucket of coal. "Senseless work," argued Father Tischner, "is the most extreme form of exploitation of man by man. It is a direct insult to the human dignity of the worker. When work becomes senseless, the strike is the only kind of behaviour which makes sense."

Between the liberating concept of this "open" Socialism, with its stress on struggle, and the Christian doctrine of forgiving love, there are obvious profound differences. But they are not irreconcilable. "The views are different . . . but the common ground is visible." In Solidarity the views seemed to coalesce. What both Father Tischner and Solidarity deplored was not the lack of consumer goods or of huge profit margins, but the way the worker was treated as a tool, a mere means to an end. As Tim Garton Ash perceptively noted[8]: "Polish Catholicism (the open Catholicism of Father Tischner) and Polish Socialism (the open Socialism of Lipiński) had come a long way from their bitter enmity of half a century before."

Through Solidarity, yet another barrier had fallen. In that thought lay hope. As the delegates rose to sing the closing National Anthem, they might have felt a deeper personal involvement than usual with the ringing words: "Poland is not yet lost so long as we shall live." They had every right to be proud of the programme they had produced, for if it could be put into effect, then Poland had a chance.

---

[1] Józef Tischner, *op. cit.* Chapter, "Polish Work Is Sick".
[2] *The Book, op cit.* Interview with the Woźniaks.
[3] Lech Wałesa interviewed in *Playboy*, October 1981.
[4] Halina Mirowska, *op. cit.*
[5] Tischner, *op. cit.* Chapter, "The Time Of Rooting".
[6] Tim Garton Ash, *op. cit*, Chapter 7: "Noble Democracy".
[7] Tischner, *op. cit.* Chapter "Socialism".
[8] Tim Garton Ash, *op. cit.* Chapter 7: "Noble Democracy".

21   THE BEGINNING OF THE END

I once heard about some kind of giant sea-anemone that commits
suicide by swimming right up to the beach. I have this dread that
we might be doing something similar.

Lech Wałęsa

"Don't worry," a Russian Politburo official is said to have consoled his Polish opposite number. "When we come in, we won't
hang you, we'll hang the people who hanged you."

Concern about Soviet intentions had surfaced again in the West,
alarmed by the Solidarity Congress's demands for free elections
and workers' self-government. As everyone knew, in genuinely
free elections, the Communists wouldn't stand a chance. And
then what would the Russians do? Solidarity was angrily accused
of megalomania, of overreaching itself. In Poland, however,
public opinion was solidly behind the union. The Congress had
given voice to the Poles' longing for non-violent change.

The trouble was that, though Solidarity had a popular mandate,
it had no power to act. How could the workers take control when
the system remained unreformed? All around, that system was
visibly collapsing: factories stood idle for the lack of spare parts;
farm produce rotted before it could reach the consumer; ration
cards were a sick joke since there was scarcely any food anyway;
and there was a tidal wave of strikes. It was a vicious circle: the
failure of the economic system produced the strikes, which in turn
made matters even worse.

The authorities were stricken with paralysis. Yet they would not
give in to Solidarity, and the people began to clamour for the union
to act. "And so both sides stood," wrote Halina Mirowska,[1] "opposite each other, speaking different languages. The authorities,
like an hysterical and frightened child clenching its fists and scream-
ing: 'You shan't have it. It's mine'. Solidarity leaning forward, arm
outstretched, like a cross but helpless mother."

Half-way through October, Kania resigned, and General Jaruzelski became Party Secretary as well as Prime Minister. For the

first time in the history of the Soviet bloc, the two most powerful posts were held by the same person. In addition, he was also Minister of Defence and an army General with more than three decades of military experience behind him. (The people joked that there was only one important post left for him: that of Primate of Poland!) The introduction of the military dimension into the Polish government at this critical stage clearly signalled the arrival of what one British TV commentator called "garrison Communism".[2]

With exceptional power at his disposal, therefore, Jaruzelski faced a situation in which half the provinces of the country were affected by strikes, and Solidarity seemed powerless to stop them. With the traditional admiration for the Polish Army still strong, there was a certain undeniable sense of relief that the Army was becoming involved. The belief that Polish soldiers would never fire on Polish citizens still held good. Wałęsa agreed up to a point. But ever since the Bydgoszcz incident in March, he had known in his heart that the government was preparing for a "state of war". Few of the other Solidarity leaders appeared to share this presentiment of danger.

It was widely believed, however, that the government was allowing things to slide down to perdition, so that Solidarity would be forced to react; and then the police would be able to move in and crush them. Already the police were stepping up their harassment of union activists, as the newly elected Solidarity Commission heard at its first meeting on 22nd October. The young leaders fell in with Wałęsa's suggestion of calling a one-hour general strike on the 28th, mainly as a way of imposing some sort of national control over the wildcat strikes. Though the strike did not generate much enthusiasm, and many grumbled that they couldn't see the need for it, it was nevertheless given total support. Wałęsa could still inspire loyalty. "He still incarnates the spirit of the streets," wrote Brandys in his diary.[3]

One of Jaruzelski's first moves was to send three and a half thousand army officers, conscript NCOs and men into two thousand towns and villages, ostensibly to test the food-distribution system. With hindsight this gesture was an early step in the build-up for martial law. The conscript soldiers also found that their two-year national service period (due to end in December) was extended by two months. In case of trouble in the larger cities, these young men – possible or probable Solidarity supporters – would be safely out of the way. The government was already training other, more politically reliable forces for use in any emergency. The Army Security Service and the ZOMO riot police, carefully selected, well-fed, sumptuously housed, thoroughly brain-washed, would not scruple about the shedding of Polish blood.

For the moment, however, the General was projecting himself as a man of peace. Earnestly he called for a Council of National Accord, which might create a programme for a National Unity Front gathered from all sectors of society: the government, Solidarity, the Church, the official unions, the intellectuals, the peasants, the economists. Wałęsa, who had been asking for a Joint Commission, in which Solidarity and the government would have been equal partners, was suspicious that the Front would mean a general watering-down. Solidarity, after all, had ten million members and could justly claim to represent the whole of Polish society. So why should the union agree to share decision-making about the country's welfare with "the incompetents and hacks – the central planners, the time-servers, the seat warmers",[4] in other words, with the very people who'd created the mess in the first place?

Solidarity's presidium, a much more moderate body than the National Commission, appealed for an end to the wildcat strikes which were eroding Solidarity's authority and giving the union a bad name. They could finish by destroying Solidarity completely, Wałęsa told a meeting of the full Commission. But they rejected his plea, impatient of his caution. And when at the end of this session he announced that he was off to Warsaw to meet General Jaruzelski and Cardinal Glemp for talks, a tremendous row blew up. Lech was not asking his colleagues' permission, he was telling them what he had decided. Not for the first time, he was accused of acting like an autocrat, and of playing into the hands of Jaruzelski. "We want democracy, not dictatorship," shouted one union leader. "Right," retorted Lech, "let's vote that we don't want to talk with the Primate and the Prime Minister. And then you can go out and explain that vote to the nation."

Gwiazda called him a "vain fool" and a "blockhead", with nothing above the famous moustache. But Lech was not going to let insults stand in the way of this meeting with the General, with the faint chance it offered of a better relationship with the government.

The historic Big Three meeting, between the Cardinal, the Solidarity leader and the Prime Minister/Party Secretary, without precedent in the Communist world, went ahead on 4th November and lasted two hours and twenty minutes. It was inconclusive, but further talks were promised on a wide range of social issues. Wałęsa returned to the National Commission, only to find that it had already voted (with Gwiazda in the chair) for a national strike within three months if the negotiations should fail. When Wałęsa told them they were choosing the path of confrontation, he and Gwiazda finally reached the parting of the ways. Playwright Tom Stoppard has illuminated this last argument between the two men in a revealing piece of dialogue:

WAŁESA: Yes, I know. They lie. They cheat. They kick and bite and scratch before they give an inch – but that's how we got this union, inch by inch across the negotiating table!

GWIAZDA: (shouting) We got it by going on strike and staying on strike.

WAŁESA: You're wrong. We got it because we could deliver a return to work. We've got nothing else to negotiate with, and if we can't deliver, what have they got to lose? (The applause grows.)

GWIAZDA: They've conned you, Lech! The talks are a sham. Across the table is where they want us – all the time we're talking, they're getting ready to hit us.[5]

With words such as these, Gwiazda and fourteen others resigned from the Commission. Lech Wałęsa's worst fears were coming to pass. Solidarity was moving towards confrontation, which was exactly what the hardliners in the government wanted. As the strikes continued – Wałęsa estimated that there were sixty-five of them – Warsaw TV for once voiced the nation's thoughts, speaking of "a national tragedy taking place in instalments, a conflict between the need to save the nation and the state, and a plethora of irresponsibility . . . There have been various predictions about Poland, but no one forecast the Poles would want to dig their own graves."

Although more talks with the government did take place and continued till the end of the month, events had suddenly assumed a momentum of their own and the direction was all downhill.

Significantly, in view of later events, the authorities announced that the military operational groups which had been working to some effect in the villages were to be withdrawn, and that similar larger groups would soon start work in the cities. The Warsaw daily paper commented that the Army enjoyed great popular support and that it was reassuring for the public "to know there is somebody who can be relied on".[6]

For some, it was a true comment – for the people's patience had snapped at last, and the hungry workers were beginning to make increasingly radical demands. THEY PROMISED US A SECOND POLAND BUT THEY BUILT US INTO A THIRD WORLD NATION proclaimed a banner in Łódź. The people were anxious, confused, hungry and utterly demoralised. "They keep changing Prime Ministers and First Secretaries but I'm still eating nothing but potatoes," complained a man-in-the-street in a radio programme. Women were still getting up at dawn "to buy a pair of shoes the wrong size so that they may have something to barter for a piece of meat which turns out to be rotten".[7]

Fears for the future mingled with a rising exasperation with Solidarity. "The hardest thing for people to bear," wrote Brandys in his diary,[8] "is the fear of a future that appears as a formless gloom." A saviour was needed – and if the saviour wore an army uniform, so be it. Just so long as it was a *Polish* uniform! It was not a universal view, but it was one that was gradually gaining ground.

On 22nd November, the police raided Jacek Kuroń's flat. At the Solidarity Congress in September, KOR had formally disbanded itself as being no longer necessary. Kuroń was now holding an inaugural meeting of a new Club For Self-Government, which might siphon off some of the political activity into which Solidarity was being forced. The police broke up the meeting and arrested him.

A few days later, General Jaruzelski asked Parliament for an Emergency Powers Bill. Before Parliament had considered the request, he acted. ZOMO riot police, landing from helicopters, broke up an eight-day sit-in at the Warsaw Fire Brigade College, by students who were demanding academic reforms: "It looked to me," wrote Brandys, "like a dress rehearsal for a fiery opening night. I have a feeling that the General who donned dark glasses after August will soon be taking them off!"[8]

Wałęsa sent off a telex declaring a "state of extreme emergency" in the union, and the next day the presidium held an emergency debate in Radom. The best they could manage was to threaten a twenty-four hour general strike on 17th December if Parliament actually passed the Emergency Powers Bill, and an unlimited further strike if the emergency powers were used. The government did a "Watergate" on this meeting and recorded what was said. Three days later, Wałęsa's voice was heard on Warsaw Radio announcing (among other carefully edited highlights) "Confrontation is inevitable and it will happen." A government statement accused the Solidarity leadership of breaking the 1980 summer Agreements, and of assuming the role of a political opposition engaged in a struggle for power.

Wałesa complained that he had been quoted out of context, that the authorities were the ones who were trying to provoke a confrontation – one bloodier even than the one in 1970. For the first time, the government began personal attacks on him. The army newspaper, *Soldier of Freedom*, called him "a great liar", and a "provocateur" who led a group of madmen hell-bent on chaos.[9]

Opening the National Commission meeting next day in the Lenin Shipyard where Solidarity had been born, Wałesa made a last effort to save the peace, saying: "I declare with my full authority that we are for agreement . . . we do not want confrontation."

But the appeal for a national strike on 17th was endorsed by a majority on the Commission. As the debates wore on, the telex machines in the shipyard began chattering with anxious messages from the regions – stories of unusual troop movements, of Solidarity headquarters being sealed off. The discussions went on. As Wałesa looked on helplessly, they called for a national referendum on whether the Party was fit to govern; and on free elections to the Sejm. If the referendum brought a vote of no confidence in the Party, then the union should go ahead and form its own provisional government.

Thus did they give the General in dark glasses the perfect pretext for taking them off.

At 12.30 a.m. on the night of the 12th/13th December, as the Commission members reached the end of their discussions, news came in that telephones and telexes had been cut off, that Gdańsk's communications with the outside world had been severed. A voice from the floor expressed dismay but was told not to "play Cassandra". Whereupon Lech Wałesa stood up, raised both arms in a gesture of despair: "Now you've got what you've been looking for," he said angrily,[10] and, turning his back on them, he went home.

[1] Halina Mirowska, *op. cit.*
[2] Bogdan Szajkowski on ITN News, October 1981.
[3] Brandys, *op. cit.*
[4] Tom Stoppard, *Squaring the Circle, op. cit.*
[5] Tom Stoppard, *Squaring the Circle, op. cit.*
[6] Kevin Ruane, *op. cit.*

[7] Tom Stoppard, *Squaring the Circle, op. cit.*
[8] Brandys, *op. cit.*
[9] *Time*, 4.1.82.
[10] *Time*, 4.1.82.

22   CROW (December 1981)

"In front of my window there's this dead old tree. Last winter a
small bird was perching in its branches, and a big fat one pecked
it to death."

Marek Nowakowski: The Canary

At about two o'clock in the morning, thirty or forty Solidarity
leaders and advisers returned through the frosty snowbound
streets to the Hotel Monopol, opposite the Gdańsk railway
station. Shortly afterwards Tadeusz Mazowiecki, editor of Warsaw's *Solidarity Weekly*, unable to sleep, looked out of his window
and saw a chilling sight – the hotel surrounded by a tight ring of
helmeted ZOMO riot police carrying truncheons and riot shields.
Mazowiecki felt, he said, "like a mouse watching the cat getting
ready to pounce".[1]

Moments later, the cat pounced, and caught almost all Solidarity's leadership in its claws. The ZOMO went to arrest Lech
Wałesa in his flat at about the same time, and flew him by helicopter
to Warsaw. The others were flung into police vans and taken off
to different destinations.

In Warsaw, the Army and police had started netting Solidarity
members and their supporters at midnight, and continued
throughout the night. Some were treated courteously enough and
given time to collect necessities, like warm underwear. Others
were dragged out brutally, their hands tied or manacled behind
their backs while they were still half-asleep. Some few were forced
out with tear-gas into the waiting arms of the ZOMO wielding
new lead-lined truncheons.

All the chairmen of the Solidarity factory committees throughout the country were arrested; all the organisers of peasant protests and Rural Solidarity. Using the element of surprise, and
having cut off all methods of communication, the government
hoped to trap all the main personalities in Solidarity. In this they
were only partly successful: between twelve thousand and eighteen
thousand were seized, one thousand of these being from Warsaw

alone. But the rest, including Bogdan Lis and Zbigniew Bujak, the Warsaw leader, somehow evaded capture. Some whose names were on the list of those to be arrested were (like Bohdan Cywiński) out of the country at the time; some had actually emigrated. The fact that their names were there, on lists which were printed in the Soviet Union, suggests that the swoop was premeditated long in advance.

That night, the Pope received a telephone call from the Polish Ambassador to Italy, informing him that General Jaruzelski had found it necessary to introduce "temporary emergency measures". A similar explanation was given to the Polish Primate, Archbishop Glemp, but not until much later, only one hour, in fact, before the rest of the nation heard the news.

General Jaruzelski broadcast over Polish radio at six o'clock on that bitterly cold December morning. Poland, he said, more in sorrow than in anger, was "on the brink of the abyss . . . not days but hours away from national catastrophe".

He sighed reproachfully over the recklessness of the Solidarity "adventurists" ". . . the words uttered in Radom . . . the session in Gdańsk"; and asked, with a sublime disregard for the truth of the matter: "How long can a hand outstretched towards agreement meet with a closed fist? . . . Things could have been different in our country; they should have been different . . . The steps we have taken today have as their goal the preservation of the basic requisites of Socialist renewal."

From midnight, the General went on to say, the country was under the control of a Military Council of National Salvation (WRON); the Polish People's Republic was under "a state of war". With whom, asked the Poles, were they at war? That morning, a woman in a taxi heard the news over the driver's radio. "What's all that about?" she asked him. "It's war," he said. "Where's the war?" she asked. "Here in Poland," he replied. "But who on earth can have invaded Poland?" The man was silent.

There was no mention of Solidarity being banned, in Jaruzelski's speech. But any early hopes were dashed in the course of that day as, punctuated by solemn or martial music, a military announcer spelled out what martial law would mean: a curfew from 10 p.m. to 6 a.m.; all gatherings, except for religious services, all demonstrations banned; trade unions and student organisations suspended; the right to strike rescinded; no public entertainments or sporting events; a ban on private motoring and restrictions on all journeys away from home. The use of printing presses was henceforth illegal; all newspapers except the Army's *Soldier of Freedom* and the Party's *Tribune of the People* were proscribed; and all persons over the age of thirteen were to carry identity cards and be prepared for a search of their house or their person at any time. All telephones were officially monitored, and travel abroad was banned for the duration.

Before that day was over, the Poles had realised that all they could now legally do in company with each other was "to work, to stand in a queue and to pray".[2] And if they stood in a queue before the curfew ended at 6 a.m., as many had to, they ran the risk of being arrested.

Many factories and institutions, such as radio and TV stations, were put under direct military rule, and any disobedience was punishable by a long prison sentence or by death. Railways, transport systems, refineries, mines, telecommunications networks all came under this jurisdiction. Military commissars, responsible for discipline, were appointed to schools and universities.

In Warsaw that morning, Hanka G. picked up her telephone and found that it had gone dead. Suspecting the worst, she immediately set about hiding the Solidarity leaflets she had in her flat, before setting out to visit friends. On the way, she passed a truck full of young soldiers. "I smiled at them as usual. But their faces were dead and their eyes full of fear," she recalls.

Next day she went to the laundry to collect a heavy load of washing. "A young woman was explaining to the attendant that the receipt was in her husband's wallet and he had been interned the night before. She was quite matter-of-fact about it. The attendant made her write a statement about the missing receipt, and the long, silent queue waited as though frozen into their silence."

At this stage, General Jaruzelski was hoping to woo the people and the moderate section of Solidarity into some sort of agreement. But the Poles were not fooled. They soon realised, as Leszek Kołakowski wrote, that what was at stake was "not Communism or Socialism, not an idea, not a social order, and not economic problems, but a mortal fear of the privileged clique which suddenly realised that the power they were given by a foreign empire might not last for ever".[3]

Though Jaruzelski had made a point of arresting corrupt and incompetent Party officials – among them Edward Gierek and TV chief, "Bloody Maciej" Szczepański – adding insult to injury by equating these "enemies of the State" with the Solidarity people – there was no doubt that the hardliners had triumphed and that "the owners of People's Poland" were back in business.

It was said that half the Party's three million members resigned in protest, including all the journalists on the magazine *Kultura*, and large numbers of university professors. Despite this unprecedented haemorrhaging, the Party proceeded to deplete its numbers still further by purges. There was no longer any place for "reformers" in the Polish United Workers' Party.

Archbishop Glemp broadcast what seemed to be an appeal for peace at any price. "The most important thing is to avoid bloodshed. There is nothing of greater value than human life."

In a way he was only echoing Wyszyński's words in 1956, after the Hungarian Rising, when the Poles had been on the brink of committing mass-suicide. "It is sometimes harder to live for one's country than to die for it," he had said then. But Glemp lacked Wyszyński's charisma, his sensitivity to Polish culture, his finger on the popular pulse; and his message distressed rather than consoled his listeners. Some, perhaps, contrasted this stress on preserving life at all costs with the "better to die standing than to live on one's knees" creed of Solidarity, the spirit that had inspired the poster which Tim Garton Ash had seen during a Rural Solidarity sit-in: WE DON'T CARE ABOUT LIFE. THE PIG ALSO LIVES. WE WANT A LIFE OF DIGNITY.[4]

It was a moot moral point, and nobody could deny that the Archbishop's position was a difficult one. The kindest explanation is that he genuinely believed what he had been told: that the emergency measures would be short-lived.

Once the first surprise had passed and the full extent of the tragedy had sunk in – *our* army and *our* militia declaring war on *our* workers – the sense of being an occupied country brought to the surface all those latent talents for resistance which the Poles had learned over two centuries. "We survived the Nazi Occupation, so we can survive this," was the general feeling. When Jaruzelski had first referred to the "state of war" – *stan wojenny* which is the Polish phrase for "martial law" – the people had gone into shock. Then, realising that the description was apt, they adopted it, referring thereafter to "the war", as if there had been no other. If the General wanted war with the people of Poland, he could have it.

Active resistance was sporadic. Solidarity's back had been broken, its few remaining leaders had gone into hiding, its superb network of communications had been rendered unworkable. Leaderless now, many of the workers continued to resist the military take-over of their factories. Tension grew as the 16th–17th December anniversary drew near, the date on which only the previous year a monument had been erected in memory of workers killed by police in a workers' state. Now history was about to repeat itself.

At dawn on Wednesday 16th, a group of workers occupying the Gdańsk shipyards were driven out by the Army and police who broke through the gates in tanks. One young woman who had been there since the Sunday said that until then, in spite of the freezing cold and the presence of soldiers and tanks in the streets, they had remained optimistic. "We were frightened all the time. But it was not until the ZOMOs began to attack the yards in force that we understood they had won. Our dream was over. It was terrible."

The remembrance service at the Monument that evening was broken up by ZOMOs with tear-gas and water-cannon. In rioting next day, more than three hundred people were injured.

Similar tragedies were reported all over the country. The following graphic account speaks for itself:

Armoured vehicles drove through the steel-mill in a show of force. Riot police came out in droves, armed with shields and truncheons and also with tear-gas and gas-masks . . . not everybody managed to run away. The police chased people towards the recreation building and there, against the wall, they beat people, while forcing them to kneel in the snow with their arms raised . . . people were chased out of the factory showers, naked, barefoot, on to the snow, and dispersed in every direction with truncheons.[5]

But the worst news of all came from Katowice where, on the 17th, at the Wujec Colliery, eight miners were shot dead by the police. (There were persistent reports that the casualty figure was far higher than eight.) A tape smuggled out of Poland a year later told a moving story about these miners. It appears that in one of the encounters between them and the riot police, a group of ZOMOs were captured, "put on trial" and found guilty. While the miners were arguing about what to do with them, one miner stood up and reminded them that they had heard Mass and received the eucharist that morning. "Can we take vengeance on these people with Christ in our hearts?" he asked. Ashamed, the men released the incredulous policemen unharmed.[6]

The pattern was always the same: the Army would surround the works and then cajole or threaten the workers into coming out. If they did not, the ZOMO would move in, forcing the workers out and arresting the leaders. At the Katowice steelworks, more than two thousand men held out till 23rd December, but after helicopters dropped leaflets threatening the use of chemical weapons, they finally gave up.

The last heroic stand was made at the Piast mine near Katowice, where on the 14th, thirteen hundred miners had voted to stay underground until the Solidarity leaders were set free and the war was brought to an end. For five days their families were allowed to send down food; then permission was withdrawn. By Christmas Day, the miners were starving and scavenging for food on the pit floor. Two days later they surrendered. The surrender marked the end of all active resistance.

Confusion and insecurity reigned. It took time to adjust to the omnipresence of soldiers and armoured cars and tanks; of militia keeping a constant check on identity papers and swooping on any group of people larger than four. The curfew was strictly, even violently, enforced. Houses were searched, telephones cut off; teachers and students in high schools and universities mercilessly weeded out. Small factories and businesses whose personnel were suspected of Solidarity sympathies were liquidated, their employees then unable to find work elsewhere. And since in a Communist state, there is "no such thing" as unemployment, there is "no such thing" as unemployment benefit either. Hardship was very real.

The courts swung into action, passing summary sentences on all who violated martial law, treating the accused like criminals with no right of appeal. The air of hopeless, incredulous misery was conveyed by a taxi-driver in one of Marek Nowakowski's "snapshots taken in haste" of martial law, smuggled out of the country and published abroad:[7] "The cold is cruel. The old are going under, a lot of funerals about. With telephones cut off, you never get an ambulance in time. Streets full of tanks, police vans, all sorts of army vehicles. Gangs of militia, swarming, nosing. Enough to choke you."

Nowakowski's "snapshots" brilliantly convey the desolation: the police harassment, the house-searches, the danger of making a careless remark in public, the vettings at work; the re-emergence of informers, the petty officials who turn other people's misery to their profit; the monitored telephone conversations; the shortages, the shoe-soles nailed on or held on with wire, the absence of soap; the lying television bulletins, which were now given by poker-faced Army presenters, and which most people tried to avoid hearing. "I switched the telly on for the news. Just pressed the knob out of habit and away we went. Seemed worse than ever somehow. The newsreaders' ugly mugs were solemn, unctuous. They mouthed their words lovingly, uttering slanders, insults and threats with pedantic care . . . Must be two realities: one on the telly, the other in real life. It's unbearable!"[7]

One of the worst things was the pressure to sign a loyalty pledge to the regime – which amounted to a disowning of Solidarity, on pain of losing one's job, or worse. One woman, arrested while at the bedside of her mother dying of cancer, was told[8] "there will not be so much as a lame dog to make your mother a cup of tea". She signed, and was released. Another young mother was threatened with having her children taken away and brought up in a State orphanage. She signed too. Some of those who thus publicly disowned Solidarity were paraded on TV to confess their "errors". An article written by a Solidarity activist and published in an underground newspaper in February, said that because the aim of this "loyalty pledge" was to induce despair, "the act of signing deserves understanding, always sympathy, but never praise. By refusing to co-operate you are preserving hope . . . You know, as you stand alone, bound in handcuffs and with tear-gas in your eyes . . . that 'the avalanche changes course according to the stones over which it passes'. And you want to be the stone that will change the course of events."[9]

The internees – leaders, intellectuals and workers all mixed up together in forty-nine different detention centres – resisted from the start, keeping up a demand for a chaplain, clean clothes, greater hygiene, contact with their families, contact with Wałęsa. (Later they discovered that the prisoners had all been demanding the same things at the same time.) In many of the prisons conditions were inhumane in the extreme. A letter from the Białołęka prison, twelve miles outside Warsaw, revealed that the internees were treated like criminals, kept in close confinement in rat-infested cells, denied proper medical care or hygiene, condemned to exercise in "a very small space in which people can hardly shuffle, surrounded on two sides by walls and on the other two by a net next to the dustbins".[10]

Tadeusz Mazowiecki kept a prison notebook, which provides invaluable information about the life inside.[11] The prisoners weren't allowed to speak to each other, but they found various means of communicating. Three times a day, at a given moment, they sang hymns together, through the windows of their cells, and at midday they recited the Angelus prayer. "It was those hymns, that prayer," said Mazowiecki, "which gave us strength to survive, even though we had no news of our families, our dear ones, our friends. We had to save the most precious thing of all – hope – by our own efforts."

The close contact between workers and intellectuals in prison was mutually enriching. When, therefore, Mazowiecki and some of the other intellectuals were moved to the plushier army camp at Jaworze, they formally protested, believing, probably rightly, that the authorities were trying to drive a wedge yet again between the two groups.

At Jaworze, Mazowiecki realised that the young conscript soldiers who served the prisoners' meals were themselves under great pressure and were closely watched by the regular militia and by the hated ZOMO troops. (One lad who had refused to carry a lead-lined truncheon was sentenced to three years' imprisonment.) The conscripts had been ordered not to talk to the prisoners, but many of them broke the rule, explaining that they were acting under compulsion. One young guard in particular spoke freely, and stirred Mazowiecki's compassion: "One of his remarks remained in my memory because it reflected a bitter truth and also revealed the core of that hellish machine that held us both enslaved. 'There will always be someone to stand up for you,' he said, 'but who will there ever be to stand up for us?'"[12]

The prisoners did not forget their leader, Lech Wałęsa, now being held in solitary confinement. A group from Jaworze wrote to him:

> The blow which the nation suffered on 13th December will not break us. It will not destroy the feelings of unity between the workers and the intellectuals. These bonds will endure. You are the symbol of the values for which we all fought. In solidarity with all those arrested, interned and in hiding, our thoughts and our hearts are with you.[13]

Arriving for interrogation (one of several) before a military procurator in Warsaw on 10th February, Lech had announced to the people who stood outside: "I shall never bear witness against my friends." If the General had hoped to suborn him into co-operating with the military regime, he had far underestimated his opponent. Lech's famed willingness to compromise stopped short of the big moral issues. Lech stood firm, resisting all blandishments, all requests to bless the new official "branch" unions which were now replacing Solidarity but gaining few recruits.

(Many Party members were ordered to join. People on the edge of retirement were threatened with the withdrawal of benefits if they did not join; and already-retired pensioners were drafted to swell the numbers.)

Lech would consider no proposals unless and until martial law was brought to an end and the prisoners were released. Until then, his response would be silence. A silence that became a symbol of Polish defiance. Isolation would not break him, as it would soon break young Jan Kułaj, the Rural Solidarity leader, and lead him to "confess" his crimes on TV. Later he would claim that he acted under duress, but it was too late. As a colleague bitterly said: "Jan gained his freedom, but lost everything else."

Not everyone expected that Lech would hold out. When Andrzej Celiński, his secretary on the National Commission, found himself in a cell in the Białołęka prison, another prisoner jeered: "Well, what price Lech now? I'll bet he'll soon be playing along with the General." Celiński flew into a rage. "You can criticise Lech for all sorts of things. But of one thing I'm certain: he'll never betray us."[14]

Thousands were sacked for their part in the strikes, and the organisers received severe prison sentences of as much as seven years. More Party members resigned. In many factories and offices, bucketsful of returned Party membership cards were collected. It was said that in Katowice, for example, a large trunk was left outside Party headquarters. Fearful that it might contain a bomb, the frightened apparatchiks called in the Army to defuse it. When the trunk was opened, it was found to be full of Party membership cards returned by the last workers still to have belonged.[15]

International support was also forthcoming. (Lech Wałęsa had appealed for help in October 1981 when Poland's plight became desperate.) Seeing a convoy of one thousand lorries leaving in heavy snow for Poland, with a cargo of food, medicines and clothing, a woman in Holland was heard to remark, "Christmas this year is a Polish Christmas." Gifts poured in from West Germany, Austria, Denmark, Sweden, France, the UK, and from all over the world people rallied in their thousands to show "solidarity with Solidarity". It was generally understood that the issues went beyond the simple existence or non-existence of free trade unions in a totalitarian state. It was a battle for human dignity at the very heart of Europe.

On this wave of popular sentiment, governments also gave their support: materially, with shipments of some of their reserves; and politically, with sanctions imposed against the Polish and Soviet governments.*

By now there was no further possibility of active resistance in Poland, but passive resistance, such as Lech Wałęsa now asked for, in a message smuggled out of prison, could be very effective. Notwithstanding Archbishop Glemp's cautious speech on the 13th, it was the Church which took the lead. In fact, now that all legitimate opposition had been stifled, the Church had no option but to become the "voice of the voiceless". It was not so much that the Church stepped into politics, as that politics imposed itself on the Church. Glemp had a difficult tightrope to walk between trying to maintain the spirit of Solidarity and avoiding a head-on clash with the military authorities.

One week after the "war" was declared, the bishops issued a statement, far stronger than the Primate's sermon, calling for a restoration of civil rights, the release of all prisoners and the renewal of dialogue between the government and Solidarity. Then they turned their attention to practical matters. Priests were asked to extend their pastoral work by setting up permanent centres for legal, medical, spiritual and material aid and counselling – to internees, prisoners, those thrown out of work, and their families.

One of the Warsaw priests who threw himself wholeheartedly into this work was the young Jerzy Popiełuszko, an assistant priest at the parish of St Stanisław Kostka. Because of poor health, he was unable to have a parish of his own, but was a very busy medical chaplain in Warsaw. During August 1980, when all over the country workers were striking in support of the Gdańsk shipyard demands, the men from the Warsaw steelworks (Huta Warszawa) had asked Cardinal Wyszyński to find a priest to say Mass for them.[16] He found Father Jerzy – a young man quite uninterested in politics – and the steelworkers adopted him as their chaplain. During the recent sit-in by students at the Firemen's College, he had acted as *ex officio* chaplain, slipping in and out of the besieged school, to bring spiritual and moral help.

* These sanctions partially collapsed in the summer of 1982, when Western European governments decided, against American opinion, to provide the Soviet Union with vital parts for a gas pipeline from Siberia. Later that year, the US government allowed large shipments of grain to be resumed to the Soviet Union. These actions meant that sanctions were more symbolic than effective. They were progressively withdrawn, as some of the repressive measures in Poland were relaxed; and were virtually removed with the amnesty of 22nd July, 1983. It is on record that their removal was publicly recommended by both Cardinal Glemp and Lech Wałęsa.

When "the war" started, many of the steelworkers were arrested, tried and sentenced, and Father Jerzy went to their assistance. "The duty of a priest," he said, "is to be with the people when they need him most, when they are wronged, degraded and maltreated."

He attended the trials of the steelworkers, sitting at the front of the courtroom with their families – so that the men would know that their families had a friend who would care for them. He brought practical help, providing money, food, clothing, much of which came in from well-wishers in other countries. As a medical chaplain, he had been entrusted with medical arrangements during the Pope's 1979 visit; and now in 1981 he was put in charge of the first medical charitable centre in Warsaw – at the church of St Stanisław Kostka, which stored the medical and other supplies coming in from Western Europe and America. At home, Father Jerzy roved far and wide in search of help, persuading the better-off to give, and encouraging the workers in industrial plants and factories to contribute to the support of the old, the sick, large families, and the totally impoverished.

As the Church alone was exempt from the ban on assemblies, it remained the only outlet for public anguish. Already on the first Sunday, a Warsaw church had changed the last line of the hymn, "*God who dost defend Poland*", from the standard, politically acceptable, "Lord, keep our country free", to the defiant version sung in the old days of Czarist oppression, "Lord, return our homeland to us free", the version which the Polish exiles in the West had continued to sing. Much to the annoyance of the authorities, the new version was taken up on all sides, and everywhere sung with passion.

Christmas cribs abandoned tradition in favour of relevance. Sixty-eight-year-old Father Stefan Dzierzek was arrested for politicising the Christian message. His crib showed a Virgin Mary weeping beside a crib which had been overturned by tanks; the Infant Jesus on the ground wrapped not in swaddling clothes but in barbed wire; and, instead of shepherds, eight workers who represented the murdered miners from Katowice.[17] The priest was charged with publicly displaying a crib whose contents "abused freedom of religion and threatened law and order". At his trial he defended himself with spirit:

What I have tried to stress is that Jesus lives, that He is born today . . . into our circumstances. I have placed Him in the realities of AD 1981–2 in Poland. The police and all those who maintain that Christ has no right to interfere in the affairs of the contemporary world, reacted violently. For my accusers, Christ is dead. For me, He is eternally alive.

At St Stanisław Kostka in January, Father Jerzy Popiełuszko said the first of his *Masses for Poland* which would make him known and loved throughout the land. With the death penalty facing anyone rash enough to make an "anti-State" pronouncement, the parishioners deluged him with advice and warnings about what to say in his sermon. "The church was packed that night," said Hanka G., "but I could see his face as he spoke – just one sentence: 'Because freedom of speech has been taken away from us,' he said, 'let us therefore pray in silence.' And we stood silent for what seemed an eternity. Those were my first tears of the war. On the way home, I cleared a patch of snow from the windscreen of my car (there was no petrol available for private use) and scraped off the Solidarity sticker with a penknife. I was still crying. 'Dear God,' I prayed, 'just let me stay on the right side of the prison wall long enough to hear his next Mass for Poland.'"

Masses for those suffering under martial law would become a regular feature of life from now on; but the Mass for Poland at St Stanisław Kostka, on the last Sunday of every month, was the most renowned. Workers, intellectuals, artists, actors, university professors, crowded this small church, and stood in their thousands outside. People came to pour out their anguish and sorrow, but also to hear Father Jerzy tell them that the Church could not be neutral in the face of injustice and suffering but must become the true protector of the oppressed.

From "underground", the Solidarity leadership called for some sort of symbolic protest on the 13th of every month – the wearing of armbands and Solidarity badges, lighted candles to be placed in windows. On 13th February, a Mass was said in a large Warsaw church for the intentions of Solidarity and the internees. The packed congregation sang the National Anthem with new words. The old chorus, with its rousing: "March, march, Dąbrowski, from the Italian mainland to Poland", had referred to the country's Napoleonic past; but now the words were changed to:

> Lead us, Wałesa, from the sea-coast to Silesia;
> Solidarity will rise again and be victorious.

They also sang: "to reduce us to silence, you will have to kill

us", and a crowd of two thousand chanted: SO-LI-DA-RI-TY
. . .WA-ŁE-SA. . .BU-JAK.

Outside St Stanisław Kostka, where a similar service was held, truckloads of militia ringed the church, but the people dispersed quietly. Elsewhere in Warsaw, a crowd of three thousand shouting JUNTA OUT were dispersed by ZOMO using water-cannon.

> The Church is a time-bomb [complained the colonel in charge of radio and TV personnel].[17] To me it is clear that the Church's activity all in all is decidedly anti-State . . ., aimed against the current system in our country . . . All the cribs in the churches now have a uniquely political character. Religious symbols of the Home Army, emblems of Fighting Poland, banners spattered with blood . . . Just as it was during Hitler's Occupation.

In fact there was a widespread belief that the authorities now wanted a showdown with the Church, so that the people would be left defenceless. Hostile measures were being urged by the hardliners (known from now on as "*betons*" or "concretes"), with the backing of Moscow which with some justification saw the Church as the prime cause of Socialism's failure in Poland.

It was also the sole source of hope, as the people withdrew into a state of total alienation from the government. Under house-arrest outside Warsaw, the imprisoned Wałęsa appealed for a passive, non-violent resistance. People responded by refusing to read the Party press or watch TV; by going for walks *en masse* at TV news time, or putting their TV sets in the windows facing outwards. Once again they turned to Radio Free Europe and the BBC for a true picture of events; and once again the Polish joke, that cynical expression of impotence and despair which had not been needed in the Solidarity era, became a major popular industry: "What is the numerical strength of your opposition?" General Jaruzelski is supposed to have asked while on a visit to China.

"About thirty-five million people," he was told.

"Ah!" returned the General, "about the same as us."[18]

People drew closer together for mutual consolation, protecting each other from discovery, closing ranks against the oppressors. WRON, Jaruzelski's Military Council, had been immediately dubbed WRONA, which is Polish for "crow". No crow can defeat an eagle, they said. And, to the tune of a patriotic song used during the Nazi Occupation, they sang: "Before us is the crow, green and decked out in uniform. Whoever refuses to caw just like him, has to be put away."

Graffiti appeared on walls: WINTER IS YOURS BUT

SPRING WILL BE OURS; leaflets bore the logo of a snail or of a tortoise, symbols of slow, step-by-step resistance or of go-slow industrial action. Marshal Piłsudski's words, inscribed on his tombstone, "To be defeated and not to surrender, that is victory", became a watchword for the young. All in all, General Jaruzelski's *blitzkrieg* had succeeded only on the physical level. His victory was a hollow one. It must have been an appalling thought for him that the young were almost totally against him. "Polish youth," wrote Norman Davies, "looks neither to Lenin nor to Leftism, but to Piłsudski, Poniatowski and the Pope."[19]

With none but the Party and Army newspapers being printed, the following ironic announcement appeared in a kiosk:

> *Soldier*: plenty.
> *Life* (i.e. the usual Warsaw daily): none.
> *Culture*: suspended.
> *Perspective*: lacking.
> *The Republic*: sold out.

But by March there was an incredible flowering of underground newspapers and literature. About one hundred and fifty independent publications appeared, in spite of the fact that "all" printing materials had been seized by the security police.

It was the underground press which revealed that Archbishop Glemp's nightmare was coming true. They had managed to get hold of documents concerning Operation Raven, which had been put into effect in March to introduce and spread the notion of the "extremist" priest.[20] In view of what later happened to Father Popiełuszko, "Raven" is of exceptional interest. It used set-ups, provocations, scandals blown up out of all proportion to the facts, false accusations – all the classic blackmailing ploys. The priests on the authorities' black list (Józef Tischner was one; Henryk Jankowski another) were surrounded by specially trained informers. "Raven" intended "to set the clergy at variance with each other by singling out those who are 'loyal' and the 'extremists'. The latter are then to be isolated from the churchgoing public and, once alone and at bay, they are to be destroyed. Aim: to prepare the ground for a general confrontation with the Church."

Here were essentially the same plan, the same methods, the same dirty tricks with which the Stalinists in the late 1940s had sought to destroy the Church, and had almost succeeded. That they had failed was largely due to that tough old warhorse,

Wyszyński. But where was a Wyszyński for the 1980s? Few could see Glemp in the role.

Using much the same tactics of "divide and conquer", the authorities poured scorn on the "anti-Socialist garbage" who had joined Solidarity. Ten million of them! Among this "garbage" was, of course, Lech Wałęsa, a man recognised and admired not only in Poland, but by people of many political complexions, creeds and colours. For the Poles, he epitomised strength of conviction, high moral principles and enduring courage. And his stature grew even as his freedom diminished.

After his various interrogations in Warsaw, they had moved Lech to the hunting-lodge of Arłamów, near the Soviet border, where he was given a room thirteen feet square. "It's in a forest," reported Danuta, in an interview for *Spectator*, one of the underground papers. "Wherever you look there's only forest. It's such a lonely place, and terrible for him to sit there with no one for company but security guards who write reports on everything he does and says, and who even keep a camera in his bedroom. But Lech has to talk to them, or he'd go mad."

Lech and Danuta's seventh child, Maria Wiktoria, had been born at the end of January, and the christening at St Brigid's church in Gdańsk in March was attended by fifty thousand people. Lech was not allowed to be there: the authorities feared an insurrection if they let him out. In fact, at this time there was a move afoot to persuade the Solidarity leaders to go into voluntary exile in the West, a move frequently interpreted in the West as a sign of General Jaruzelski's generosity of heart, but deeply resented in Poland. A popular joke showed mistrust as well as resentment. Lech Wałęsa is being interrogated:

"Well now, comrade, where would you rather we sent you – East or West?"

"West, of course," says Wałęsa.

The colonel turns to his secretary and says: "Write it down – West Siberia." (In another variation on this theme, a woman approached a police patrol and asked if there was really a war on, just like Hitler's? "Yes," said the policeman. "In that case," said the woman, "can we please be sent to work in Germany?")

A few Solidarity people accepted the offer of emigration for themselves and their families, but Lech would not even consider it. When Deputy Prime Minister Rakowski raised the matter, he met such an explosion of rage that he hastily retreated from the room.

Lech, with time on his hands, spent much of it reading.

Although he had told Oriana Fallaci that he had never read a book, that was just inverted showing-off. On other occasions he had been more explicit: "I take a book, read two pages, understand what the author wants to say, check the end to see if I'm wrong, and if I am, check the middle to see why. Then I say to myself: well, why read the whole thing when I already know the answer?"

He asked now for Cardinal Wyszyński's prison memoirs, and for a variety of books on the Church's social doctrine, including John Paul II's encyclical on workers' rights and duties. He read these works right through, and when he'd finished with them he passed them on to the guards to read!

The only exercise he took was walking round and round the thirteen foot room, because whenever he went out into the garden, the guards came too. A picture of him taken in April showed him with a bushy beard, a pasty complexion and a paunch. When the guards reproached him with not exercising enough, he told them: "Just open that gate, and I'll show you just how fast I can run." "Your husband is lucky," said a police colonel to Danuta, "he lives in reasonably good conditions." "Yes," replied Danuta, "like a sheep among wolves." Among all the people she talked to, there was no one, she said, who would have changed places with him, for all his supposed "luck".

Yet he said he was never bored, nor did he waste time regretting the past. However gregarious he may have seemed, he had always described himself as a loner. "Internment was good for him," said Father Jankowski.[21] "It gave him the opportunity and the space to think a lot of things out and to learn about people. Much as he may have disliked being surrounded by security police, he is quite incapable of hating anyone."

Lech endorsed this view, saying:

Forgiveness is always necessary. I don't look on anyone as an enemy, though we may have different aims and purposes, and they may regard me as a pest. In my mind, I always see the cross of Christ. He seemed to lose everything and fail. But He forgave His enemies just the same. And He didn't fail – two thousand years later, he's still winning.[21]

"Internment," he claimed later, "was just one more school of life which it was necessary for me to attend . . . In many ways it was good for me to go through it. We have to take whatever comes to us in life and make the best possible use of it. If we've failed, then we must simply start again. Nothing is ever final. Life is all fresh starts."[21]

Violence grew in intensity. As Underground Solidarity called for a boycott of the May Day parade, a crowd of fifty thousand attended an alternative demonstration of their own in Warsaw's Old City. (And in other cities too.) Two days later, on 3rd May, ZOMO riot squads wearing gas-masks attacked a crowd of demonstrators with firecrackers, missiles and tear-gas. Many were hurt and over a thousand arrested. At midday on the 13th – a day on which there was a "staggered" stoppage of work throughout the country – all traffic came to a halt, and pedestrians wearing Solidarity badges stood still with their hands outstretched in the V-for-Victory sign. During the afternoon, the ZOMO attacked anyone standing around on the public squares with gas, clubs and water-cannon. The most serious incidents were reported in Kraków, Warsaw, Gdańsk and Szczecin, with heavy casualties and numerous arrests in each case.

Although July brought a partial relaxation of martial law, trouble flared again in August, when the anniversary of the signing of the Gdańsk Agreements (31st August) came round. In Przemyśl, for example, a small town in the south-east, people were attacked by police and beaten up on their way to Mass; a man returning peacefully from his vegetable plot was beaten and thrown to the ground; and gas-canisters were thrown at a group of women with prams. Similar events were reported from all over the country. The bishop of Częstochowa complained to the authorities that schoolchildren had been arrested and cruelly ill-treated by militia.[22] More seriously still, in Lubin and Wrocław police opened fire and killed a number of demonstrators; and the official press admitted similar deaths in Gdańsk and Częstochowa. (It was almost impossible to find out the exact numbers, since only those who died in hospital were admitted as statistics. Those killed outright on the streets were removed by the military, and their families were bribed or threatened into silence.)

As a poem circulated by the Underground noted, it seemed as though the government regarded the men in armoured tanks and ZOMO helmets as the only genuine "workers"; while the ordinary man-in-the-street was automatically a "hooligan" or a "scoundrel". The people's bitterness was undeniable. Yet it is significant that they did not offer violence for violence. In Poland there was no terrorism: no bombs, no sabotage. Throughout the world, there were those who interpreted this as a sign of weakness. But to the Poles, it was a sign of honour, a proof that they had learned well the lesson taught them by Solidarity and the Church. They could hold their heads high, even though the happy Solidarity baby of the 1981 I AM ONE YEAR OLD TODAY poster now had a successor, a wretched, sad-eyed little waif who proclaimed AND NOW I AM TWO.

[1] Tadeusz Mazowiecki, *Internowanie*, Aneks, 1982.

[2] Tim Garton Ash, *The Polish Revolution, op. cit.* Chapter 9.

[3] Preface to Nowakowski's *The Canary* (see below).

[4] Tim Garton Ash, *op. cit.* Chapter 3, "Inside The Rzeszów Commune".

[5] *Poland Under Martial Law*, a report on Human Rights by the Polish Helsinki Watch Committee 1984.

[6] Grażyna Sikorska, *A Martyr for the Truth*, Fount 1985.

[7] Marek Nowakowski, *The Canary and Other Tales of Martial Law*, Harvill Press, 1983.

[8] Norman Davies, *Heart of Europe, op. cit.* Chapter 6.

[9] Norman Davies, *Heart of Europe, op. cit.* Chapter 6.

[10] Statement made by the internees of Białołęka and addressed to Amnesty International, The International Red Cross etc. Published by Solidarity Information, Warsaw, 12.1.82.

[11] Tadeusz Mazowiecki, *Internowanie*, Aneks, 1982.

[12] Tadeusz Mazowiecki, *Internowanie*, Aneks, 1982.

[13] As note 1: *Letter to the Solidarity Leader, Lech Wałesa, From The Internees in Jaworze*, 22.1.1982.

[14] Pawlak and Terlecki, *Każdy Z Was Jest Wałesa, op. cit.*

[15] Tim Garton Ash, *The Crow and the Eagle, Spectator* 6.2.82.

[16] Grażyna Sikorska, *A Martyr for the Truth*, as above.

[17] *The Church in Poland under Martial Law*, booklet published by Voice of Solidarność, London, 1984.

[18] *Wojna Polsko–Jaruzelska W Karykaturach I Rysunkach*, Kopenhaga, 1982.

[19] Norman Davies, as above.

[20] *Wojna Polsko–Jaruzelska W Karykaturach I Rysunkach*, Kopenhaga, 1982.

[21] Personal interviews with the author.

[22] Sermon by Bishop Tokarczuk, Czestochowa, 5.9.82.

23 "THERE WILL BE NO RETURN TO ANARCHY" (1982)

No one expected that they would impose such suffering on the nation during the state of war. They seem to want to impose the maximum suffering on us; they want to see the workers on their knees.

Danuta Wałesa

For a brief moment the scene shifts to Rome, where, on 10th October, 1982, the bells peal out in welcome to hundreds of thousands of pilgrims – mainly Polish – from all over the world. On this day a new saint is to be canonised – the Polish priest, Maximilian Kolbe, who in 1941 had voluntarily taken the place of a man condemned to die of slow starvation in Auschwitz concentration camp. The example of Father Kolbe's heroism had brought new heart to the prisoners and his fame had spread not only throughout the camp but later, when the war was over, throughout Poland and throughout the world. By a strange historical irony, it was the German bishops who, more than any others apart from the Poles themselves, had pressed for Father Kolbe's canonisation. And now the Poles were to have at last their twentieth-century martyr-saint, and their rejoicing should have been great.

Should have been! Coachloads of pilgrims had been given special visas to come to Rome, and the huge Orbis coaches now perched on St Peter's Square, as though keeping a watchful eye on their passengers. But the previous day, the Polish Sejm had outlawed Solidarity, declaring its statutes null and void. It was part of Jaruzelski's "normalisation" programme, which also recreated the old transmission-belt trade unions against which at least ten million people had rebelled. For how could Poland be returned to its "normal" state of subservience to the Party and to the USSR, while a free trades union continued to exist, even if only in name?

Just how "normal" the Poles felt this action to be could be

judged by the tens of thousands who came out on strike in protest. But by now, the strike weapon was scarcely even a paper tiger. It could be easily destroyed by a combination of water-cannon, tear-gas, the threat of dismissal, and the possibility of a five-year prison sentence.

Although the strikes were put down, the situation in Poland remained so volatile that the Primate, Cardinal Glemp, did not feel justified in going to Rome for the canonisation. At a special Papal audience for Polish pilgrims in the Nervi audience hall on the day after the ceremony, the air was electric with emotion,[1] and the applause which greeted the Pope's arrival was tinged with desperation. As John Paul did not fail to notice. Close to tears himself, he addressed his compatriots: "When I was passing through the hall, I heard and saw many tears. What has happened to our country that our fellow-countrymen arrive for the canonisation of a compatriot with their eyes brimming with tears? These were no tears of joy . . ."

Turning to the official government delegation, he said sternly: "Let there be no more tears. Polish society does not deserve the fate of tears of despair and resignation. It deserves something else – to be allowed to build a better future for itself."

It seemed appropriate then that having finished his address, the Pope went down from the rostrum to greet a group of former prisoners from Auschwitz, in their striped twill prison attire and carrying their own flag: a Polish eagle dominated by a cross and a crown of thorns.

Father Kolbe, the new saint, was Jerzy Popiełuszko's ideal, but the young priest was not in Rome for his canonisation. Ever since his first Mass for Poland in January, he had been singled out for special intimidation and harassment by the police. The clergy house where he lived had been broken into and vandalised, his car had twice been smeared with white paint, his telephone was tapped, and two "guardian angels" followed him wherever he went. He was accused of inciting people to violence; and the increasingly popular Masses for Poland, attended by people from all walks of life and from all over the country, were denounced as "rallies hostile to the Polish state".

It was true that the authorities had good reason to fear Jerzy Popiełuszko, in that he was a fearless exponent of the evils that afflicted Poland, and spoke of things which others dared not mention. He spoke openly of "a nation terrorised by military force"; of people detained and brought to trial for being faithful to the ideals of Solidarity; of the beatings and ill-treatment of prisoners, of attempts to send healthy detainees to psychiatric hospitals. He laid bare the sickness of soul from which his country suffered. But he did not, as his enemies alleged, preach hatred. On the contrary. "Let us be strong through love," he pleaded in one of his sermons, "praying for our brothers who have been misled, without condemning anyone, but always condemning and unmasking the evil that they do, Let us pray in the words of Christ on the cross, 'Father, forgive them, for they know not what they do.'"

The crucial need, he said, was to overcome fear, and "we can do this only if we accept suffering in the name of a greater value. If the truth becomes for us a value worth suffering for, then we *shall* overcome fear."

Everyone remarked on the extraordinarily prayerful silence which prevailed at these services. But the authorities saw them as political demonstrations and determined to silence Popiełuszko. They tried first through the Church, asking the hierarchy to deal with this "turbulent priest". When the bishops took no action, they took matters into their own hands. When Father Jerzy in September referred to Poland as "a nation hanging on the cross with Christ", they refused him a passport for Rome, and drew up plans for a new campaign against him.

Like Lech Wałęsa, Jerzy Popiełuszko articulated the hopes and fears of almost an entire nation, and gave them a moral direction. "We are called to the Truth," he said in October. "We have to witness to the Truth with our whole lives." And in February 1983: "Let us put the Truth, like a light, on a candlestick. Let us make life in Truth shine out . . . Let us not sell our ideals for a mess of pottage. And let us not sell our ideals by selling out our brothers."

Witnessing to his own kind of truth, in early November Wałęsa wrote to General Jaruzelski with a new proposal for dialogue: "It seems to me that the time has come to clarify some issues and to work for an agreement . . . I propose a meeting and a serious discussion of the problems, and I am sure that with goodwill on both sides a solution can be found."

His guards at Arłamów had repeatedly urged him to write such a letter, assuring him that it would bring about his release. Wałęsa had consistently refused, pointing out that since he had not asked Jaruzelski for his arrest, he would not ask him for his release either. He had frequently told Father Orszulik, a representative of Cardinal Glemp who was allowed to visit him, that he would stand firm until martial law was abolished, since he had no wish to be released before all the other internees.

However, in November, he wrote the letter asking for dialogue and signed it "Lech Wałęsa, Corporal". Four days later, he was released from internment – an unexpected turn of events which caused many internees to accuse him of buying his way out; especially when they heard about the "Corporal" signature.

It was the first time he had put a foot wrong since martial law began; and, if it was a mistake, it remained the only one. General Jaruzelski was, in any case, considering a partial relaxation of martial law in December, and Wałęsa's release may have been a calculated ploy to convince world opinion that Poland was returning to "normal".

The ordinary people were delighted about his release. When he arrived home, he found the words WELCOME HOME, LESZEK painted in huge white letters on the street in front of his apartment. Banners streamed from the windows of the Zaspa estate: LECH, WE WANT ONLY YOU AND SOLIDARITY. Thousands of supporters gathered to see him, and the police stayed at a discreet distance. He was fatter (there were dark rumours about his having been forcibly drugged in prison); his face was rounder and puffier, his voice weaker. He was obviously a sick man. He greeted the people, but without his usual exuberance. And when he met the press, he asked them to leave him alone to reflect: he had been eleven months out of touch with reality, and needed time to readjust.

The Party newspaper, *Tribune of the People*, carried a non-committal nine-line paragraph about his return, and Jerzy Urban, the government press officer, describing Lech as "the former leader of a former union", added dismissively, "I do not feel called on to comment on any statements made by Citizen Wałęsa, a private citizen." (To underline what the people thought of this cavalier dismissal of their hero as a non-person, a portrait, recognisably of Wałęsa, was soon circulating in Warsaw, entitled, Portrait of Ordinary Citizen With Moustache.)

Wałęsa was well aware of the pitfalls that faced him. As he told a friend: "I have been released on to a tightrope stretched over a prison-yard. The rope is greased, but I do not intend to fall off it."

He was right about the greasy rope. Almost immediately, a Canadian news agency reported that a smear campaign was under way against the unimportant "private citizen". Just before his release from prison, security agents had handed to Church officials pictures of Lech in allegedly compromising pictures with women. For good measure, there were also documents accusing him of financial misconduct.[2] When told about this, Lech was un-impressed. "Attacks like that are a bonus," he shrugged. "Nobody will believe them."

To escape from such sordidness, Lech, with Danuta and a number of other recently-released internees, set off at the end of November on a private pilgrimage to Częstochowa.[3] Presenting to the Prior a bronze medal depicting a bleeding heart and the words *Poland 1982*, he prayed at the shrine:

My heart I submit to thee from this day forth . . . To thy care, Mother, I commit both myself and Poland . . . Shield us in our strivings to defend the rights and dignity of all who labour. I beg thee to embrace our country with thy care, so that Poland may be truly a home to her people . . . a place where justice, peace, freedom, love and solidarity shall triumph.

Guide me, Mother, that I may be a worthy tool in thy hands, to serve the Church, my country and my neighbour. Look with love upon the workers and peasants of Gdańsk and upon all thy people in Poland. Sustain them and strengthen their hearts in the struggle for justice and freedom.

It was a dreary existence to which Lech had returned, a travesty of his former hectic life. He was out of work, and the authorities would not recognise his status, though his stock was high in the country, and he was still the acknowledged leader. The people did not realise how powerless he now was. For them he was still the saviour, and many of them still beat a path to his door, bringing him all kinds of problems. "The neighbours don't go to the militia when their husbands get drunk and start throwing things," he sighed. "They come to me."

At least he now had a chance to get to know his children. Bogdan, Sławek, Przemek, Jarek, Magda, Ania, and the baby, Maria Wiktoria, knew him mainly as an absentee father.[4] The boys, he said, were all: "awkward buggers, like their father. The oldest one wants to go on strike, and they all want to change the director of their school."

They were, in fact, cheerful, attractive, lively youngsters, but being Wałęsa's children had given them a certain notoriety and often made them aggressive and imprudent. Danuta had her hands full with them, and she was not beyond using the belt to show who was boss. Lech was aware of his inadequacies as a father, and was content to leave the discipline to Danuta. But he did have his ambitions for his children: that they would "learn to

253

distinguish truth from lies, and become real human beings". Danuta shared this hope: "I don't want my children to have the same sort of life as Leszek and I have had. I wish they could live in a free country, without this awful feeling of helplessness."

"Danuta is more of a hero than I am," he would often say. During Lech's long internment, she had shown herself to be immensely competent, strong-minded and good-humoured. "A woman always finds the necessary strength when she is forced to face the unexpected," she says modestly. But Lech did not undervalue her achievement. He had been inclined to take her for granted before, but his admiration for her had grown during the last difficult months. "It's a strange marriage," he mused. "We don't discuss things, and we don't quarrel. People tell me that those who love each other quarrel a lot. Well, we don't. But we do love each other, I think. I have an old-fashioned attitude to marriage: a wife's a wife for ever. She'll bury me, or I'll bury her."

He did not, he said, want a wife who went out to work – "I'd hate to be married to a woman-welder in overalls." For Danuta, with seven young mouths to feed, it was scarcely even a temptation.

Life for women was exceptionally hard, whether they went to work or not. There were few of the labour-saving devices which ease the life of women in the West, and their lives were reduced to a series of "queue, wait, queue, wait, hunt, look, barter, bargain, bribe, queue".[5]

Prices had risen during the "war" by 400 per cent, and many families could not afford to feed themselves. About thirty per cent of all Polish families were living below the accepted minimum standard which was itself not far above the biological survival level.[6] A butcher in Warsaw displayed his entire stock (for a month) of six salami sausages, which his customers bought in thin slices. He was using the meathooks as supports for climbing-plants. Fathers bartered live rabbits for food for their children. Miners in Silesia were exchanging a ton of coal for two tons of potatoes. More and more city-dwellers travelled to the country to deal direct with the farmers, though this was illegal. Farmers and their wives travelled to the cities, with pieces of meat hidden under their coats.

Because of the poor diet, there was an epidemic of viruses stemming from malnutrition. Lack of medicines and of even the most basic facilities for hygiene added to the hopelessness. In the appallingly overcrowded hospitals, patients had to be responsible for their own hygiene. Since detergents and disinfectants were unavailable, hospital laundries were being closed down, and nurses were washing dirty linen by hand in small washbasins in the wards. Many doctors had no surgical gloves, sutures, masks, bandages, plaster of Paris, or apparatus for blood transfusions. Cross-infection was rife, and the danger to life enormous.

Soap was so scarce that not even doctors could wash their hands properly. One of Marek Nowakowski's "snapshots" of life under martial law (later described by Wałęsa as "the best account of that tragic time to have been written") tells of a shop assistant announcing to the queue that there is no more soap:

> The queue started to disperse. Some cursed their luck. The face of the fat woman grew red, and she gasped soundlessly like a fish out of water. With shaking hands she took from her bag a small piece of grey soap wrapped in newspaper:

> "It stinks! They allowed us a hundred grammes each at work, and the cleaner won't even scrub the lavatory with it."

> She threw the soap down on the pavement and stamped on it in a rage. "Stinks like rotten fish!" she kept saying, her voice hoarse from her exertions.[7]

To combat their tragic demoralisation, the people instinctively turned to the Church as their only hope. Churches were packed day and night. In an effort to reduce tension, the bishops had asked the people to refrain from making the V-sign in church and to hold a cross in their hand instead. The people responded by holding a cross in one hand and making a V-sign with the other! Many churches had their own Solidarity altars where weekly all-night vigils were kept. In Radom, a banner over a church read DO NOT BE AFRAID, FOR BEHOLD I AM WITH YOU. And because a "cultural cold shower" prevented not only foreign but any new Polish books, films, poetry and paintings which did not advance the Socialist cause, the churches had taken to staging exhibitions of Polish culture.

There was, of course, a price to be paid by the Church for this solidarity with the people. The attacks on "extremist" priests were being stepped up. In Gdańsk, Wałęsa's priest, Henryk Jankowski, was subjected to a campaign of vilification in the Party press – "my role is to keep Wałęsa's spirits high," he once said. "And I succeed. That's why the authorities hate me." In Warsaw, on the night of the 13th–14th December, "hooligans" hurled a brick containing a detonator through the window of Jerzy Popiełuszko's room. The bomb did not go off; but the priest now realised the kind of danger he faced. After this, the Warsaw steelworkers organised round-the-clock protection for him.

At the beginning of December, Wałęsa again wrote to General Jaruzelski. The crisis in the country, he wrote, could only be overcome by the whole of society pulling together in an atmosphere of mutual trust. And this could only be achieved on the basis of the Gdańsk Accords of 1980. Three conditions were fundamental to agreement: an amnesty for those arrested during martial law; the reinstatement of those who had been deprived of their jobs; and a recognition that Polish society needed some kind of pluralism. He ended the letter with the words, "I am ready to take part in any work to this end." There was no reply to this letter, but the authorities circulated a scurrilously distorted version of it which made it seem as though Lech was abandoning Solidarity and making a bid for power on his own account.

Wise after the event, Lech would not be caught in the same way again. Before the 16th December, he took the precaution of releasing in advance his intended speech at the Monument. It was just as well he did, as early on that day a group of six armed militia pushed their way into his flat and took him away for questioning. They then drove him up and down the motorway for eight solid hours, to prevent him from keeping his appointment at the Monument. But his speech was read for him. "We have been hurt again," it said:

> But our cause is still alive, and a victory will one day be ours. What can I say, as leader of this great union which officially does not now exist? I say that it exists within us, even within those who seem to have abandoned it . . . I believe we have sown a seed that lies deep. We are not the people that we were before August 1980. We know now what we are striving for. The question is, how do we set about it?

Although he was continuing to keep a low profile, Wałęsa gave numerous interviews to Western journalists in this period. His message was always the same: the demand for an amnesty, the cessation of reprisals, the need for free trades unions, and his own willingness to take part in a dialogue. But by March, when there was still no response to any of his overtures, he was beginning to get exasperated. He realised, moreover, that if he didn't exert some sort of pressure on the authorities, he would soon be losing his own credibility as a leader. The government was making an all-out effort to coerce people into the new unions, and the repression was becoming more severe. It was the trials of two Solidarity leaders: of Anna Walentynowicz; and of six internees which brought him out of his quasi-retirement. Though Walentynowicz had little time for him these days, and openly queried his right to be leader, Lech attended the opening of her trial and later promised some "hard action". As he left the court, passers-by shouted encouragement at him, and gave a hurried V-sign.

The promise was followed by a meeting between Lech and the Solidarity leaders who were still in hiding. When Lech announced that this meeting had taken place, the authorities were furious. But no amount of questioning could make him divulge where it had taken place or what had been said. From now on, however, he would be followed by police wherever he went; a security police family would occupy the floor below his; his telephone would be tapped and a complex surveillance system installed. "My telephone and my walls are all ears," he would warn visitors. "It's not pleasant, but you can get used to anything."

A week later, as he and Father Jankowski drove from Gdańsk to Warsaw, to lay a wreath at a memorial service for the victims of the 1943 Ghetto Rising, they were stopped on the road by the police and held in detention. Presumably the authorities feared that Wałęsa's mere presence at such an emotive occasion would provoke a riot.

So perhaps it was to keep him off the streets that in April – one week before the expected public outbursts on May Day – they gave him back his old job as an electrician at the Lenin shipyard. It said much for his strength of character that this man, so recently the uncrowned king of Poland, admired all over the world, could accept, without any inner turmoil, a return to the role of an electrician working shifts. For all his surface vanity, Lech had never ceased to regard himself as a worker first and foremost:

I am a worker and that's all I ever want to be. It doesn't mean I have no ambition to learn, or to improve myself. But to the end of my days I shall be a working man. And why? Because, in my kind of work I repair tools old and new, from the East and from the West, from simple hammers to highly complex machines. Now, *there*'s a job which expands a man's mind.

Solidarity had, in fact, *not* asked for any demonstrations to mark May Day. Instead they had asked the people to boycott the parade, and on the 3rd to go to work in their best clothes and observe one minute's silence at some time during the day. But there were some localised protest rallies on May Day: in Kraków, for example, where a demonstration passed off peacefully, and in nearby Nowa Huta, where at least one man was killed when the police moved in to break up the crowd. On the 3rd, spontaneous demonstrations burst out in various cities. It was the largest display of public opposition since the declaration of war over a year earlier. In Warsaw a crowd of eight thousand heading for the Party building were dispersed by water-cannon and many arrests were made. As night fell, a group of security men disguised as thugs raided a convent attached to St Martin's Church and with cudgels beat up a group of volunteer helpers who were making up parcels for the families of internees. Among them was the poet and Solidarity activist, Barbara Sadowska. After wrecking the premises, the thugs took four of the injured to a forest outside Warsaw, and left them to walk home. (A favourite ploy of the police.)

Next day, the official press made a casual reference to "a few isolated incidents" involving "a handful of extremists".

Worse was to come. Grzegorz Przemyk, Barbara Sadowska's nineteen-year-old son, having passed his school-leaving exams, went to a wine bar to celebrate with friends. On the way out he was stopped by the police who kicked and beat him so brutally that he died two days later in hospital. In an open letter to General Jaruzelski, a Polish writer who was also a friend of the family reported that the boy's insides were "a bloody pulp", and that there was "not a centimetre of undamaged intestine". "It is not often that surgeons cry," he wrote, "but these did, as they left the operating theatre."[8]

The people cried too. The Przemyk affair stirred them up again, and ten thousand attended the funeral mass at St Stanisław Kostka. A telegram from Wałęsa stated that: "Every death is painful, but this one is especially brutal. It must not be forgotten." All emotion spent, the mourners walked the two miles to the cemetery, their numbers doubling on the way, their faces frozen in silence. After seeing those faces, an eye-witness confessed to feeling fear: ". . . fear of that stony silence, for what it might mean some day in the blood and death of those young people, when the silent scream was cried aloud."[9]

When Pope John Paul again visited his native land in June to pay tribute at the shrine of Our Lady, Queen of Poland, at Częstochowa, there was none of that hopefulness that had marked the earlier visit. In those long-ago days of 1979, he had persuaded them to pick up their courage and try to save their world. Four years later, they had made the attempt and failed. Hope was in limbo. "Even their expectations are tired," said Józef Tischner. "All they can pray for is a miracle."

Nevertheless, hundreds of forbidden Solidarity banners fluttered in the breeze to greet the Pope, and hundreds of thousands of hands raised in the V-sign showed the world that Solidarity was not yet dead. But, to prevent any spontaneous outburst against the regime large numbers of militia were deployed at every event. The authorities clearly felt even less secure than in 1979, when the policing of the visit was left entirely to stewards appointed by the Church.

It was a difficult journey for the Pope. He too was being asked to walk a slippery tightrope. In government eyes, he was there to bestow authenticity on them, to consult and confer with them as the legitimate rulers of the land. But this he refused to do. Instead he constantly urged Jaruzelski to make good the Gdańsk Agreements, to restore civil liberties and initiate genuine dialogue as the only sure path to social harmony. He was prepared to respect the existence of military rule, but denounced the misery it had inflicted on the people, "the bitterness of disappointment, humiliation, suffering, loss of freedom, injustice, the trampling of human dignity underfoot".

Nearly one million people crowded John Paul's large outdoor Mass in Warsaw, to hear him tell them that "at this particularly difficult moment in the country's history", only a moral victory over themselves could help to heal the divisions in society.

It was a visit which underscored the yawning gap between the entire people and the government which claimed to rule in their name. Yet he did not mention politics, and when he used the word "solidarity", it was in lower-case type, and in the ordinary, human sense of the word. In effect, all he could do was raise morale and preach endurance. It was, said someone, "a call to faith not arms". He did not raise hopes, because he could not. But he did, nevertheless, breathe hope into the people, "not because he suggested that anything could be done, but because he showed us a way of living with the situation, by overcoming hatred and returning good for evil".

To the Polish bishops he threw out a challenge which many of them welcomed. It was necessary, he said, now that the people had no spokesmen of their own, for the Church "to defend every citizen, to protect every life, to prevent any injuries, particularly to the young and weak" – an obvious, even if sideways reference to the police murder of Grzegorz Przemyk.

Lech Wałęsa had been refused holiday leave from the Lenin shipyard for the duration of the Pope's visit. The Pope had asked to see him, but the authorities were most unwilling to give such prominence to this "former leader of a former union", and indeed had been keeping Wałęsa under close surveillance throughout the Pope's visit. John Paul, however, insisted. The two men met in the Tatra mountains near the Czech border and talked for two and a half hours. What they talked about has not been revealed, though an article next day in the Vatican's *L'Osservatore Romano* gave rise to speculation that the Pope had asked Wałęsa to step aside and leave the Church and the authorities to sort things out. Lech himself gave no hint of what passed between them on this score, revealing only a more general comment made to the Pope by himself:

> During my meeting with the Holy Father, I said that our situation is in many ways what we make it. As a nation we Poles are always being forced by circumstances to examine ourselves and our capabilities. This means that we are constantly being driven back to bedrock, to seek and find the most basic truths about ourselves. We have no shoes for our feet, and rarely have enough to eat. But we do ask ourselves questions about what really matters in life. Do other richer nations have such opportunities? In this sense, I believe that Poland is the richest nation in the world.[10]

Meeting the Pope revived at least some of Lech's wounded self-esteem: "I watched him getting in the plane and saw his big shoes and giant clip-clopping stride. Each step seemed to express peace and faith . . . I felt as though I had received an electric charge . . . as though he had passed some of his own peace to me."[10]

But there was not to be much peace in the months ahead. Lech returned to the hurly-burly of a life in which he never had any time left to himself. There was no privacy, and Danuta felt herself a prisoner in a flat where, in spite of the conspicuous police presence outside, people were always dropping in unannounced.

> How can one describe this place [wrote a friend],[10] which for some is a family home, for some a place of work, and for others a cross between a theatre and a zoo? How does the host feel when he returns tired from the shipyard and after a short nap has to divide himself up between his family, the office, visiting journalists, and several million others? How can one calculate the stresses of a life in which if he says something stupid, gets drunk or whispers I love you to his wife, there's a listening microphone to pick it up?

Though he had a better flat than most of his fellow-workers, few of them would have exchanged their lives for his. As he said:

> I have to get up at five to go to work. I can't drive fast because I have a police car on my tail. At home, five hundred letters are waiting to be answered, so I stay up till midnight or later, and then have to be up at five again. Even if I do have more things to eat, I don't have time to eat them. What's more, I never know whether someone is planning to hang me, beat me up or just arrest me.

In July, the "war" officially came to an end. But "there will be no return to anarchy", Jaruzelski warned. By which he meant that there would be as much repression as ever, if not more. New laws required employees to give six months' notice before changing jobs, while facilitating the expulsion of unruly students and dissident academics without any notice at all. The right of assembly continued to be restricted: only church gatherings or meetings of the official unions could be held without prior permission. All printing equipment was to be registered and anyone connected, however remotely, with any underground publication was liable to imprisonment. Those Poles who continued to belong to "secret unions or those that have been dissolved" could be put away for three years.

At the same time, a partial amnesty was announced for all but sixty or so internees and prisoners. Partial, because they were to remain on probation until the end of 1985. Hundreds of internees accepted, for the sake of sparing their families further hardship. Bujak, the Warsaw leader, ignored the amnesty, and preferred to stay underground to ensure the continuance of what was left of Solidarity. As for Wałęsa, he didn't listen to the General's speech, but spent the day fishing.

When he returned to work in August after a break, he was wearing a T-shirt imprinted with the Solidarity logo. By this time, many of the released internees had already been re-arrested for such crimes as scrawling Solidarity slogans on walls. Wałęsa said the new laws meant a return to Stalinism, and the bishops wrote a stiff note to the Sejm to this effect. The Sejm managed to modify a projected new law which would have made "spreading false information" (whatever that might be construed to mean), a crime punishable by prison. But the Sejm's powers were very limited and apart from that one concession, the rope round Poland's neck continued to be pulled tighter.

On the third anniversary of the Gdańsk Agreements, a cordon

261

of armed ZOMO ringed the shipyards, blocking the path to the monument outside the gate. As Lech and two thousand of his workmates approached the gate, the ZOMO parted momentarily to let Lech through, then immediately closed ranks to keep the others back. Wałęsa, a lonely figure, placed his bunch of flowers beneath the crosses and stood for a minute in silence. But few had come to support him, and fewer still of the shipyard workers had observed the Solidarity call for a go-slow.

The largest response had been, not in Gdańsk, but in the steel town of Nowa Huta outside Kraków, purpose-built as a stronghold of Socialism. Here riot police scattered ten thousand demonstrators with their usual brutality. The ZOMO were now using paint mixed with the water in the cannon. This ruined the clothes and took a week to wash off the face. In Nowa Huta too, militia forced their way into a church where about 300 people had taken sanctuary. Unable to deal with them in the church, the militia went outside again and simply waited till the three hundred came out.[11]

The authorities were jubilant, claiming "a boycott of the boycott". But Wałęsa was reasonably content that, however limited the boycott had been, it had at least proved that Solidarity was still breathing. At the same time he realised that in view of the inevitable reprisals, the time for public demonstrations was past. A new more forward-looking programme of social structures needed to be worked out, covering every area of national life. Doctors, he said, should work out their own programme for a future health service, teachers one for schools, economists for industry: "Sooner or later talks with the government must take place. And whoever represents our side must have behind him a massive, detailed and readable programme of reform. We must be ready and waiting for the new August."[12]

It was a new attempt to show the world that though Solidarity had been stifled, the social conscience which it had awakened lived on. In Warsaw, Jerzy Popiełuszko was making the same point. He too saw the enduring legacy of Solidarity as the awakening of the nation's conscience, the restoration of human dignity to the working people of Poland. He had been impressed by the Pope's references to a "solidarity of hearts". "Solidarity," said Father Jerzy during his August Mass for Poland, "is the unity of hearts, minds and hands rooted in ideals which have the power to change the world for the better . . . Solidarity means that we must overcome the fear that paralyses us . . . and bear witness to what we believe and to the truth which is in our hearts."[13]

Such "anti-State" sentiments were too much for the authorities, who now began legal proceedings against the priest. In September during a workers' pilgrimage to Częstochowa, he had accused the authorities of violating human dignity and depriving the people of freedom of thought and action. Three days later an official investigation was ordered into the priest's "abuse of freedom of conscience and religion".

It seemed as though the authorities had declared open season on their major opponents. For their slander campaign against Wałesa too was moving into overdrive. Throughout the summer, the media had been indulging in character assassination, endeavouring to portray Wałesa as an "enemy of the people", who had led the country into bankruptcy and civil war![14] The Party newspaper, *Tribune of the People*, drew public attention to the numerous gifts he had received from Western admirers, and sneeringly dubbed him "the Yank from Gdańsk". In September, with a great deal of advance "hype", a special thirty-minute TV film, *Money*, "exposed" him as a fraud and an embezzler. The film, which reproduced an alleged conversation between Lech and his brother, Stanisław, a year earlier (when Stanisław had visited Lech in prison), claimed to prove that he had over a million dollars-worth of ill-gotten gains salted away in the Vatican Bank. Unfortunately, the tape was of such poor quality that it was impossible to hear who was saying what, so an "interpreter" had to be used. A note of farce was injected into the proceedings when the presenter unctuously warned: "Because the heroes of this programme use vulgar expressions, we ask children and very young people not to watch. We also inform you that we have removed from the conversation . . . remarks which are insulting to the Pope and the Church . . ."[15]

Next day, the specious government spokesman, Mr Jerzy Urban, assured foreign journalists that Citizen Wałesa was certainly not the target for a propaganda campaign, since he was of no importance in Polish politics. The people had their own opinion about that. They did not need Lech to assure them that the programme had been a tissue of lies, a hotch-potch of various tapes sewn together. At the European Cup-Winners Match in Gdańsk next day (between Lechia Gdańsk and Juventus Turin) about forty thousand soccer fans suddenly realised that Lech was amongst them. Rising to their feet, hands held high in the V-sign, they roared LESZ-EK, SO-LI-DAR-NOŚĆ, LESZ-EK, while the stadium managers turned up the music on the loud-speaker system as loud as it would go, to drown the din. But nothing could have drowned a din as loud as that.

[1] I was there.
[2] *Newsweek*, 29.11.82.
[3] *The Church Under Martial Law*, op. cit.
[4] The rumour that the children were not all his, that he had adopted two children of one of the workers killed during the riots of 1970, was absolutely untrue.
[5] A. M. Rosenthal, *New York Times* Magazine, 7.8.83.
[6] *Uncensored Poland*, 22/83.
[7] Marek Nowakowski, *op. cit.* "A Short Street".
[8] Polish Affairs III. Summer/Autumn 1983.
[9] A. M. Rosenthal, as above.
[10] *Każdy Z Was Jest Wałesa*, op. cit.
[11] Eye-witness account told to the author.
[12] Interview with Lech Wałesa in *CDN* underground publication, 8.9.83.
[13] Grażyna Sikorska, *A Martyr for the Truth*, op. cit.
[14] *Uncensored Poland*, 16/83.
[15] *Uncensored Poland*, 19/83.

24   GOLD . . . (1983)

> I have always believed it to be my duty to help others and to serve
> them as far as I can. I did that before August, during Solidarity
> and still today. Sometimes I can help a large number of people,
> sometimes only a few. The numbers aren't important. As for
> rewards – one day they give me the Nobel Prize, and on the next
> they'll probably put me in prison.
>
> Lech Wałęsa, 1984

Ashes and diamonds, gold and tears. If such dramatic paradoxes
lie at the heart of the Polish experience, they were never more
graphically illustrated than in the twelve-month period between
the Octobers of 1983 and 1984. For it was in October 1983 that
Lech Wałęsa won the golden Nobel Prize for Peace and in October
1984 that the murder of Father Jerzy Popiełuszko plunged the
nation into yet another deep collective trauma.

Wałęsa had been nominated for the Nobel as early as 1981, and
two years later his name was on the short list along with the Pope,
Anatoly Scharansky, Philip Habib and Bishop Desmond Tutu.
(General Jaruzelski had been on the list of nominees!) Having
been unsuccessful earlier, Lech was not particularly hopeful this
time; and his own government was extremely anxious that he
should fail. On 5th October, 1983, *The Times* (London) carried
the following brief paragraph:

> Anticipating the possibility that Mr Wałęsa might win the prize, the
> Polish government spokesman in Warsaw said yesterday that the
> nominee is still under investigation for illegally holding bank accounts
> in the West and for evading Polish taxes. It is clear that the authorities
> in Warsaw are nervous about him winning the prize, for that would
> undo most of their attempt to discredit him at home.

Warsaw Radio announced on the same day that it was doubtful
if the prize would be awarded that year. Presumably the candidates
were not of a high-enough standard!

It was a Wednesday. Lech, who had been off work with stomach ulcers, had decided to spend the day in the lake district around Gdańsk, fishing and gathering mushrooms with a few friends. At 11 a.m. they heard the news on the car radio that he had won the Nobel. Passing cars honked their congratulations, and his friends tossed him up in the air with delight. Lech, they noted to their surprise, was "pleased but tight-lipped. Definitely tight-lipped".

Back at the flat, Danuta was being deluged with flowers, telegrams, telephone calls, foreign journalists and camera crews. By 5 p.m. there were two thousand people waiting outside for Lech to return. On the police radio frequencies, voices could be heard discussing this build-up:

> *First voice*: How many are there?
> *Second voice*: A lot. They're standing there, shouting.
> *First voice*: Shouting what?
> *Second voice*: They're shouting: Long live Wałęsa.

When Lech put in an appearance, the cheering began: WA-ŁĘ-SA SO-LI-DAR-NOŚĆ, LE-SZEK. He came to the window, gave a twin-fisted salute, thanked them and shouted: "This prize is for all of us. I didn't consult you, but I've decided to give the money to the bishops for their Private Farmers' Fund."

"Everyone is pleased," he said, at a press conference in the flat immediately afterwards, "but not all are equally so. Many people are in prison, many have been thrown out of their jobs. Many nameless people have deserved this award, and I feel ashamed that at present I am so powerless to help them."[1]

Would the award be a shot in the arm for Solidarity, wondered the pressmen? "Well, winning a prize like this puts us all under an obligation for the rest of our lives. We must never forget why it was awarded." Was he scared by his new international status, asked a French journalist? To which Lech replied: "I'm scared of nothing and nobody but God. I am only a man who belongs to his own time and his own place, and who tries to solve problems as they come along. Unlike some of my colleagues, I believe there's always a solution to every problem, if one tries hard enough."[1]

The official media were less enthusiastic than their foreign counterparts. They did not mention the award until late that night. When they did so, their displeasure was obvious. Mr Urban said the award was nothing but Western propaganda against People's Poland.

Outside of Gdańsk, the people were not sure how to react.

Nobel was the first thought in everybody's mind and heart, but they were not free to give vent to spontaneous enthusiasm. The writer of this book was in Kraków when the news broke, and four times was taken behind closed doors to be told about it – in a muted whisper. *A teraz co?* mused one lady – and now what's going to happen?

In Warsaw, Jerzy Popiełuszko was delighted by the award, which he too saw as an international acknowledgment of Solidarity's admirable record of non-violence. He praised Wałęsa's role since internment: "He does not say so much now, but what he does say is always good and well thought out. He has the appearance of a man with a deep living faith, who gets his strength from God."

Father Popiełuszko was under great strain. He already knew that the State prosecutor was preparing a case against him and would soon charge him with "abusing the role of priest . . . turning churches into places for anti-State propaganda, harmful to the interests of the Polish People's Republic."

It was a charge that could send him to prison for fifteen years. "If they put lies in my mouth, will you tell them in the West that my only concern was the truth?" he asked the author. And in answer to the obvious question about whether he was afraid, he replied: "Yes, I am afraid. But I could not act otherwise. I must continue to protect those who are helpless and have no one else to defend them. That is my pastoral work. As a celibate priest, with no family dependent on me, I must use my freedom on their behalf."

So, what if "they" decided to kill him? He didn't so much as blink. "I live with that risk every day," he admitted. "On one level it terrifies me, the human level. But for the Christian, death is not the end of the story. I would rather die a violent death in the defence of human freedoms, than save my life by opting out of the struggle against evil."

Lech Wałęsa would have agreed that for Father Jerzy there was no real choice. Speaking of the Church's role in society as being "beyond politics", he explained. "The Church may not say that she 'belongs to Solidarity'; but she *must* stand up for the fundamental human values which Solidarity embodies. She may not intervene directly in politics, but it is her duty to speak out in defence of those basic human values."

Since martial law had begun, Lech had spoken in public only a handful of times. That he was able to do so now was almost entirely due to the fact that the world spotlight was on him, and the authorities would not dare prevent his speaking out.

LECH WAŁĘSA AND HIS POLAND

Accordingly, on 14th November, word went out that Lech Wałęsa was to speak at a church hall in a Gdańsk suburb, and about fifteen hundred people made their way through the dark streets in order to hear him.[1]

They saw the same, straightforward honest human being that he had always been, but they saw too that the experience of internment had deepened and matured him. He had always told them the truth, but often in the past his oratory had been stumbling, and his thoughts had lacked the words to express them adequately. But this evening it was obvious that here was a speaker of consummate power. "We had a great and beautiful programme for self-government," he told the audience, "but it was too vague and we used too many slogans. So . . ."

Here he threw the ball right into their unready laps, and refused to take it back again. A new programme must be worked out, and *they* were the ones to do it. They must go home, form small groups, throw ideas around, patiently and slowly.

First of all, he told them, they must decide on the kind of society that was possible. The ideal society was unattainable, but "a better Poland" *could* come about. As they were stuck with a Communist bureaucracy, they might as well try and find a way of humanising it. Next, they must find a way of ensuring that their trade unions were both self-governing and united with each other – acting mainly in their own workers' interests, but capable of acting on behalf of the others. Thirdly, the economy: perhaps it could be made to work, if every work-place was well-run and efficient, and was also geared to the general good. And lastly, Truth. Let them go home and reflect on how to create a community which would preserve Truth and resolve its internal conflicts without resorting to violence.

Sooner or later, insisted Wałęsa, there would be another genuine working-class revolt, and they must be ready for it, with their blueprints worked out. "We are three years older now, and next time round we must do better." No, this did not mean that he was abandoning Solidarity. "This new programme is still Solidarity, a more experienced and therefore wiser Solidarity."

"Every one of you here is Wałęsa," he barked at them, refusing to let them off the hook. "We have been humiliated and insulted. Let us all see to it that we are humiliated no more. None of us has any excuse. Solutions *must* be found. Agreement *must* be reached. Everyone here lives in a family and in a factory. Very well, then, let everyone find the truth about his country in the context of his or her own family or factory. If we can solve our

268

own problems in that smaller sphere, we shall be able to solve them in the larger one."

As the audience sat stunned, feeling they had been turned upside down and shaken, he rammed the point home. "I cannot decide for you. But decisions are vital. Each of us must decide according to our own conscience. And each of us is responsible for what he decides."

There must have been many present that night who had once criticised Wałęsa for being undemocratic. But many also had long ago understood their mistake. Lech's understanding of democracy went beyond the mere licence to pull in a dozen different directions at once; it involved the patient harmonising of many voices. Since martial law, they had realised that Wałęsa was essential to the survival of Solidarity. His patient refusal to give in to the authorities had saved the movement. "If it hadn't been for him," said a former critic, "we'd have had a pseudo-Solidarity today, led by a 'liberal Democrat' like Rakowski. That's what the government wanted, to destroy the movement by taking it over."[1]

But the movement was alive, and Wałęsa had just thrown down a powerful challenge to its rank-and-file. For a moment, said a participant that night, "we could believe that we were living in a free country. Each one of us *was* a Wałęsa. Of course we were."

Between then and the Nobel ceremony in December, the knowledge that the outside world had appreciated their struggle was some consolation in the worsening atmosphere of "normalisation". A letter from Jacek Kuroń,[2] in prison again, spoke of a people which was "hungry, exhausted and poor" and of the "psychological terror" being practised in factories and firms, where every day there were wholesale sackings. One plant manager had lost his job for taking part in a Mass at which the factory's Solidarity banner was blessed; another for being reported in conversation with a former member of Solidarity's National Commission. The pressure to join the new unions was considerable and involved not only threats but bribes – the offer of coupons for washing-machines or colour TV sets, for example. Kuroń begged that both sticks and carrots be rejected. "When the regime tries to persuade us to collaborate with the security police, when we experience doubt and fear, let us remember those who sacrificed their lives, health and youth for our cause."

Wałęsa was in two minds about going to Oslo in person. In the end, two factors persuaded him not to. The first was the possibility of not being allowed to return to Poland; the second the conviction that to go and be wined and dined in Norway while his companions

269

rotted in prison, would be immoral. He decided to send Danuta and thirteen-year-old Bogdan, their eldest son. "When the press find out," he sighed, "they'll say I want Danuta out of the way so that I can play around with other women." Tadeusz Mazowiecki was to go too, to read Lech's Nobel address. But the authorities refused Professor Mazowiecki a passport, and Bohdan Cywiński, now living in Switzerland, stepped into the breach.

On 10th December, at Oslo University, Egil Aarvik, the Chairman of the Norwegian Nobel Committee, presented the $195,000 cheque and the golden Nobel award to Danuta.[3] Lech Wałęsa, he said, had "raised a burning torch . . . and lifted it unarmed", his chosen strategy being that of peaceful negotiation. The determination to resolve conflicts by means of a mutually respectful dialogue was the recognised hallmark of Solidarity. Lech Wałęsa had shown courage when he leaped over that steel fence into the shipyard in August 1980, and his courage had been rewarded by the "millions of Polish workers and farmers who had joined him in the struggle". Mr Aarvik regretted the circumstances which prevented Lech from being present and made it necessary to listen to "a silent speech from an empty chair". But, he asked:

Is Lech Wałęsa really so silent? Are he and his cause really defeated? Many are of the opinion that his voice has never been stronger nor reached further than at the present moment. The electrician from Gdańsk, the carpenter's son from the Vistula valley has managed to lift the banner of freedom and humanity so high that the whole world can once again see it . . .

. . . Lech Wałęsa has made humanity bigger and more inviolable. His two-edged good fortune is that he has won a victory which is not of this, our political, world. The presentation of the Peace Prize to him today is a homage to the power of victory which abides in one person's belief, in his vision, and in his courage to follow his call.

Danuta, who, as the time for her journey to Oslo had drawn near, had become increasingly nervous, even to the point of praying that she wouldn't be given a passport, rose to the occasion magnificently, reading Lech's acceptance speech with such poise and calm dignity as to win all hearts. Lech, watching a video-recording of the event, on TV in their flat, "fell in love with her all over again", though his friends insist that his admiration was not without a distinct tinge of jealousy.

The theme of reconciliation and of Peace to Men of Goodwill characterised both this and the more important Nobel address delivered next day by Dr Cywiński.[3] The forty years of his own life, Lech reflected, had surrounded him with "violence, hatred and lies". But the lesson he had learned was that "we can effectively oppose violence only if we do not resort to it". The Gdańsk Agreements of 1980 – "a great Charter of workers' rights which nothing can ever destroy" – remained the only possible springboard for a way forward. The Poles, he said, wanted dialogue not confrontation with their government. "Dialogue is possible and we have a right to it . . . But it is impossible to be constructive if frustration, bitterness and helplessness prevail."

Yet, in spite of martial law, about which he preferred not to speak, the people were still vowed to "the defence of our rights and our dignity; as well as efforts never to let ourselves be overcome by feelings of hatred".

A day or so earlier, at a press conference, Wałęsa had called for an end to the Western sanctions against Poland which had been introduced at the time of the imposition of martial law. In this he had the support of underground Solidarity. For the government was now blaming sanctions for the forthcoming spate of price rises and were attacking Solidarity for continuing to support them. Now Wałęsa went further and, as a gesture of good-will towards the regime, asked that Poland should be given a massive transfusion of aid. "We must not close any doors or do anything that would block the road to an understanding," he concluded, making it clear that he was addressing not just Poland but the whole world community. "But we must remember that only a peace built on the foundations of justice and a moral order can be a lasting one."

He might have added, "and based on freedom". That very day, Adam Michnik was writing one of his many letters from prison, this time to General Kiszczak, the Minister of the Interior, accusing: "It was not I who was proscribed that December night two years ago – it was Freedom. It is not I who am in prison today – it is Poland."

Next day, 12th December, Father Jerzy Popiełuszko was ordered to the Public Prosecutor's Office in Warsaw, where he was confronted with "documentary evidence" of his anti-State activities: cassettes of his sermons, photographs, and a video-cassette confiscated from a foreign TV crew. After three hours' interrogation he was taken to the flat which his American aunt from Chicago had recently bought for him and where, by an amazing coincidence the police, within seconds of their arrival, found a cache of gas-canisters, explosives, rounds of machine-gun ammunition, over fifteen thousand copies of underground publications, and leaflets calling for an armed uprising on the 13th and 16th December.[4]

He spent the night in a police cell with a group of convicted murderers, one of whom asked him to hear his confession. Next day, on the intervention of the bishops, he was released – pending investigations. The allegations were on a par with those against Wałęsa, and few believed them. On Christmas Eve, Father Jerzy's parish priest pointed out the absurdity of such accusations against a man who so consistently preached the message of overcoming hatred by love. And on Christmas Day, when Father Jerzy said the December Mass for Poland, the crowd of fifteen thousand who packed the church, the square and the surrounding streets, showed by their mere presence that the attempt to smear a much-loved priest had decisively failed.

[1] Pawlak A. and Terlecki M., *Każdy Z Was Jest Wałęsa: Nobel 1983*, *op. cit.*
[2] *Newsweek*, 28.11.83.
[3] *Uncensored Poland*, 24/83.
[4] *Author's Note*: When I met Father Popiełuszko in October 1983, he was fully aware of the case being prepared against him and equally aware of the probability that false evidence would be produced from somewhere. In order to make absolutely sure that there could be no genuine evidence against him, he was going through all his papers and possessions and discarding anything that could be considered even remotely "subversive", in the government's sense of the word. In view of that, it is hard to believe he was so careless as to overlook the large cache of arms etc. which the police later found in his flat – within seconds of their arrival.

25 . . . AND TEARS (1984)

Let us lie in wait for the virtuous man, since he
annoys us and opposes our way of life,
reproaches us for our breaches of the law
and accuses us of playing false to our upbringing.
Before us he stands, a reproof to our way of thinking;
the very sight of him weighs our spirits down . . .
Let us test him with cruelty and with torture . . .
and put his endurance to the proof.
Let us condemn him to a shameful death.

from The Book of Wisdom

General Jaruzelski's government maintained a stony indifference. Nobel or not, they did not intend to admit Wałęsa into partnership on *his* terms. The accusations concerning his tax evasions and foreign bank accounts continued, and by pointing to all the money he had gained the government hoped to drive a wedge between him and the ordinary worker.

> The ordinary worker? [snorted a woman in Warsaw]. My God, he earns money but has nothing to spend it on. He has to wait fifteen years for a flat and if he already has one, he can't buy a bigger one because there aren't any. He can't buy a dress for his wife, because they're all so revolting she wouldn't be seen dead in any of them. He can't buy food because it's rationed or because there's none to be had. If his wife has a baby, she'll probably have it without anaesthesia in a filthy overcrowded ward, and when she comes home she won't find a baby food that doesn't make the baby sick. The ordinary worker is up the creek without a paddle. He has no hope.

An article in *Mazowsze Weekly*, the underground Warsaw Solidarity paper with a national circulation, claimed that conditions were now as bad as in the chaotic post-war years, except that then wages had been higher. "We started near the bottom, but we've managed to get even lower."

Many Poles were getting out of Poland if they could. The Stefan Batory boat which plied the Baltic routes was constantly full of

273

"tourists" who had no intention of returning. It wasn't only economic hardship that drove them away. Magda, a teacher in a town in western Poland, sought refuge with her children in West Germany because she had reached the end of her endurance. She and several other teachers at her school had refused to join the new teachers' unions and were being victimised. Magda herself was under investigation for anti-State activities; her flat had been ransacked several times. But it was the bleak prospect for her children which finally broke her. During martial law, her twelve-year-old son, Marek, and many of his friends had been arrested and taken to a state "correction house", where they had to stand to attention for twelve hours at a stretch. Since coming out, Marek had been nervy and unable to concentrate on anything for long. His crime had been to ask for the replacement of the old Stalinist text-books in the school library with newer, more truthful books. "How could I remain in Poland?" Magda wrote from Germany to a friend in England. "The children have no future there. They're already on the police black list, which means that the road to higher education will be closed to them."

Cardinal Glemp continued to appeal for calm and to rely on a successful outcome of his own negotiations with the General. He was hopeful that the Private Farmers' Fund which he had mooted two years earlier* would be operative by the end of 1985. The public were inclined to think he was too soft on Jaruzelski, and that his views coincided too often with government propaganda. Cruelly, they coined a new Polish verb: *glempić* – to glemp, which meant: to say nothing, at great length, but soothingly.

The people's suspicions were deepened when in March the Cardinal was reported as saying, during a visit to Brazil, that though a section of the Polish Church had retained close links with Solidarity, he himself had chosen "a different, more difficult and more just path – the true pastoral path". The Cardinal's remarks caused undisguised fury at home and earned him for some time to come the sobriquet of Comrade Glemp. Devout, elderly ladies on their way out of Mass could be heard wishing to string him up to the nearest lamp-post.

But, if the Cardinal seemed remote from the actual views of

* The Nobel Prize cheque which Lech Wałesa still intends to hand over to the bishops for the fund intended to help private farmers with much-needed equipment and supplies, is still in Norway, since the government has not yet allowed the fund to get off the ground. The diploma and medal etc. were taken by Wałesa to the monastery at Częstochowa where they are being held in trust for the nation.

the people, a large number of parish clergy were very close indeed to those views.

> It was they [wrote Bogdan Szajkowski], who had to cope with the real everyday sufferings of the faithful, the miseries of life in prisons and internment camps, where they went to offer spiritual solace; they who experienced the plight of families deprived for long months of their fathers and of any means of livelihood; they who had to celebrate memorial masses for those killed and injured during the rallies and strikes; and who sheltered the fugitive Solidarity supporters.[1]

At a stormy meeting earlier in the year, Cardinal Glemp was taken to task by a group of about seven hundred younger priests from his Warsaw diocese. But he offered no explanation of his attitude; nor was he prepared to enter into discussion. He merely invited the priests to pray along with him. The special Religious Affairs Office within the Ministry of the Interior now had a black list of eight hundred "subversive" or "strongly anti-State" priests. Their "anti-State" activities covered such misdeeds as organising courses of lectures for workers or for farmers; allowing their churches to be used for performances of underground theatre or for the exhibition of forbidden books or paintings; or even putting on Saturday night discos in the crypt for the young.

Father Henryk Jankowski from St Brigid's church in Gdańsk – which had set up a Solidarity altar and was known as the "shipyard church" – was under interrogation for anti-State activities. As was Jerzy Popiełuszko: between January and June 1984, he was interrogated thirteen times; his friends and even casual callers were threatened; cars parked outside the clergy house were vandalised. When he kept the appointment with the police, a large crowd of well-wishers would escort him to the Ministry of the Interior and wait outside till he was released. This enraged the authorities, who accused him of "using the interrogation as a means of inciting public unrest"!

Troublemakers would regularly be planted in his Masses to try and turn them into the political circuses the authorities declared that they were. Though no one could fail to notice the strain it put him under, Father Jerzy was ready for them and would appeal for self-restraint. No songs or slogans outside church, he begged: "Let us show our maturity and force the troublemakers to go home without achieving what they came for." He would appeal to the provocateurs too: "And you, brothers, who were ordered to come here by others, if you want to serve the truth and regain your self-respect, let the people go in peace."

The ZOMO would be waiting outside, ready to pounce, but the people would disperse quietly, as he had asked. It was said that some of the militia refused to act against him, and that replacements had to be brought in from outside. Perhaps some of the local men remembered that first Christmas of "the war", when Father Jerzy had gone to break the Christmas wafer with the ZOMO patrol outside the church. (The curfew was abolished for Christmas Eve, the traditional time for breaking the wafer, and for midnight Mass.)

"What I do is not political," he continued to insist. "It is my simple duty as a priest. My fight is against hatred and for the dignity of human work; and the only weapons I have are truth and love."

He asked the people to pray for those who had "sold themselves into the service of lies, hatred and violence". There was never any question of his inciting them to violent action. "Jerzy's very careful," a friend in Warsaw assured the author at this time. "He knows how far he can go, and doesn't overstep the mark."

But that was May 1984, and emotions were running high. There was the anger and frustration over the "war of the crosses": the authorities' persistent removal of crosses from schools and public places, no matter how many times the citizens put them back again. Police broke up the resultant protests and sit-ins with truncheons. There was fury over the downward-spiralling living-standards: even the official press now admitted that children were suffering from lack of vitamins and protein. The situation in the hospitals had gone from disastrous to catastrophic. IF YOU NEED AN INJECTION, BRING YOUR OWN SYRINGE, read a notice in one Warsaw hospital; and the spread of scabies and hepatitis was not unconnected with such an appalling lack of basic facilities. The medicine cupboards were all but bare.

A new offensive had been launched against Polish culture, marked by the arrest of Marek Nowakowski for "slandering the State". Once again, only writers who toed the Party line could hope to be published. Add to all that the continued persecution of Solidarity, with scores of Poles being arrested on the strength of their underground connections. "You must realise," Magda had said in the letter referred to above, "there are many supporters of Solidarity, but there are many spies and stool-pigeons too, who track them down and betray them."

Since the much-vaunted amnesty in July 1983, the prisons, with far less publicity, had been quietly filling up again with political prisoners, and there were horrific stories of abductions and torture used to force witnesses to testify against Solidarity. Kuroń, Michnik, two other KOR members and the seven Solidarity leaders – including Andrzej Gwiazda and Bogdan Lis – who had not been released in July, were still awaiting trial after two and a half years. The group was known collectively as the Solidarity Eleven.

Some of those who had been amnestied reported continuing persecution. One man who wrote to thank a Western agency which had helped him with food and clothing, told them:

> I find myself on the right side of the prison wall, but don't be fooled. From the moment of leaving prison, I have been hunted and followed like an animal. I have to move on, changing my address in order to avoid re-arrest and thus jeopardising my sick mother and my brother's family . . . After sixteen years as a miner, I now have nothing, neither a job, nor a home, nor any income, nor freedom. The only freedom I know is carried inside me. Thank you on behalf of my brother's children for the baby food and other wonderful things you sent, which are impossible to get here.

It seemed as though the regime had no idea how to deal with either the economy or the opposition, and resorted to the only procedure they understood: repression. If they could browbeat the people into giving up hope, they might yet numb them into docility.

But May Day killed that hope and brought protest back on to the streets, when thousands of Solidarity supporters infiltrated the official parades. Squeezing themselves in between two factory groups and pretending to be an official delegation, Lech Wałęsa and several hundred Gdańsk supporters disrupted the parade by flashing V-signs, unfurling anti-government banners and chanting FREE THE POLITICAL PRISONERS as they passed the rostrum. ZOMO dispersed them with tear-gas broadsides, rubber truncheons and high-pressure jets of water, whereupon some of the protesters retaliated with stones. That afternoon, the police brought a huge water-cannon, "like some prehistoric animal", and stationed it outside Wałęsa's flat. "I'm surrounded here," he reported on the telephone. "They're chasing people all over the place with water-cannon. They've just hosed my windows down, and they're drenching anyone who attempts to look out."

Near the old Solidarity headquarters in Gdańsk, street-fighting was heavy. Youths tore up stones from the railway tracks to defend themselves against the ZOMO,[2] who, by most eye-witness accounts were more brutal in Gdańsk than elsewhere.

But tensions were just as high in Warsaw – and police scattered a crowd which had assembled after the nine o'clock Mass at St John's Cathedral. The crowd then walked to St Stanisław Kostka to hear Jerzy Popiełuszko speak. After that service too they were assaulted by police. They came back again on the 18th, on the anniversary of the murder of young Grzegorz Przemyk. Those responsible for his death had been arrested and even tried. But the trial had turned into an attack on the murdered boy himself. Two of the four accused were acquitted; the two others were sentenced to a mere two and a half years' imprisonment and were, in fact, released on amnesty in July 1984. On that occasion, Father Jerzy said: "We do not want punishment of the guilty. We yearn for something that stirs the conscience and generates the courage to say, 'It was my fault', and to ask forgiveness."[3]

It was probably two weeks later, during the May Mass for Poland, that Father Jerzy sealed his fate. Local government elections were coming up in June, the first since martial law, and the government was hoping that a high turn-out (however it was achieved) would convince the outside world that "normalisation" was proceeding. Solidarity, on the other hand, called for a boycott. Father Jerzy stepped feet first into the arena, warning:

> We ourselves are responsible for our slavery, when, either through fear or the desire for a quiet life, we elect authorities who proceed to promote evil. If we vote such people into power, then we have no right to condemn the evil that results, as we ourselves are helping to create it and make it legal.[4]

In the event, the government claimed a seventy-five per cent turn-out. (Much less than the usual norm of ninety-eight per cent in a country where the people have much to fear from reprisals. It is no small matter to accept being put back to the bottom of the housing list, for example.) Solidarity, which tried to monitor the results at several polling stations, put the average national turn-out figure at sixty per cent. Whichever way one looked at it (and both sides claimed a victory), between six million and ten million Poles found the courage to boycott the elections, an astonishing figure in a Communist society.[5]

On 12th July, Father Popiełuszko was indicted on the basis of the charges laid against him in December. Ten days later, to celebrate the fortieth anniversary of the Polish People's Republic, General Jaruzelski announced an amnesty for more than six hundred political prisoners, and many common criminals. Father Jerzy was not among them. The following Sunday, his parish priest, Father Teofil Bogucki, took the unusual step of defending his assistant priest from the pulpit: "Just as no one can forbid the sun to shine," he told a packed congregation, "so no one can forbid a priest to speak the truth. Preaching the divine message is not politics."

Father Jerzy, he assured everyone present, was "the best type of priest and the best type of Pole . . . a man who makes people face up to the truth about themselves and society . . . Everyone here knows that he has never preached hatred or revenge . . . On the contrary, he comforts those who are distressed in mind."

Then he added, putting into words the fear that gripped his listeners: "All of us pray night and day for Father Jerzy, trusting in God that no one in Poland will ever do him serious harm."

The 1984 amnesty let General Jaruzelski neatly off the hook as far as the remaining Solidarity prisoners (the Solidarity Eleven) were concerned. Trial dates had been fixed, and indeed the trial of Kuroń, Michnik and company had already started. But it could have been extremely embarrassing to the regime if such fluent and articulate men had been allowed to have their say in court. Attempts had been made to persuade them to emigrate, or to forswear any further political activity. But the prisoners were not to be bought. Releasing them now was the safest course. In any case, they could easily be picked up again, the moment they resumed their "anti-State" activities. They were warned that there would be no leniency, should there be even the slightest return on their part to the "paths of crime". "Urban says I'm free," shrugged Andrzej Gwiazda, "but three police cars follow me wherever I go."

As far as the General was concerned, the amnesty introduced an apparently more normal atmosphere, which permitted him to make overtures to Western bankers again, in the hope of Western credits being renewed. The way was open for Western ministers to begin visiting Poland for the first time since the declaration of martial law. Yet the third report by the Polish Helsinki Committee on Violations of Human Rights in the country told a very different story – of a fierce and bloody struggle against all opposition. The report gave chapter and verse for a horrifying list of kidnappings, beatings, torture of individuals and groups. It also instanced a series of killings by unidentified police officers throughout the year. These crimes *always* went unpunished; and all appeals for justice failed.

It was not until the end of August that Jerzy Popiełuszko learned with relief that his case was after all to be covered by the amnesty.

279

That week saw the fourth anniversary of the Gdańsk Agreements and also the fortieth of the Warsaw Rising. Lech Wałęsa was allowed to place a bouquet of flowers at the Monument in Gdańsk; but in Wrocław, two members of the recently-released Solidarity Eleven were jailed for two months for making a similar gesture.

The Church marked the anniversaries by calling for a month's abstinence from vodka. Although the sale of liquor before 1 p.m. had been made illegal, there were five million problem drinkers in the country, many of whom manufactured their own hooch, using anything from potatoes to anti-freeze. Solidarity supported the Church's appeal, asserting that alcoholism was one of the weapons with which a totalitarian regime was able to keep a whole people enslaved.[6] Deputy Prime Minister Rakowski marked the anniversaries by warning the clergy not to meddle in politics. In an interview published on the 31st, he said: "One's hair stands on end when one hears what is being said in some pulpits." Jerzy Urban, the government spokesman who wrote for the magazine *Tu I Teraz* (*Here and Now*) under the pen name of Jan Rem, singled out Father Popiełuszko in particular. In an article entitled "Sessions of Hate", he described the priest as "the Savonarola of anti-Communism", "a manipulator of collective emotions" and "a spreader of political rabies".

Adam Michnik was to reproach himself afterwards for not having seen the writing on the wall for Father Jerzy when that article appeared. "If I had had more imagination and had publicly accused Urban of incitement to murder," he wrote, "I might have been sentenced for slandering a minister, but Father Jerzy might still be alive."[7]

In fact, the steelworkers who protected Father Jerzy *were* alarmed, and they asked the bishops to remove him from the scene for a while, for his own safety. The bishops took the request seriously, and plans were made to send him to Rome to study. But the steelworkers had made their move too late. Other people had made plans too. Or perhaps – an even more sinister possibility – these "other people" were so determined to settle accounts with Jerzy Popiełuszko that, rather than let their prey elude them, they brought their own plans forward in time.

The first warning came on 13th October, as the priest was being driven from Gdańsk to Warsaw by his friend and bodyguard, Waldemar Chrostowksi. A man suddenly emerged from the forest bordering the road, and threw a heavy rock at the car. Chrostowksi took successful avoiding action and drove on. Both men decided that the man with the rock was someone deranged.

But that had been Plan One for the disposal of Jerzy Popiełuszko. In the Interior Ministry it had already been decided that the anti-State priests were to be dealt with, and Popiełuszko's name headed the list.

There is considerable confusion about who actually gave the orders and what the orders were. But sadly there is no confusion at all about what was actually done.

Early on the evening of 19th October, Jerzy Popiełuszko took part in a special workers' Mass in the northern town of Bydgoszcz. In the previous nine months, several Solidarity sympathisers had been abducted from the surrounding area. There had, in fact, been so many kidnappings that the oppositionists had nicknamed the area Poland's Bermuda Triangle!

The parish priest of the church to which Father Jerzy had been invited, had been threatened with reprisals if he allowed his visitor to preach. So there had been no sermon. Instead, Father Jerzy prayed with the people after Mass, on the theme of overcoming evil with good. His last words were: "Let us pray to be free from fear, but most of all to be free of the desire for violence or revenge."

Outside, in a Fiat car, his three murderers, Piotrowski, Chmielewski and Pekała, all from the Religious Affairs department of the Interior Ministry, were already waiting. Their executioners' tools were prepared: two clubs hacked from the trees outside Bydgoszcz and wrapped in an old T-shirt brought specially for the purpose; lengths of rope, gauze, sticking-plaster, bags of stones . . .

At ten o'clock, with Waldemar Chrostowski again at the wheel of the VW, Jerzy Popiełuszko set off back to Warsaw. Not far from Bydgoszcz, however, the car was stopped by a "traffic policeman", who ordered Chrostowski out to take a breathalyser test. In the front seat of the police car, he was held at gun-point, bound and gagged. While one man stayed in the car with Chrostowski, the other two returned to the VW to deal with the priest. They ordered him out, dragged him to the Fiat, beat him unconscious with the two clubs, threw him trussed up and gagged into the boot and drove off, telling Chrostowski as they did so to prepare for his "last journey".

Seizing a moment when another Fiat was overtaking them, at a spot where two men were standing by a motorcycle on the left – Chrostowski hurled himself at the car door and threw himself out on to the road, rolling to safety on the verge. The handcuffs came off in his fall, and he managed to escape and raise the alarm.

Had he not done so, the murderers would never have been

281

caught, for nobody would ever have known what had happened. Father Popiełuszko's body (and Chrostowski's too) would have been fished out of the Vistula dam, and, no matter what anyone might have suspected, would have been attributed to yet another "unfortunate accident". After all, there had been ninety-three such "accidents" since the end of martial law.

The actual events of that dreadful night did not emerge until the trial of the murderers four months later. On the evidence of the accused at that time, Father Jerzy had regained consciousness as he lay tied up in the boot of the Fiat, and began banging on the lid. They decided to stop and tie him more securely, but by the time they had got out of the car, he had somehow got free and was running away calling for help. They caught up with him and Piotrowski began to belabour him with the club on his back and chest. When the priest was unconscious again, they tied him more firmly and pushed a towel in his mouth before putting him face upward in the boot. But again he recovered consciousness and began prising the lid open. Outraged, on his own admission, by such lack of co-operation on the part of his victim (he said aggrievedly in court that "if the priest had obeyed orders, we shouldn't have had to hit him at all"), Piotrowski was "forced" to stop the car and beat him again while he was still lying in the boot. Then, for good measure, he dragged him upright and beat him senseless. Tightening the ropes and pushing the towel further down the priest's throat, he gave orders to drive on a little way, until they came to a wood. Here, they laid their victim on a blanket and tied his legs separately and together in such a way that escape would be impossible. A second rope was attached to his legs at one end and his neck at the other, so that any movement to straighten his legs would have strangled him. That being done, they put more gagging material in his mouth and over his nose, securing the lot with gauze and sticky tape. As a final insurance, they tied bags of heavy stones to his legs, before returning him to the boot one last time.

Waving a phoney traffic pass at a patrol which tried to stop them, they drove straight to the huge dam on the Vistula at Włocławek, where they flung the body into the icy water. Experts who examined the body later said that the priest had already died from suffocation by the time he entered the water.

For ten days after the news of his abduction broke, the people waited and prayed in a kind of stupor. Many spent all their free time, night or day, in the churches, and thousands gathered each evening for Mass in Father Jerzy's Church, St Stanisław Kostka.

Letters of sympathy poured in. Lech Wałęsa came to Warsaw a few days later and warned that "if a hair of Father Popiełuszko's has been harmed, somebody will have a terrible lot to answer for".

It was an explosive situation. The bishops appealed to the authorities to find the missing priest with all possible speed. Thousands of uniformed and plain-clothes police using helicopters and sniffer-dogs scoured the country in search of him. General Jaruzelski denounced the kidnapping and hinted that it was a deliberate challenge to his authority and to his policy of pursuing national accord. Solidarity was convinced that those responsible for the kidnapping had the backing of hardliners extremely high up in the security police who were intent on showing that the General was incapable of keeping order in the country. It was common knowledge that Jaruzelski had lost control over the Party "betons" and the security apparatus which they controlled. The police, it seemed, were above the law and safe from it, just as they had been in Stalinist times.

On 24th October, Polish TV announced that five men were being questioned in connection with the priest's disappearance; and on 27th their identities were divulged. The Minister for Internal Affairs announced the names on television, "with the utmost sorrow", and appealed for public help in the continuing search for Father Popiełuszko.

Throughout the country, the tension was becoming unbearable, and many workers wanted to call strikes or organise marches, in order to relieve pent-up feelings. But Solidarity called for caution. In Gdańsk, Lech Wałęsa persuaded a crowd to disperse quietly after warning them: "We must take care not to be drawn into their internal power struggle. If they want to play musical chairs, they must do it without us."

All over Poland, masses were being said for Father Jerzy's safe return. A banner outside St Stanisław Kostka proclaimed: WHEREVER YOU ARE, JUREK,[8] CHRIST IS WITH YOU, AND OUR PRAYERS.

Then, on the 30th, at eight o'clock, just as the evening mass was finishing, a priest came out . . . "Nobody who heard it," wrote a British journalist who was present,[9] "will ever forget the awful howl of agony that rose from the thousands waiting in the church of St Stanisław Kostka when a priest announced that Father Popiełuszko's body had been found, a cry which went on for many minutes until it was joined by the tolling of the bells."

"Outside," another writer[10] said, "the people . . . were visibly stunned and helpless. They stood with pale, shut faces, with forgotten, folded hands."

There was some pressure on the murdered priest's parents to take his body and bury it quietly in his own home village. But Father Jerzy's mother resisted: "Years ago I gave my son up to the Church. I am not going to take him back now." After much hesitation, it was agreed that he should be buried in Warsaw, where he belonged, in the grounds of St Stanisław Kostka church.

On 2nd November, friends of the family went to identify the body, and then the true horror of his murder was at last exposed:

> The whole body was covered in brownish-grey bruises. The face was deformed. The nose and areas round the eyes were black, the fingers were brown and dark red, the feet greyish. His hair was much thinner, as if some of it had been pulled out. Large areas of the skin on his legs seemed to have been torn away . . . When the mouth was opened, they saw a piece of pulp in the place where the tongue should have been.[3]

"Passivity is no way of combating the present evil," cried Andrzej Gwiazda, calling for a one-hour strike to coincide with the time of the funeral. But Lech Wałęsa, while insisting that the whole truth be told, asked for calm and for a resumption of talks with the government. "This death," he said, "must become the cornerstone from which social peace may be built. Let the silence of mourning reign throughout Poland. But let it also be the silence of hope."

Honest dialogue, he urged, was still Poland's only chance. He begged the Church to give a moral lead at this painful time, and asked the people to trust to the wisdom of Cardinal Glemp. But it was his own influence which carried most weight: "If the Poles stay off the streets in the next few days," suggested a leading article in *The Economist*,[11] "it is because they still give Mr Wałęsa the respect they deny to the government."

Wałęsa's advice prevailed. But the murder had blown a hole the size of a dead priest in Jaruzelski's claims about "normalisation".

Tens of thousands of mourners had been waiting at the church since dawn for the body to arrive. Patiently and sadly they filed past the coffin as it lay in the church. Flowers, candles, lamps were everywhere, and farewell notes were pinned to the surrounding fence. There was one from Solidarity which mourned, "We could not defend the man we most loved"; one from a group of non-believers to say that they too would join the all-night vigil at Father Jerzy's coffin; and one which proclaimed the message he had lived by: FORGIVE US OUR TRESPASSES AS WE FORGIVE THOSE WHO TRESPASS AGAINST US.

The church was cleared at five in the morning. But by seven the crowds had returned, to begin another long wait. With them now were delegations from all over Poland. Every big industrial centre sent its Solidarity delegates. They had hitched a lift or travelled by overnight train, then walked from the city centre, their Solidarity banners held high. It was the largest, most confident Solidarity turn-out since martial law, and it was as if the movement was coming alive again after a long concussion. And in the popular response, there could not have been a more resounding affirmation of support for the banned union which many of them had been forced to abjure.

The funeral Mass was celebrated by Cardinal Glemp with six bishops and six priests on the balcony and over a thousand other priests inside and outside the church. A wreath of thorns lay on the catafalque. The crowd was later estimated at between three hundred and three hundred and fifty thousand, and their self-discipline and restraint were amazing. In the overpowering silence, it was as if the whole assembly had been, as one woman put it, "touched by a visible wave of grace".

During the farewell speeches which followed the Mass, Lech Wałesa expressed the general emotion when he said simply: "Solidarity lives today because you, Father Jerzy, gave your life for it. A Poland that has such priests and such people has not perished and will never perish."

But the most moving and heart-felt tribute came from one of the steelworkers from Huta Warszawa, whose voice was hoarse with grief as he cried out: "Jurek, our friend, you are still with us . . . Can you hear the bells tolling for freedom? Can you hear our hearts praying? . . . Your ark, the good ship Solidarity Of Hearts drifts along, carrying more and more of us on board . . . You have already won with Christ . . . and that was the victory you most longed for."

When the coffin was sealed, it was carried to the waiting grave. Flowers, wreaths and candles which covered not only the grave but the church, the forecourt, and the squares and streets beyond were indication enough that Solidarity had a new martyr and that the pilgrims were already at his shrine.

*   *   *

Piotrowski, Pękała, Chmielewski and their immediate superior in the Interior Ministry, ex-Colonel Adam Pietruszka,[1] were brought to trial. That at least was an achievement. And though arguments raged about the whys and the wherefores, most people were inclined to give Jaruzelski the benefit of the considerable doubt. He was, it was agreed, showing his respect for the rule of law, and at the same time showing his hard-liner rivals that there were limits beyond which they could not go. But would the regime really dare sentence four of its security police to death? Or would the whole affair turn out to be the travesty of justice that the Grzegorz Przemyk trial had been? There were grave fears that Father Popiełuszko's death may have been the opening salvo in a new campaign against the Church.

In court number 40 at Toruń, these fears were borne out. The trial took place in a fanfare of publicity, and the four pawns were duly sacrificed as a sop to public outrage. But the question of where the buck stopped was not resolved or even sincerely tackled, and all evidence which might have pointed the finger at anyone higher than Adam Pietruszka was rigorously suppressed. Though ex-Lieutenants Pękała and Chmielewski were visibly suffering from remorse, ex-Captain Piotrowski was unrepentant.[12] Piotrowski was allowed to indulge in an impassioned tirade against the Church in general and Father Popiełuszko in particular, whom he held responsible for all the social unrest in Poland. Ex-Colonel Pietruszka, who was palpably more upset that the good name of the Interior Ministry had been besmirched than by the murder of the troublesome priest, said bitterly that Popiełuszko was one of a number of priests in Poland who "wear a cross on their chests and carry hatred in their hearts". The State Prosecutor suggested that the "extremism" of Father Popiełuszko had given birth to "a no less damaging" (but, by implication, more excusable) extremism on the part of his murderers.

All these attacks were given widespread coverage by the media. But the words of Mr Olszewski, the auxiliary Prosecutor who represented the Church, were not reported at all. Mr Olszewski who was given only a brief time in which to make his reply to these dumbfounding accusations protested that: "This is supposed to be the trial of the murderers of Father Popiełuszko. I never thought I should have to stand in court and defend the innocent victim of the crime."

And, he added heavily: "History alone will reveal whether all the guilty men were in the dock."

The trial lasted twenty-five days. In his summing-up, Judge Kujawa explained that the death penalty was not in order, since the accused had not acted "from base motives" but merely from "excessive zeal" for eliminating "an enemy of the State". Nevertheless, a crime had been committed and he pronounced a sentence of twenty-five years for Pietruszka and Piotrowski (with ten years' loss of civil rights); fifteen years for Pękała and fourteen for Chmielewski.

Severe sentences certainly, but even these could be seen as no more than a symbolic gesture. The manner in which the trial had been conducted caused consternation. Jerzy Popiełuszko's brother said there had been three trials: of the accused, of his brother and of the Church. Waldemar Chrostowski, the driver who had escaped to give the alarm, and whom the State Prosecutor had done his best to dismiss as an unreliable witness, said the trial had been used "to spit on the Church". It was Leszek Kołakowski's opinion that the trial had represented "a clash between two worlds", the one brought up to hate, the other to respect human dignity. "Even now one must forgive," said Lech Wałęsa. "But forgiveness for the cruel and premeditated murder of Father Popiełuszko will make sense only if our determination to resist evil is thereby strengthened."

Cardinal Glemp, in an unwontedly (for him) strong sermon, protested at the implications of the trial and insisted that the Church must have the right to protect the people from injustice.

If General Jaruzelski had hoped that the trial would appease society, he could not have made a bigger miscalculation. The way it had turned out, it had driven Solidarity, the Church and all the independent social forces in the country closer together in a more determined effort and integrated opposition to the regime than at any time since 1981. The war between the General and the Polish nation entered a new and bitter phase.

[1] Bogdan Szajkowski, *Next to God . . . Poland, op. cit.*, Chapter 4, "Tribulations Under Martial Law".

[2] *The Times*, 2.5.84.

[3] *The Tablet*, 26.5.84.

[4] Grażyna Sikorska, *op. cit.*

[5] Tim Garton Ash, *op. cit. Postscript 1984.*

[6] *The Tablet* 8.9.84.

[7] Interview with Tim Garton Ash, *Communists Should Not Believe in Miracles*, November 1984.

[8] Jurek is a diminutive of Jerzy.

[9] Neal Ascherson, the *Observer*, 11.11.84.

[10] Tim Garton Ash, *op. cit. Postscript* as above.

[11] *The Economist*, 3.11.84.
[12] All four accused had been demoted after the crime.

Note: On the site where Father Jerzy had been kidnapped, the villagers set up a birchwood cross surrounded by flowers and candles. In April 1985, they applied for permission to build a permanent memorial. Permission was refused on the grounds that "the Toruń trial showed that Father Popiełuszko was not worthy of a monument". The authorities then proceeded to put up road signs forbidding cars to stop anywhere near the site, which is, however, still marked by its wooden cross.

26 "THEY'VE PRACTICALLY DECLARED CIVIL WAR ON US . . ." (1985)

Whereas the seed which falls into the ground but does not die remains alone, without value, the seed which dies when it falls to the ground brings forth great fruit. And the death of Father Jerzy is for us a sign that we have not been mistaken, that we chose the right path, the path which sooner or later will be fruitful. Let us humbly pray God that it will be so.

Sermon by Father Paweł Piotrowski at the church at St Stanisław
Kostka, Warsaw, June 1985

The murder of Jerzy Popiełuszko was really only the tip of the iceberg, just one chilling proof that the regime would stop at nothing – not even brutal murder – to stamp out opposition to its policies. In an interview given to an Italian newspaper in February, Adam Łopatka, the Minister for Religious Affairs, insisted that government leniency was responsible for Father Popiełuszko's death: they should have acted against him immediately the cache of arms and leaflets had been discovered. Now, said Mr Łopatka regretfully, they would have to take more rigorous measures against "priests who deliver sermons which violate the laws".

This was no idle threat. 1985 saw a spate of attacks against the clergy. The "war of the crosses" became more vindictive, with participators sentenced to imprisonment, heavy fines and dismissals from work. (Religious tolerance in Poland, said Cardinal Glemp in August, applied only to atheists, and the authorities would not get the support of believers until they began acknowledging their rights. He was speaking at the monastery of Jasna Góra and was cheered by two hundred thousand pilgrims.)[1] Stones were thrown at the car of Father Kazimierz Jancarz,[2] a parish priest in Nowa Huta, as he drove from Gdańsk to Warsaw to take part in a Mass for the Country at St Stanisław Kostka. In April, one of his assistants, twenty-nine-year-old Father Tadeusz Zaleski[3] was attacked in his parents' house late at night, dazed by a chemical spray and burned on his hands, face and chest with

V-shaped burns. The official media put it about that Father Zaleski was mentally disturbed and had inflicted the burns on himself, "by pressing a burning coat-sleeve against his body". But two separate commissions of doctors, one set up by the Cardinal of Kraków, the other by the Kraków medical fraternity, dismissed this possibility as extremely unlikely, and found no evidence whatever of psychological instability in the priest.

At this point it must be explained that after Jerzy Popiełuszko's death, small human rights groups had come into existence to monitor the activities of the police and to collect information about disappearances and unexplained "accidents". These Citizens' Committees Against Violence were known by their (somewhat unfortunate) acronym, KOPPS. They had naturally enough become a new target for police activities and many of them had already been disbanded, their members arrested. The Kraków KOPP was still functioning, however, and now suggested[4] that Father Zaleski had been chosen as a victim because he possessed evidence about the death of a Solidarity activist, which might incriminate the police. The body of this man, a research student, Tadeusz Fraś, had been found in a Kraków street in September 1984. Apparently he had jumped out of the window of a flat belonging to a total stranger! A verdict of suicide was returned. The police made no effort to take photographs of the body or to determine the position in which it was lying. They also conveniently lost the post-mortem documents until well after the suicide verdict had been given. The documents revealed a punctured carotid artery and other injuries which could indeed have resulted from a fall but were just as likely to have been caused by a blow on the head with a heavy object.[5]

Fraś was one of four cases of political dissidents who had met similar deaths in that year. In none of them were suspects either sought or apprehended. The eleven-year-old daughter of Jan Budny, who had died of head injuries after a short spell in police custody, was pressurised again and again to make a false statement about her father's death. The official verdict was that he had sustained the fatal injuries by falling down the three steps leading to his house![6]

Apart from these killings, at least three murders by unidentified policemen had also gone unpunished, while house searches, kidnappings, burglaries and violence against known activists became the norm.[7]

More and more frequent forty-eight hour detentions were followed increasingly by summary court procedures and the convic-

tion of the detainee on trumped-up criminal charges. Maria Jedynak, wife of a member of the Solidarity underground leadership
was evicted from her home, and threatened with having her child
abducted, with being run over by a car, and with rape, if she
refused to divulge the whereabouts of her husband, Tadeusz. In
vain did she insist that she did not know where he was; and when
she complained to the Ministry of the Interior, she received no
reply to her letter.[8]

The political climate had not been more arctic since Stalinist
days. In December 1984, riot squads in Gdańsk, armed with
truncheons, flares, smoke bombs and the inevitable water-cannon,
had squashed a demonstration of about two thousand people at
the Monument. Lech Wałęsa, who in 1980 had sworn always to
be present at the Monument on 16th December but who had been
prevented ever since from keeping his promise, broke through
two police cordons, but gave up at the third and dropped the
flowers he was carrying at the feet of the police. Gdańsk was "a
study in blue" that day, with ZOMO and militia in every niche
and opening. Andrzej Gwiazda was arrested at the Monument
and sentenced to three months in prison. When he appealed
against the sentence, it was not only upheld but extended for
another two months.

During February and March, the confrontation between
government and opposition intensified, over government proposals to raise food prices on 28th February. (It was an observable
fact that as prices went up, quality went dramatically down!) A
Solidarity report on the economy noted that the poor were getting
poorer and that a quarter of the population lived in grossly
overcrowded and insanitary conditions.

On 13th February, just one week after the end of the Toruń
trial, and two weeks before the new price rises were due to come
into effect, Lech Wałęsa held a meeting with a group of Solidarity
activists in a private flat in Gdańsk, to discuss the catastrophic
economic situation. There was some talk of calling a fifteen-minute
protest strike on 28th February. At this point the meeting was
invaded by twenty plain-clothes and uniformed police who detained everybody present. Some, including Wałęsa, were later
released, though placed under police investigation. Three were
held and charged: Bogdan Lis, Adam Michnik and Władysław
Frasyniuk (a bus-driver and Solidarity's regional chairman in
Lower Silesia).

In one swoop, the authorities had thereby netted a representative of the three different strands of the opposition. Lis, from the

old pre-Solidarity workers' Free Trades Unions groups; Michnik, from the hated KOR; and Frasyniuk, from the younger generation that had come to political awareness through Solidarity itself. The message was plain enough: Popiełuszko trial or no, the secret police were still on top.

Since the Toruń trial, Lech Wałęsa, so restrained at Father Popiełuszko's funeral, had adopted a much tougher stance and was therefore drawing more flak from the authorities. As he wrote, in a letter to the European Trades Union Federation in May[9]: "The demands and goals that Solidarity set for itself are not easily achieved in a country where every single act of independent organisation is immediately thwarted and where every single attempt at social self-organisation is regarded as anti-State agitation."

Interviewed for the underground *Solidarność* in March,[10] he said disgustedly that government propaganda had gone beyond the bounds of common decency and had turned into "a ruthless struggle against any reconciliation or agreement. We are faced with propaganda terrorism . . . They have practically declared civil war on us."

Wałęsa believed that the authorities were using the opposition as scapegoats on whom to lay the blame for the appalling mess the country was in; and also that they were seeking to counteract the shock of the Toruń trial. The frenetic propaganda, the accusations hurled against the social activists were an attempt to distract public attention away from the guilt of Father Popiełuszko's murderers, and indeed to play down the latters' guilt:

> There is a deliberate campaign to equate the crimes of the activists with those of the police. We must clearly and decisively protest against such cynical scheming. This wave of black propaganda must be stopped, not least because the dividing line between psychological terror and actual physical terrorism is a very shadowy one.

Bishops were being asked to remove outspoken priests to country parishes where they could do no harm. This did not mean that the authorities then left them in peace. Father Mieczysław Nowak, whom Cardinal Glemp, as a result of official pressure, had removed from the parish serving the industrial complex of Ursus in Warsaw, narrowly escaped death in July 1985 when the wheel of the car he was driving suddenly fell off. (The mechanic who repaired the wheel said it had been tampered with.) Nor were bishops any more immune than their clergy. The new bishop of Gdańsk was attacked in front of his own cathedral. He managed to reach his car, and the attacker ran off to the police station directly opposite, dropping his identification papers as he ran. Two young girls who had witnessed the incident picked up the papers and took them to the clergy house. As they left, they were detained, charged with prostitution and locked up. They were released when the policeman's identity papers were returned, but neither explanation nor apology was given.

On 23rd April, 1985, the feast of St George, the name day of the late Father Popiełuszko, a crowd of about twenty thousand gathered in or around the church of St Stanisław Kostka for the evening Mass. Outside the church, a huge poster depicted Father Jerzy as St George, plunging a sword into a red dragon. The crowd sang the Solidarity theme song, "Let Poland Be Poland".[11] Father Teofil Bogucki, the parish priest, said that Father Jerzy's death "was intended to extinguish the flame of love for the country that burns in this church. But, on the contrary, it has resulted in that flame spreading all over Poland."

May Day that year brought demonstrations in thirteen cities, described by the authorities as "senseless aggression against the process of normalisation". In Gdańsk, there were thousands of police and soldiers on the streets, and in an angry telegram to the Sejm, Lech Wałęsa asked if this was what "normalisation" was supposed to look like. Police prevented him from joining in the official parade, and marched him home under escort, cheered all the way by people standing in the streets, in doorways or at open windows.

When a march of about ten to fifteen thousand in Warsaw threatened to turn ugly, Jacek Kuroń and Seweryn Jaworski stepped in to cool things down and persuade the marchers to disperse peacefully. Having succeeded, they came forward to negotiate with the police – and were promptly arrested for causing the disturbance! Next day, a court sentenced them both to three months in prison. When they appealed, Kuroń's sentence was quashed, but Jaworski's was not.*

In spite of these disturbances, General Jaruzelski claimed on television that the May Day atmosphere had been much pleasanter than in previous years. "What great things we have achieved. How much calm and hope have come to Poland!" (Did he, one wonders, know of the "souvenir" banknote being circulated by

* In August 1985, the judge who quashed Kuroń's sentence was removed from her post and the Warsaw Prosecutor demanded that the case be re-opened.

underground Solidarity? The note was for "fifty pieces of silver". What, one was supposed to ask, had Jaruzelski done with the other twenty?)

When the trial of Lis, Michnik and Frasyniuk opened in Gdańsk on 23rd May, 1985, the accused, who all faced a possible five-year sentence, were charged with attempting to incite public unrest – though the fifteen-minute strike had been called off after the government had second thoughts about the price rises – and with occupying leading positions in an illegal union.

From the start, the trial was, in Michnik's words, "a classic example of police banditry", lacking even the appearance of legality. Such was the authorities' fear of free expression that no foreign journalists or observers were allowed; counsels were searched as they entered the courtroom; and the court was packed with UB security policemen only. The defendants were not allowed at first to speak with their lawyers privately, away from the ears of the police – so they refused to testify. When that ban was withdrawn, the defendants were repeatedly prevented from stating their case: they were allowed only to answer "yes" or "no". When they tried to do more, they (in particular Adam Michnik) were expelled from the court. Defence lawyers were not permitted to question police witnesses; and all embarrassing questions were disallowed, while prosecuting counsel and police witnesses were given free rein.

Much of the evidence was fabricated, the main case against Bogdan Lis, for example, depending on a recording which was easily exposed as a fake. The judge's sole aim, it seemed, was to have the defendants pronounced guilty and given as stiff a sentence as possible.

By the fourth day, Lech Wałęsa, who was under orders not to leave Gdańsk without permission, issued a statement saying that the trial was "an insult to justice". "The law in Poland has been trodden underfoot," he said. "Its place has been taken by brute force."

When Wałęsa was called as a witness on day seven, he showed his feelings by appearing in court wearing his T-shirt, with the Solidarity logo. Questioned about the meeting on 23rd February, he admitted that he had arranged it, and invited the guests: "Private meetings among friends are considered normal in civilised countries, and the police don't usually go and break them up," he commented.

When asked what sort of people he had invited, he looked pointedly round at the rows of police in the courtroom and said that he wouldn't have considered inviting any of the present company. The judge warned him not to be offensive, and Wałęsa apologised.

Wałęsa's testimony lasted fifty minutes. Towards the end of the session, Adam Michnik asked if he could make a statement in Wałęsa's presence. His request was refused and Wałęsa was escorted out of the courtroom. Michnik raised his fingers in the V-sign and shouted to his retreating figure: "Don't worry, Lech! Solidarity will win in the end."

Whereupon (for the fourth time in the course of the trial), he was expelled from the courtroom.

> Whatever sentence is passed on us [Michnik wrote in his diary], it will be a sentence on Jaruzelski and his cohorts rather than on us. They will incur the odium of the world for their lawlessness; whereas they will have offered us the priceless gift of dignity, which is inseparable from faithfulness . . . The functionaries think that by gagging us they have deprived us of our dignity. But this is the one thing they cannot do.[12]

Frasyniuk got three and a half years, Michnik three and Lis two and a half. With breathtaking mendacity, the judge said this was a criminal not a political trial, for the crimes involved were against public order. The same double vision was exhibited by Major Wiesław Górnicki, a government spokesman being interviewed for a British TV programme.[13] He quite seriously compared the accused, with their call (later rescinded) for a fifteen-minute protest strike, to the Brighton Bombers who, the previous autumn, had attempted to blow up the British Prime Minister and most of her government.

In an eloquent statement smuggled out of prison, Michnik drew attention to the fact that a police note on his file described him as being "of Jewish nationality":

> The staff-sergeant has applied here the very same Nazi criterion which was applied by the Hitlerites when they exterminated my father's family . . . Of course, Communist anti-semitism is nothing new in Poland. Imported from Stalinist Russia, it has always had a dual purpose: to serve as ideology for . . . political police incapable of absorbing anything more complicated, and to blacken the name of Poland in the eyes of the world. A despicable tool.*

* *Uncensored Poland* 17/85. As a matter of interest, by 1985 there were only between three thousand and five thousand Jews still in Poland. It is also worth noting that, in September 1984, Polish and Jewish scholars from all over the world held a week-long Congress in Oxford, England, in an attempt to overcome some of the historical differences which have divided them.

In this same message, Michnik expressed his fervent belief that Jaruzelski's totalitarian regime in Poland was in its death-throes. Unlike the comparable regimes of Hitler's Germany and Stalin's Russia, it was almost totally without popular support, and was thus "Communism with its teeth knocked out". The only course left to it was repression. But "the resistance offered by Solidarity is too strong, the pressure of authentic public opinion too powerful, for the authorities to succeed in the long run."

Lech Wałęsa was no less forthright. When he presented himself for investigation a week later at the Gdańsk Prosecutor's Office, he did not speak, merely bowed and placed a written statement on the Prosecutor's desk. In it he had written that, after such a trial, the only way to preserve one's human dignity when dealing with courts, prosecutors or police, was to be silent.

[1] *Uncensored Poland*, 17/85.
[2] *Uncensored Poland*, 6/85.
[3] *Uncensored Poland*, 9/85.
[4] *Uncensored Poland*, 6/85.
[5] *Uncensored Poland*, 8/85.
[6] *Uncensored Poland*, 17/85.
[7] Polish Helsinki Committee's 4th Report, Sept.–Feb. 1985. See *Eastern European Reporter*, Volume 1, Number 1.
[8] Tadeusz Jedynak was arrested on 19th June, 1985.
[9] *Uncensored Poland*, 11/85.
[10] 23.3.85.
[11] *Uncensored Poland*, 9/85.
[12] As above 17/85.
[13] *Newsweek*, BBC 2. July 1985.

27 THE CRYSTAL SPIRIT

Reason has won through in Solidarity. The non-confrontational policy has prevailed. It seems to me that in Solidarity the dominant view is that we are already building the framework for an independent and democratic Poland . . . The only alternative would be desperate actions directed against the political banditry of the security apparatus. And that's precisely what I'm afraid of. In my view, we should not pay them back in kind – we should not kidnap, execute or murder our opponents. Let such methods remain *theirs*. We are not fighting for power, but for a democratic form for our country. Any kind of terrorism necessarily leads to moral abasement and spiritual degradation.

Adam Michnik (talking to Tim Garton Ash in 1984)

Wałęsa was warned to stop making public attacks on the authorities – or take the consequences. But threats like that have long been a factor in the equation of Lech's life; his inner resources enable him to take them in his stride. "I am a normal worker, an abnormal husband, the leader of a union that doesn't exist but that is stronger than ever before, the father of seven children, and a man with a load of troubles," is how he introduces himself. If they arrest him, that's just one more trouble. "I do what I have to do, regardless of consequences," he says simply. He believes in facing trouble when it comes, not in meeting it halfway:

Obviously, some people will not like what I say or do, and may decide to put me behind bars. But if you're free inside yourself, it doesn't matter what they decide. The most important freedom of all is inner freedom, and in that sense I am the free-est man in the world. I say and do what I believe is right. Nobody is free just to act in his own interest; our human freedom is to act within and on behalf of society.[1]

This "free-est man in the world" is followed by police wherever he goes, whether on foot, by bicycle or by car. His flat is bugged, and electronic surveillance monitors his every action. He has no time for himself, no time to get away from it all, to pick mushrooms

297

LECH WAŁĘSA AND HIS POLAND

or go fishing. And he has too little time for his children, though he is quite clear about what it is he wants to pass on to them:

> We cannot behave in the twenty-first century as we did in the nineteenth. That means we should destroy or demolish as little as possible, but build, transform and adapt the present reality to our needs. We should not pass on to our children less than our parents gave to us.

> If your own father gave you a bicycle and taught you how to make the sign of the cross, you should give *your* child a car, and also teach him to say a prayer . . . If you give him a car and don't teach him to say a prayer, you make a fatal mistake.

Though his name appears less in the Western media than formerly, he is "not ready to be a museum exhibit yet". But he does not worry about whether his fame will outlast him: "Will people even know where my grave is? Or will they tear my grave apart because everyone wants a piece of it? Perhaps even then they won't leave me in peace."[2]

Patiently he works on "building, transforming and adapting the present reality", on preparing blueprints for a "better Poland". "We want to change things so that the system becomes more efficient and our lives become more bearable."

The echoes from the distant past are uncanny; the wheel seems to have come full circle. Like his great-great-grandfather who, over a century ago, longed to "build a better Poland", but who was realistic enough to recognise that the moment was not his to choose, Lech also works and waits. If Solidarity ever comes out again into the sunlight, he may or may not be its leader. "I am not irreplaceable," he admits, for all his so-called vanity. "Someone will eventually take over from me." Zbigniew Bujak perhaps? That will be for the workers to decide. For Lech Wałęsa, what the workers want has always been the overriding factor.

"Wałęsa's an extraordinary man," says Father Jankowski (who is himself being threatened with dire consequences, if he does not desist from preaching "anti-State sermons". "He always stresses the importance of human dignity, especially that of the workers. He could have been just a face in the crowd; or he could have bought himself a comfortable life. Instead, he saw that there was a need, and he gave his life to doing something about it."[1]

> It wouldn't have been possible without faith [admits Lech]. Without faith I wouldn't be where I am now, and I wouldn't have the strength to go on. Nothing would have any sense. I suppose it might have been

easier to have an uncomplicated life. But I have always believed that I'm the steward of whatever talents I've been given and have to use them to the best effect. I'm an average man, a "sinning believer" with many faults. I wasn't prepared for great tasks. But life put me in this situation, and I have had to do what I can with it.[1]

It is above all his simplicity and transparent truthfulness that have made him indispensable. In a world of appalling mendacity, people know they can trust what he says. And what he says now is that Poles must work at their future themselves. "I do not hand solutions out on a gold plate. Everyone must search his or her own conscience and discover how he can best contribute. The community wisdom is the real wisdom."[3]

In a statement issued for the fifth anniversary of the signing of the Gdańsk Agreement, Wałęsa stressed that in 1985, the need was no longer for millions of demonstrators fighting the police – "no one in his right mind is keen to take on tanks with his bare hands" – but for small groups of wise men and women patiently preparing a programme for the future – so that when the time comes, everybody will know what to do. To a French Press Agency, he said: "The biggest battle is yet to come . . . It will be without fireworks, unspectacular, but much more interesting."

It would in fact not be a battle at all, but "a long march into the future". On this march, political and economic concerns would be given equal priority, since "it is hard to be a political militant if you have nothing to eat".[4]

A five-hundred page report issued by Solidarity on 31st August to mark the anniversary and popularly known as the "Wałęsa Report", filled out Lech's statement. Commissioned by him, it was written by lawyers, doctors, economists, sociologists and university professors; and it represented a plea for a new kind of society in Poland. It suggested that the East–West divide brought about by the Yalta Treaty did not mean a stark choice between, on the one hand, abject submission to a totalitarian system, and, on the other, the complete breakdown of social order. In between those two polarities, there was room for the ideas of Solidarity. The report asked for market forces to be allowed to play a role in the economy, and for an end to those piecemeal items of reform which merely get sat on by those who will go to any lengths to prevent change. It asked for the reform of the judicial system, with judges being allowed genuine freedom; for trade union pluralism; and for workers' councils in factories to be free of management (i.e. Party) interference.

As the report pointed out, the 1980s are witnessing an unprecedented decline in the standard of living in Poland. One family in three has no accommodation of its own; and thirty per cent of the population are officially in the poverty belt. Infant mortality has increased by nearly a third, and life-expectancy generally has decreased. Working conditions are more hazardous than ever, and pollution has reached the danger level. The handicapped and elderly suffer from undernourishment, and the whole country lives with bad sanitary conditions and a poor diet which contains few vitamins. Almost all Polish children have some kind of spinal defect and traces of rickets; all young pregnant women develop anaemia; every third drug in circulation is unavailable in sufficient quantities; and every fourth person who enters a pharmacy leaves it empty-handed.[5] Health care is twenty years behind that of the West. In spite of the many heroic doctors who battle against intolerable odds, the medical profession is demoralised, and the patient often bears the brunt. The Church cannot offer the real help it would like to, for even its long-hoped-for agricultural fund has not yet been given the government go-ahead. Polish life is a no-go area; a seed-ground for despair.

Yet for all this, the deepest cause of the Polish crisis, said the Solidarity report, was "the destruction of the elementary mutual trust between people and the authorities".

Lech Wałęsa continues to believe that the search for this lost mutual trust is the only possible path for Poland to tread: "One day, maybe, the authorities will understand that they must choose between two alternatives: ours, which is non-violent; and the other, which is fraught with danger and could lead to incalculable consequences."

Confrontation does not figure in his plans:

> People on our side are convinced that nothing will be achieved by raised voices and violent actions. Some of the other side know it too. When the moment comes for dialogue, we must be ready, and we must be united. We must return to our work-places, for that is where our strength lies. We must struggle there for rights which it will later be impossible to withdraw . . . I am convinced that it is simply not possible for us not to win . . .

Not possible? Is Wałęsa then simply an incurable optimist? 1985 has been a bad year for optimists. The trials, the kidnappings, the police brutality, the unexplained murders. There are between two hundred and two hundred and fifty political prisoners in Poland now and the number increases steadily. The fines imposed get more prohibitive, with the result that many are imprisoned now for debt. There is a clearer than ever dichotomy between "us" and "them", between the vast majority and those who are unequivocally dubbed "the Reds". The system, corrupt to the core, has become psychologically intolerable.

It is the young who are in the vanguard of the revolt. The heirs to the spirit of Solidarity, who did not previously suffer the spiritual desolation of what Miłosz, in Stalinist days, called "ketman" – the survival technique of thinking and believing in one set of values while being forced to act in accordance with another. The young have had better models than that, and they do not want to let them go. They are intelligent enough to understand that a corrupt regime contaminates society with the fall-out of its own corruption. Lies become too easily accepted, for the sake of a quiet life; work is too easily devalued, the natural environment degraded, science and culture dehumanised.

One recent law has tightened censorship; another has made singing hymns outside church a punishable offence; a third has eroded any hope of trade union pluralism for the foreseeable future; and yet another threatens to do away with academic freedoms and reduce the universities to the level of tied Party schools. Professor Bronisław Geremek, a respected member of the Polish Academy of Sciences for thirty years, was dismissed after meeting with the British Foreign Minister, Sir Geoffrey Howe, in April 1985. But Poland, as an industrial nation at the end of the twentieth century, cannot afford to muzzle its universities and research institutes, and thus erode still further its economic competitiveness and render it even more incapable of repaying its foreign debts. Such a short-sighted course is an invitation to economic catastrophe, for the sake of short-term political point-scoring. The "grand old man" of the Academy, ninety-six-year-old Professor Lipiński, goes further in his condemnation. He speaks of a return to Stalinist practices and warns: "The threat to Polish science and learning does not come from 'troublemakers' at the universities but from the numerous attempts made to limit freedom of thought. Science ends when a political muzzle is put on mouths and thoughts."[6]

So does freedom. And trust. And spontaneity. With the return of informers and the increased feelings of insecurity, the Solidarity days of mutual trust have for the moment gone. "What has happened to the days when everyone seemed like a member of the family?" they ask mournfully. Shop assistants are bored and

301

rude; the endless queues and shortages make people short-tempered and weary.

Yet miracles have happened in the past, and the Poles are not beyond hoping for one now. It may even be that one has already happened. As recently as 1977, Adam Michnik remarked disconsolately to a friend in Paris that the Poles were concerned only with their creature comforts and were utterly conformist. Yet today, however grievous the pain of living, what Michnik, Kuroń, Gwiazda, Walentynowicz – and Lech Wałęsa – were working towards then has actually happened. Despite the frustration and the hopelessness – and they are undeniable – the Poles are aware of their situation now, and aware that that awareness is generally shared. 1980 was not a brief interlude but a turning-point. As Wajda said, at the conclusion of *Man of Iron*: we have seen this truth and there is no going back on it. There *is* no going back on August 1980.

However many may now belong to the new unions[7] – said by Wałęsa to be workers' unions in name only[8] – their deeper allegiance is almost certainly elsewhere. The spiritual strength of the people, severely taxed by the grinding everyday reality, cannot be entirely crushed.

The government professes to believe that "normalisation" has been restored. But what is "normalisation"? If, as Wałęsa suggested, it means more troops and police on the streets to maintain the power and privileges of the ruling elite; more people like Adam Michnik behind bars, then indeed normalisation has come about. (Some would perhaps call it pacification!) But it is an illusion. For the true normalisation would be what Lech Wałęsa and his colleagues are still striving for, a dialogue between rulers and ruled, enabling a common effort for the good of Poland.

In many, perhaps the majority of, world societies, it would already be too late. The spiral of violence, in which one violent act begets another even more violent, would already be too tightly coiled, ready to spring back with destructive force. That is the way things have happened in Northern Ireland, in Lebanon, in Uganda, in South Africa. It has come to seem the only possible way out of impasse. But Poland is different. The Poles have shown in the past that they are capable of overcoming their prejudices and of swallowing their wholly-justified grudges. They are romantics, but they have learned realism in a hard school and with it has come maturity. There have been isolated instances of violence in some of the street demonstrations, but these have never been encouraged or condoned by the majority. The record of non-violence in the Polish struggle is impressive. The ultimate crime in Polish eyes is that brother should be killing brother. Where else could one have come across a leading article[9] entitled "How Can We Love the ZOMO?" and justifiably expect it to be taken seriously? The Poles may find it hard to love the ZOMO, but they know the effort is important. "Ours are spiritual values which we can never lose," says Lech Wałesa, "they form us and explain us, which is why the West finds us difficult to understand."[1]

The people do not want to overthrow the system under which they live; they want to humanise it and make it work. They might want to have more to eat and a reasonable share of the basic consumer goods, but there is no hankering after capitalism in Poland; no desire to return to the pre-war *ancien regime*; egalitarian sentiments are almost universal. There would be no takers for the privatisation of heavy industry, though some call for more private enterprise in other areas. Socialism is what they want, but it must be open not closed Socialism, one with a human face and not the version exported from the Soviet Union.

It follows that they want someone to overhaul their disastrous economy without ideological spectacles on. Such a move would require imagination and courage on the part of the government, because it would involve moving power away from the centre, and this in turn would mean a genuine democratisation of social and political life. The alternative to this – a society perpetually alienated and hostile – may prove too grim to live with, however little the regime seems to care about public good-will. In a stalemate situation, in which the government has power but no popular mandate, while Solidarity has the mandate but no power, something will have to give. Solidarity has gone underground and is biding its time. After all, the Poles are used to waiting. They have waited for two hundred years, and the lessons of those years have not been wasted on them. But how long can a bankrupt regime afford to wait? How much time does it have?

Lech Wałesa has no doubts at all about the eventual outcome. "Like all the world's major battles, it will end at the negotiating table. Sooner or later there will be an agreement with the authorities. I have held out the hand of friendship, so far without response. But in the end, I shall not have waited in vain."

There are many on "the other side", he claims, who want accord. Even the militia. In so doing, they admit their guilt, but Wałesa for one will not let past grudges prevail over the need for reconciliation. The revealing and rather touching story is told that one day Lech was found at home drinking vodka with six members of the ZOMO riot police. They were six young conscripts who had hated what they had to do, and this was their last night in the service. They were celebrating by visiting Wałęsa, drinking his health and explaining their conduct.

The incident brings to mind the young prison-camp guard who said to Tadeusz Mazowiecki: "Who will there ever be to stand up for *us*?" The militia men with "dead eyes full of fear" seen by Hanka G. on the day martial law was declared and the internment camp commandant in a moving short story by Andrzej Szczypiorski: a good man whose moral sense has been buried deep with the passing years, yet who is aware of something seriously wrong with his life. He attempts to avoid facing the truth about himself by drinking, but the placebo doesn't work. "Every drink lessened the pain a bit, but after a time it hurt more again. I don't mean a pain in the chest, something more general, maybe not even a pain, more like a burden . . ."[10]

It is Wałęsa's strength, not, as some would say, his weakness, that he can understand the nature of such a burden, and is unwilling to judge anybody as "the enemy". The future will be built by everybody pulling together, or it will not be built at all: "We must forgive. We should listen to everyone we meet, even those we do not like or who do not like us. Every single person has something to teach us, but so often we are deaf and blind to what that something is."[1]

Jerzy Popiełuszko preached that message too. The truth is that the religious faith of the Poles is not just a political safety valve (though it is that too) but a real dynamic force. The gospel of Christ is taken seriously in Poland: not for nothing did a nineteenth-century poet call her the "Christ among nations".[11] The Christmas 1984 crib in St Stanisław Kostka church was a car boot filled with straw, on which lay the mangled body of a young man. The gospel story is a living reality. The Poles understand about crucifixion, because they have lived the experience many times.

But they understand about resurrection too. Today and every day Jerzy Popiełuszko's shrine is visited by thousands, and ablaze with lights and candles. In the church, people pray not for vengeance but for the strength to overcome hatred. The words from the Cross, often repeated by Father Jerzy, FATHER, FORGIVE THEM, still flutter on their banner outside the church. Learning to forgive is an uphill struggle, but if reconciliation is to take place and brother is to stop killing brother, it must be won.

"It's a bit like learning to do the long jump," says Wałęsa

typically. "First a little jump, then a little bit further. We thought we could do more than we were capable of doing, and we were beaten back. But we'll try again. You *must* have hope."

On 31st August, 1985, the fifth anniversary of the founding of Solidarity, workers, farmers, housewives, students, the old, the young, went to church. One poster produced by the underground for the occasion showed a large fist crushing a prison; another showed the defiant five-year-old that the 1981 happy Solidarity baby had become. The crushing grip and the uncrushable defiance: those are the twin realities of Poland today. The defiance may be non-violent, but it is not to be underestimated. A poignant new hymn, popularly attributed to Father Popiełuszko himself, begins sadly and plangently:

> Oh my country, how long you have been suffering,
> How deep your wounds today.

But it ends on a note of hope. The white eagle of Poland, chained now by the foot, will break its chain "when the freedom bell shall ring".

Until that day, the people turn for solace to the source that has never failed them: "Mary, Queen of Poland, grant us freedom, peace and loving hearts, that we may stay true to you and your Son." Listening to them sing, reduced to helpless tears by the passion in their voices, one senses something of the underlying spiritual force as well as the anguish of this much-tried people; the "glory of the starlike diamond" among the ashes of their lives.

As the birthday Mass in St Stanisław Kostka draws to a close, a voice, powerful and resonant, comes through the loudspeakers: "Let us swear to make Solidarity live."

Thousands of fists shoot into the air, and thousands of voices shout as one: "We swear it."

Outside, in front of the banks of fresh flowers which permanently cover the grave of Jerzy Popiełuszko, a group of Silesian miners have laid a wreath in the shape of an anchor. The ancient symbol of undying hope. As Lech Wałęsa says: "You *must* have hope."

---

[1] Interview with author.
[2] Interview with Lech Wałęsa by Aimé Lemoyne, for *La Croix*, October 1983. Reproduced by *Reader's Digest*.
[3] *Każdy Z Was Jest Wałesa*, op. cit.
[4] *Uncensored Poland*, 14/85.

[5] Tygodnik Mazowsze, number 129, 16.5.85. Article by member of Solidarity's independent Voluntary Health Commission.

[6] *Uncensored Poland*, 12/85.

[7] The government claims five and a half million, which is still only half the Solidarity figure.

[8] *Uncensored Poland* 11/85.

[9] Józef Tischner, Jak Kochać Zomowca – interview reproduced in Dziennik Polski, 4.8.84.

[10] Andrzej Szczypiorski, *Confession of A Child Of Our Time*, Index on Censorship, Volume 14, Number 4, August 1985.

[11] Juliusz Słowacki, nineteenth-century Polish Romantic poet.

See also East European Reporter, Spring 1985 and Summer 1985.

POSTSCRIPT: January 1987

A great deal has changed in Poland since September 1985 when this book was finished; though it must be said that for Lech Wałęsa personally there has been little to attract the world's attention. His eighth child, Brygida Katarzyna, was born in December 1985, but otherwise he has faded from sight. He is still in his job at the Lenin Shipyards, still officially an "ordinary citizen." His hopes of donating the money from his Nobel Prize to the Church for its projected Farmers' Fund have been frustrated. The Church had high hopes for this potential revitalisation of Polish agriculture; but after three-and-a-half years of argument and discussion, it became clear that the government had no intention of letting the plan get off the ground. At this stage, the Church reluctantly—and to the surprise and disappointment of many—abandoned the idea. Wałęsa's money went instead to providing medical supplies for the sorely beleaguered hospitals. In 1981, when Poland was starring nightly on the TV screens of the world, it was Lech Wałęsa's appeal for help that set the lorry-loads of much-needed supplies rolling into Poland from all over the West. The situation in the hospitals is as bad as it ever was, or even worse, but the West has now lost interest and the incoming relief-lorries are increasingly few and far between.

"Crisis is too weak a word to describe the economic situation of the country," Jacek Kuron wrote in September 1986. "Everything is in ruin, everything has to be rebuilt at once, and that in the framework of a system that is virtually incapable of doing anything at all." True, there are many more goods in the shops in 1986, but the prices are set so high that few can afford more than the barest necessities. People are overworked and exhausted, the economy is in spinning decline, not least because Poland's external debts have gone from twenty-six-billion dollars in December 1981 to somewhere near the thirty-five-billion mark at the time of writing. Some of this increase is undoubtedly due to new debts, but most of it stems from the continued inability to repay the interest on the old ones. To make matters worse, the Poles find it increasingly difficult to stay afloat in the export market. World markets are becoming vastly more competitive, and only the strong survive: the demand for coal, always Poland's staple export, is slackening.

More and more, Poland is finding its only reliable markets to be with the Eastern bloc countries, in particular the USSR.

This unhappy situation has not been helped either by rampant pollution or by the disaster at Chernobyl in the Ukraine. Poland, the country closest to the Ukraine, was affected by high levels of radiation. Just how high has never been, nor is likely to be officially disclosed. Among the many imponderables in the post-Chernobyl situation, one economic result is only too painfully clear: the West has stopped buying Polish agricultural produce, its cheese, milk, meat, fruit and vegetables, and Poland is poorer to the tune of about one million dollars a day.

The repercussions from Chernobyl will rumble on for years to come, and nobody knows what they will be. But it is possible that the disaster had one good result. The much-vaunted Amnesty for political prisoners in July 1986 may have had its origins there. For the already bad and dramatically worsening economic situation made it more imperative than ever to seek an end to American sanctions, as a prelude to a fresh supply of credits from the West. "For the moment at least," wrote Kuron, "they do not want to put people behind bars – they want to be rid of the image of a gendarme." (At the same time, the authorities appear to have realised that crippling their opponents financially by means of un-payable fines is an effective punishment that does not incur the wrath of other nations.) At the time of writing, sanctions are still in place; but the Polish government is hopeful that they will soon be withdrawn. Perhaps the Americans want to be sure that the released prisoners are not to be rearrested once the short-term economic objective has been attained. They may also have felt an understandable alarm at what has been happening in the universities, where the regime has determinedly reestablished control over a milieu they had decisively lost. Not only have all the Rectors and most of the Deans (all elected in the heady days of freedom in 1981) been removed from their posts, but new rules about the ratio of teaching-staff-to-students means that many of the former are in danger of losing their jobs. It goes without saying that those who are "difficult" will be the first to go.

Repressive measures of this kind are aggravated by the random and arbitrary way in which the regime habitually imposes them. Nevertheless, in spite of the constant serious violation of human rights, the Poles seem to be calmer than before. One of the objectives of the Amnesty, in fact, was to achieve this calm, to weaken social resistance and convince the mass of the population that "normalisation" has prevailed. But "pacification" remains a truer description, and what prevails is not true calm so much as apathy. The authorities are well aware of this, of course. They know as well as anyone that they have not won over the people, and have brought utter chaos to the economy. "If only we could persuade people to work harder," complained one top-ranking official to a Western colleague, "we could change so much. But we can't bring the people with us, we don't generate confidence."

Few would disagree with that assessment. But the Poles have accepted – out of sheer weariness – that the time for dreaming is over and that they are stuck with their unreformable regime for better or for worse. They have stopped gazing upward and outward to far-off horizons and are getting on with their lives as best they can. Some, alas, have fallen into a moral malaise, their earlier sense of social responsibility replaced by a new venality and corruption. Alcoholism, fueled by lack of hope, is once again rampant. Others, however, are rising to the challenge. A new realism, pragmatic and without expectations, has set in. The majority are distancing themselves more and more from the Party, and even, to a certain extent, from Solidarity. Mutually supportive neighbourhood groups are springing up, inward-looking but each in its own way dynamic. These are the backbone of the "alternative society," and one of their major charms is that they are not centrally organised from above. To counter Marxist-style unemployment – the refusal to reemploy released internees or dismissed university teachers – there has come into existence a whole network of small workshops run on cooperative lines. These groups manufacture products that are scarcely to be found in Poland: spare parts for agricultural and industrial machinery, chemicals, agricultural implements, household goods and clothing. Many of them owe their existence to capital supplied by Polish émigrés in the West.

Such links with the West are constantly being strengthened, more easily now than before. Automatic subscriber dialing, for example, has made telephone conversations more difficult to monitor and control – and therefore freer and less inhibited. The constant flow of Polish pilgrims to see Pope John Paul II in Rome has provided its own brand of assurance, and given an added spurt to the spirit of independence. Most significant of all, perhaps, are the new burgeoning Peace movements. These are unlike their counterparts in the West in that they are less concerned with nuclear weapons than with the continued insistence on the military oath to the Soviet Union. But these groups have their clear links with the West, notably with the Greens of West Germany. The Polish government dislikes this new development, and is ruthless in tracking down the peacemakers. It is a sign of the times that, although Solidarity leaders like Bujak and Michnik qualified for release under the terms of the latest Amnesty, the members of the peace organisations did not.

The people have not forgotten the murder of Jerzy Popieluszko, and thousands still beat a regular path to his grave. The Roman Catholic Church retains its hold over the Polish national psyche, and has become the representative of the "alternative society." Polish culture is flourishing under the aegis of the Church, and specially sponsored art exhibitions, concerts, recitals, poetry readings and film showings abound. The Church has turned into Poland's main patron of the arts, supporting and sustaining those creative artists for whom the regime's "socialist realism" can find no place.

In this flourishing alternative society, the number of Catholic publishing houses has greatly increased, and so has the number of KIKs, the Catholic Intellectual Clubs which enshrine the Catholic sense of responsibility for society. The allocation of paper is as restricted as ever, censorship is as intense; but there is now a much wider available range of opinion. There is a growing and eager market for the new publications.

Solidarity itself has come out into the daylight, although it has not completely abandoned its underground structures. (In a country as unpredictable as Poland, that would be folly indeed.) But since the Amnesty, its leaders have taken the momentous decision that, as a prerequisite for rebuilding the country, the Independent Trade Unions will operate freely and in full view of everyone. They are therefore back in business, with their own publications and information network. Pluralism has been reasserted. Lech Wałęsa has set up a new Provisional Council, together with a system of regional councils working openly. This openness may yet prove to be foolhardy and mistaken, even dangerous; but it has the expressed aim of making dialogue with the regime a possibility. "The purpose," says Adam Michnik, "is to initiate the process of changing confrontation into dialogue." In a recent issue of the independent magazine, *Tygodnik Mazowsze*, Lech Wałęsa reminded his readers yet again that Solidarity does not exist, never did exist, for its own sake, but for the sake of Poland.

Time is not on Poland's side. She grows weaker by the day, and drastic measures are needed to save her from economic and social collapse. The hour is late. As an article in the revered Catholic *Tygodnik Powszechny* recently spelled out, even if all Poles decided to rally to the common cause of national salvation, all that can be hoped for would be to slow the rate of decline.

However limited the possibilities, General Jaruzelski cannot be unaware of the advantages of having the whole of Polish society pulling together in the same direction. It is in the interests of Poland's survival that some form of pluralism be injected into a stagnant society. In fact, at the beginning of December 1986, the Government took a tentative step forward. It announced the setting up of a new Consultative Council, to consist of fifty-six members representing the Party, certain Catholic circles, and some non-partisan intellectuals. The Church, though invited to take part, declined to do so, on the grounds that this was a purely political initiative. But she did not overtly oppose the idea and did nothing to dissuade Catholics from taking part. Here at last then is an embryonic "experiment in dialogue" with society at large, but as neither the content nor the scope of the Council have been finally decided, it is far too early to judge its possibilities of success.

One thing is certain, however. Solidarity must have more than a token presence in any such dialogue if it is to have any meaning at all. The presence of Wałęsa, Bujak, or Frasyniuk – to say nothing of Adam Michnik – would greatly enhance the prospects of success. Though there are many today who curse Solidarity for intransigence, or dismiss it as a stumbling block to real social peace, the Solidarity movement continues to provide a unifying and protective framework for society. Without it, all dissent would be fragmentary, isolated, and hopeless. "One cannot speak of an opposition in Poland," says Professor Geremek, "in the sense that there exists a force waiting to take power. More accurately, there is a certain state of alertness in society – an all-embracing state of communion." Perhaps the Pope's third visit to Poland, scheduled for June 1987, will make this potential "state of communion" a reality. Perhaps John Paul II will provide the impetus for the much-needed renewal of Polish society.

There are, of course, many different strands of political opinion within the Solidarity movement. It says much for Lech Wałęsa's undiminished powers of leadership that he succeeds in holding together and reconciling those different strands, and thus keeps the movement intact. He has always been aware that such unity is crucial, and if sometimes he seems to be slow in reaching decisions, it is because none but the right decision will do. As a skill, this may not be a headline-hitter, but it is of rare value. Kuron, for one, has gone on record as saying that because of it Wałęsa deserves to be awarded a second Nobel Prize for Peace.

ENDPIECE

The essential aim of any project of renewal in the world by means of a moral renaissance is not so much the construction of an earthly paradise as the fact of restraining and disarming a rampant evil. In this defence of human life against the evil that threatens it, we can discern the ultimate meaning of those appeals to brotherhood, solidarity, freedom and human dignity . . . Human history is not only a sad procession of human errors and injustices. It is also made up of courageous and wise efforts towards the common good.

The encounter with contemporary evil of an exceptionally aggressive nature awoke in Poland the will to renewal and inclined a large number of people to renounce self-interest in order to defend themselves against the suppression of human rights and against the abasement of human dignity. Their witness will become even more powerful when it moves others to defend the same values, common to us all, in all the diversity of the actual situations which confront us in our own days.

BOHDAN CYWIŃSKI, 1984

BIBLIOGRAPHY

Andrzejewski, Jerzy, *Ashes and Diamonds*, Penguin.

Arendt, Hannah, *On Revolution*, Faber & Faber 1963, Penguin 1973. (Canovan, Margaret, *The Political Thought of Hannah Arendt*, Methuen 1974.)

Ascherson, Neal, *The Polish August*, Penguin 1981.

Ascherson, Neal, *The Book of Lech Wałesa*, Allen Lane (introduction to) 1981.

Barańczak, Stanisław (Wybor), *Poeta Pamieta, Antologia Poezji Świadectwa I Sprzeciwu 1944–1984*, Puls Publications, 1984.

Bethell, Nicholas, *Gomułka, His Poland and His Communism*, Longmans 1969, Penguin 1972.

Bethell, Nicholas, *The War Hitler Won*, Allen Lane, Penguin 1972.

Bierut, Bolesław, *The Six Year Plan for the Reconstruction of Warsaw*, Ksiazka i Wiedza, 1949.

Blażyński, George, *Flashpoint Poland*, Pergamon Policy Studies, Oxford 1979.

Brandys, Kazimierz, *A Warsaw Diary 1978–1981*, Chatto & Windus 1984.

Brolewicz, Walter, *My Brother, Lech Wałesa*, Robson Books 1984.

Bromke, Adam, *Poland: The Protracted Crisis*, Mosaic Press, Canada.

Bromke, Adam, *Poland's Politics: Idealism v. Realism*, Harvard Press.

Charlton, Michael, *The Eagle and the Small Birds: Crisis in the Soviet Empire from Yalta to Solidarity*, BBC, 1984.

Davies, Norman, *God's Playground: A History of Poland*, Volume II, Clarendon Press, Oxford 1981.

Davies, Norman, *Heart of Europe: A Short History of Poland*, Clarendon Press, Oxford 1984.

Dobbs, Michael, K. S. Karol and Dessa Trevisan, *Poland, Solidarity, Wałesa*, Pergamon Press 1981.

Dziewanowski, M. K., *Poland in the Twentieth Century*, Columbia University Press, New York.

Dziewanowski, M. K., *The Communist Party in Poland*, Harvard Press 1976.

Fournier, Ewa, *Poland*, Vista Books 1964.

Garliński, Józef, *Poland, Soe and the Allies*, George Allen & Unwin, 1969.

Garton Ash, Tim, *The Polish Revolution, Solidarity 1980–1982*, Jonathan Cape 1983.

314

BIBLIOGRAPHY

Halecki, O., *A History of Poland*, with additional material by A. Polonsky, Routledge & Kegan Paul 1978, p/b 1983.

Kaplan, Chaim A., *Scroll of Agony*, Hamish Hamilton 1966.

Kapuscínski, Ryszard, *The Emperor*, Picador 1983.

Konwicki, Tadeusz, *A Dreambook For Our Time*, Penguin 1976 and 1983 (with an introduction by Leszek Kołakowski).

Konwicki, Tadeusz, *A Minor Apocalypse*, Faber & Faber 1983.

Konwicki, Tadeusz, *The Polish Complex*, Penguin 1984.

Korowicz, Marek, *W Polsce Pod Sowieckim Jarzmem*, Veritas 1955.

Krzywicki-Herbert and Rev. Walter J. Ziemba (translators), *The Prison Notes of Stefan, Cardinal Wyszyński*, Hodder & Stoughton 1985.

Lane, David and George Kołankiewicz, *Social Groups in Polish Society*, Macmillan 1973.

Lewis, Flora, *The Polish Volcano: A Case-History of Hope*, Secker & Warburg 1959.

Macshane, Denis, *Solidarity, Poland's Independent Trade Union*, Spokesman 1981.

Mazowiecki, Tadeusz, *Internowanie*, Aneks 1982.

Michener, James A., *Poland*, Secker & Warburg 1983.

Miłosz, Czesław, *The Captive Mind*, Secker & Warburg 1953, Penguin 1980.

Miłosz, Czesław, *Native Realm*, Sidgwick & Jackson 1981.

Miłosz, Czesław, *The Seizure of Power, 1955*, pub'd Abacus 1985, (sel. and ed.) *Post-War Polish Poetry*, University of California Press.

Mirowska, Halina, *Lechu*, Glos Publications, New York 1982.

Moczarski, Kazimierz, *Rozmowy Z Katem*, Państwowy Instytut Wydawniczy, Warszawa 1977.

Nowak, Jan, *Courier from Warsaw*, Collins/Harvill 1982.

Nowakowski, Marek, *The Canary and Other Tales of Martial Law*, Harvill Press 1983.

Offrédo, Jean, *Lech Wałesa. Czyli Polskie Lato*, Cana, Paris 1981.

Pawlak, A. and M. Terlecki, *Każdy Z Was Jest Wałesa: Nobel 1983, Spotkania, Paris 1984*.

Raina, Peter, *Political Opposition in Poland 1954–1977*, Poets & Painters Press, London 1978.

Raphael, Robert R., *Wojna Polsko-Jaruzelska w Karykaturach i Rysunkach*, Copenhagen 1982.

Ruane, Kevin, *The Polish Challenge*, BBC 1982.

Ścibor-Rylski, Aleksander, *Człowiek Z Marmuru, Człowiek Z Żelaza*, Aneks 1982.

Sebastian, Tim, *Nice Promises*, Chatto & Windus 1985.

Sienkiewicz, Henryk, *With Fire and Sword*, London ed. of 1898.

Sikorska, Grażyna, *A Martyr for the Truth: Jerzy Popiełuszko*, Fount, 1985.

Steiner, George, *A Reader*, Penguin 1984.

Steven, Stewart, *The Poles*, Collins/Harvill 1982.
Surdykowski, J., *Notatki Gdańskie*, Aneks 1982.
Syrop, Konrad, *Poland in Perspective*, Robert Hale, London 1982.
Szajkowski, Bogdan, *Next to God . . . Poland. Politics and Religion in Contemporary Poland*, Frances Pinter Publishers, 1983.
Taylor, John, *Five Months with Solidarity*, Wildwood 1981.
Tischner, Józef, *The Spirit of Solidarity*, Harper & Row 1982.
Tuohy, Frank, *The Ice Saints*, Macmillan 1964.
Żenczykowski, Tadeusz, *Dramatyczny Rok 1945*, Polonia 1982.

ARTICLES AND PAMPHLETS

"Dissent in Poland 1976–1977", Reports and Documents in Translation. Assn of Polish Students and Graduates in Exile, 1977.
The Church in Poland Under Martial Law, a voice of Solidarność Publication, London, June 1983.
"Solidarity Underground", A PSC special report, London 1983.
Jak Kochać Zomowca, wywiad z ks. prof. Józefem Tischnerem, Dziennik Polski, 4.8.84.
Uncensored Poland News Bulletin, Information Centre for Polish Affairs (especially 1983–1985, passim)
East European Reporter, Volume 1, Number 1 and Number 2.
Polish Affairs, Spring 1985:
Przemko Maria Grafczyński: Reflections on the Murder of Father Popiełuszko.
Janusz Bugajski: The Dead Victims of Martial Law.
Religion in Communist Lands, II, 1. Spring 1983: Grażyna Sikorska, The Light/Life Movement in Poland.
Poland One Magazine, 1984 and 1985.

INDEX

317

INDEX

INDEX

treatment of Home Army, 50
troop movements (October
1956), 99
Warsaw Rising, 50–54
winter offensive (January
1945), 56

Refugees, 56
Religious Affairs Office, 275,
281, 289
Rem, Jan, see URBAN, JERZY
Rembertów, 60–61
Renewal, see Odnowa
Ribbentrop, Joachim von, 31
Robotnik (Worker), 147
Charter of Workers' Rights,
149
*Robotnik Wybrzeża (Worker Of
The Coast)*, 149
distributed by Lech Wałęsa,
150
statement of aims, 149
Rokossovsky, Konstantin,
Marshal, 70
Rome, 249, 251
Roosevelt, Franklin D., 57, 58
Royal Palace, Warsaw, 136
Rulewski, Jan, 201, 204, 205,
219, 220, 221
Rural Solidarity, 234
agreement on, 204
arrests, 231
attacks on, 201
bishops' support for, 198
Bydgoszcz incident, 201–2
demands for, 192, 197
first groups, 190
government refusal to
acknowledge, 198
Kułaj, Jan, 239
registration, 206
Russification, 23
Russo–Polish War, 24, 90

Sadowska, Barbara, 258
St Brigid's Church, Gdansk,
172, 245, 275
shipyard church, 16
St Martin's Church, Warsaw,
146, 258
Saint Stanisław, patron of
Poland, 154
St Stanisław Kostka Church,
Warsaw, 240, 241, 242,
243, 258, 278, 282, 283,
284, 289, 293, 304, 305
samizdat literature, 206, 244,
261
Sapieha, Adam,
Cardinal-Prince, 83
Scharansky, Anatoly, 265
Sebastian, Tim, 172
Security Police, see UB
Sejm (Parliament):
bishops write stiff note to, 261
call for free elections to, 229
elections (1957), 110
modifies new law (1983), 261
outlaws Solidarity, 249
under Gierek, 136
Seminarians, 116
Show Trials in Stalinist Poland,
77
Siberia, 33

Sieńkiewicz, Henryk, 92
See also LITTLE KNIGHT
Sikorski, Władysław,
General, agreement with
Stalin, 37
Silesia, 35
Silesian Miners, 155
Six Year Plan for 1949, 79, 87
Słowacki, Juliusz, 181
*Słowo Powszechne, see
Universal Word*
Sobowo, 66, 87, 91, 138
*Soldier Of Freedom, (Żołnierz
Wolnosci)*, 229, 233, 244
Solidarity, 14, 15, 81, 83, 86,
129, 148
activists meet Wałęsa, 291
altars in churches, 255, 275
"anti-Socialist garbage", 245
appeals for May Day boycott
(1983), 257
appeals on behalf of women,
212
as trade union movement, 13
as "voice of Poland", 13
attacked by hardliners, 202
attacked by media, 214, 228
baby, 248, 305
bloodless revolution, 114
bulletin, 179
Bydgoszcz incident, 202
continuing persecution of,
276, 281, 282
demands, 192, 224
during martial law, 234, 237
enforced loyalty pledges, 237
fifth anniversary of, 305
food distribution, 213
free Saturday crisis, 198
Glemp on, 274
government plans for, 269
government urges leaders to
emigrate, 245
headquarters sealed off, 229
intensified opposition to
(1985), 291
leaders arrested, 231
lessons of non-violence,
247–8
logo, 184
Mazowsze branch, 190
moves towards confrontation,
227
Narożniak affair, 194
new martyr for, 285
Nobel Peace Prize, 266, 267,
270–71
not seeking power, 213, 214
on the Polish crisis, 300
outlawed by Sejm, 249
police harassment, 201
Popiełuszko funeral, 285
"psychological terror"
against, 269
registration crisis, 191–3
Report on the economy
(1985), 291, 299–300
seeks partnership with
government, 213
Soviet pressure, 208
talks with Rakowski, 213
theme song of, 13, 192
Tischner on, 211
threats against, 237

unveiling of Monument, 195
Wałęsa essential to, 269
Wałęsa suggests new
programme for, 268–9
Western aid sent, 239–40
witnesses forced to testify
against, 277

and associated organisations,
190
and Church, 267
See also BUJAK, FIRST
SOLIDARITY CONGRESS,
GDAŃSK AGREEMENTS,
INTERNEES, KOR, MARTIAL
LAW, RURAL SOLIDARITY,
SOLIDARITY: NATIONAL
COMMISSION, SOLIDARITY:
UNDERGROUND, WAŁĘSA,
WYSZYŃSKI
Solidarity bulletin, 178
Solidarity Eleven, 277, 279, 280
Solidarity: National
Co-ordinating
Commission, 201
appeals for end to wildcat
strikes, 200, 226
calls for national referendum,
229
chooses Wałęsa as
Chairman, 188
emergency meeting on
Bydgoszcz, 202
final meeting in Gdańsk, 229
less moderate than presidium,
226
over-rides Wałęsa, 198, 226
resignations from, 227
votes for national strike, 229
See also GWIAZDA,
ANDRZEJ, WAŁĘSA, LECH,
SOLIDARITY
Solidarity, Presidium, 204, 219,
226, 228
Solidarity, Underground, 303
attempts to monitor election
results, 278
Bujak ignores amnesty, 261
calls for election boycott, 278
calls for May Day boycott,
247
calls for symbolic protest,
242
issues Jaruzelski banknote,
294
poem, 247
proscribed, 261
supports Wałęsa's call, 271
Solidarity Weekly, 206, 231
Solidarność, 292
Soviet Union, 37, 303
allowed to keep Polish
eastern territories, 58–9
anxiety over strikes, 181
anxiety over Solidarity, 213,
219
attacked by Germany, 35
deportation of Poles, 32–4
Hitler attacks, 35
invades Poland, 32, 90
naval manoeuvres, 216
Nazi–Soviet Pact, 31
shocked by Polish demands
(1981), 194

323

INDEX